THEORY AND HISTORY

THEORY and HISTORY

*An Interpretation of Social and
Economic Evolution*

by LUDWIG VON MISES

New Haven: YALE UNIVERSITY PRESS, 1957

Contents

Introduction

1. *Methodological Dualism*

MORTAL MAN does not know how the universe and all that it contains may appear to a superhuman intelligence. Perhaps such an exalted mind is in a position to elaborate a coherent and comprehensive monistic interpretation of all phenomena. Man—up to now, at least—has always gone lamentably amiss in his attempts to bridge the gulf that he sees yawning between mind and matter, between the rider and the horse, between the mason and the stone. It would be preposterous to view this failure as a sufficient demonstration of the soundness of a dualistic philosophy. All that we can infer from it is that science—at least for the time being—must adopt a dualistic approach, less as a philosophical explanation than as a methodological device.

Methodological dualism refrains from any proposition concerning essences and metaphysical constructs. It merely takes into account the fact that we do not know how external events—physical, chemical, and physiological—affect human thoughts, ideas, and judgments of value. This ignorance splits the realm of knowledge into two separate fields, the realm of external events, commonly called nature, and the realm of human thought and action.

Older ages looked upon the issue from a moral or

1

religious point of view. Materialist monism was rejected
as incompatible with the Christian dualism of the Creator and the creation, and of the immortal soul and the
mortal body. Determinism was rejected as incompatible
with the fundamental principles of morality as well as
with the penal code. Most of what was advanced in
these controversies to support the respective dogmas
was unessential and is irrelevant from the methodological point of view of our day. The determinists did little
more than repeat their thesis again and again, without
trying to substantiate it. The indeterminists denied their
adversaries' statements but were unable to strike at their
weak points. The long debates were not very helpful.

The scope of the controversy changed when the new
science of economics entered the scene. Political parties
which passionately rejected all the practical conclusions to which the results of economic thought inevitably lead, but were unable to raise any tenable objections against their truth and correctness, shifted the
argument to the fields of epistemology and method-
ology. They proclaimed the experimental methods of
the natural sciences to be the only adequate mode of
research, and induction from sensory experience the
only legitimate mode of scientific reasoning. They be-
haved as if they had never heard about the logical
problems involved in induction. Everything that was
neither experimentation nor induction was in their eyes
metaphysics, a term that they employed as synony-
mous with nonsense.

2. *Economics and Metaphysics*

The sciences of human action start from the fact that man purposefully aims at ends he has chosen. It is precisely this that all brands of positivism, behaviorism, and panphysicalism want either to deny altogether or to pass over in silence. Now, it would simply be silly to deny the fact that man manifestly behaves as if he were really aiming at definite ends. Thus the denial of purposefulness in man's attitudes can be sustained only if one assumes that the choosing both of ends and of means is merely apparent and that human behavior is ultimately determined by physiological events which can be fully described in the terminology of physics and chemistry.

Even the most fanatical champions of the "Unified Science" sect shrink from unambiguously espousing this blunt formulation of their fundamental thesis. There are good reasons for this reticence. So long as no definite relation is discovered between ideas and physical or chemical events of which they would occur as the regular sequel, the positivist thesis remains an epistemological postulate derived not from scientifically established experience but from a metaphysical world view.

The positivists tell us that one day a new scientific discipline will emerge which will make good their promises and will describe in every detail the physical and chemical processes that produce in the body of man definite ideas. Let us not quarrel today about such issues of the future. But it is evident that such a meta-

physical proposition can in no way invalidate the results of the discursive reasoning of the sciences of human action. The positivists for emotional reasons do
not like the conclusions that acting man must necessarily draw from the teachings of economics. As they
are not in a position to find any flaw either in the reasoning of economics or in the inferences derived from
it, they resort to metaphysical schemes in order to discredit the epistemological foundations and the methodological approach of economics.

There is nothing vicious about metaphysics. Man
cannot do without it. The positivists are lamentably
wrong in employing the term "metaphysics" as a
synonym for nonsense. But no metaphysical proposition
must contradict any of the findings of discursive reasoning. Metaphysics is not science, and the appeal to
metaphysical notions is vain in the context of a logical
examination of scientific problems. This is true also of
the metaphysics of positivism, to which its supporters
have given the name of antimetaphysics.

3. *Regularity and Prediction*

Epistemologically the distinctive mark of what we
call nature is to be seen in the ascertainable and inevitable regularity in the concatenation and sequence of phenomena. On the other hand the distinctive mark of
what we call the human sphere or history or, better,
the realm of human action is the absence of such a
universally prevailing regularity. Under identical conditions stones always react to the same stimuli in the

same way; we can learn something about these regular patterns of reacting, and we can make use of this knowledge in directing our actions toward definite goals. Our classification of natural objects and our assigning names to these classes is an outcome of this cognition. A stone is a thing that reacts in a definite way. Men react to the same stimuli in different ways, and the same man at different instants of time may react in ways different from his previous or later conduct. It is impossible to group men into classes whose members always react in the same way.

This is not to say that future human actions are totally unpredictable. They can, in a certain way, be anticipated to some extent. But the methods applied in such anticipations, and their scope, are logically and epistemologically entirely different from those applied in anticipating natural events, and from their scope.

4. *The Concept of the Laws of Nature*

Experience is always experience of past happenings. It refers to what has been and is no longer, to events sunk forever in the flux of time.

The awareness of regularity in the concatenation and sequence of many phenomena does not affect this reference of experience to something that occurred once in the past at a definite place and time under the circumstances prevailing there and then. The cognition of regularity too refers exclusively to past events. The most experience can teach us is: in all cases observed in the past there was an ascertainable regularity.

From time immemorial all men of all races and civilizations have taken it for granted that the regularity observed in the past will also prevail in the future. The category of causality and the idea that natural events will in the future follow the same pattern they showed in the past are fundamental principles of human thought as well as of human action. Our material civilization is the product of conduct guided by them. Any doubt concerning their validity within the sphere of past human action is dispelled by the results of technological designing. History teaches us irrefutably that our forefathers and we ourselves up to this very moment have acted wisely in adopting them. They are true in the sense that pragmatism attaches to the concept of truth. They work, or, more precisely, they have worked in the past.

Leaving aside the problem of causality with its metaphysical implications, we have to realize that the natural sciences are based entirely on the assumption that a regular conjunction of phenomena prevails in the realm they investigate. They do not search merely for frequent conjunction but for a regularity that prevailed without exception in all cases observed in the past and is expected to prevail in the same way in all cases to be observed in the future. Where they can discover only a frequent conjunction—as is often the case in biology, for example—they assume that it is solely the inadequacy of our methods of inquiry that prevents us temporarily from discovering strict regularity.

The two concepts of invariable and of frequent conjunction must not be confused. In referring to invariable conjunction people mean that no deviation from the regular pattern—the law—of conjunction has ever been observed and that they are certain, as far as men can be certain about anything, that no such deviation is possible and will ever happen. The best elucidation of the idea of inexorable regularity in the concatenation of natural phenomena is provided by the concept of miracles. A miraculous event is something that simply cannot happen in the normal course of world affairs as we know it, because its happening could not be accounted for by the laws of nature. If nonetheless the occurrence of such an event is reported, two different interpretations are provided, both of which, however, fully agree in taking for granted the inexorability of the laws of nature. The devout say: "This could not happen in the normal course of affairs. It came to pass only because the Lord has the power to act without being restricted by the laws of nature. It is an event incomprehensible and inexplicable for the human mind, it is a mystery, a miracle." The rationalists say: "It could not happen and therefore it did not happen. The reporters were either liars or victims of a delusion." If the concept of laws of nature were to mean not inexorable regularity but merely frequent connection, the notion of miracles would never have been conceived. One would simply say: *A* is frequently followed by *B*, but in some instances this effect failed to appear.

Nobody says that stones thrown into the air at an angle of 45 degrees will *frequently* fall down to earth or that a human limb lost by an accident *frequently* does not grow again. All our thinking and all our actions are guided by the knowledge that in such cases we are not faced with frequent repetition of the same connection, but with regular repetition.

5. *The Limitations of Human Knowledge*

Human knowledge is conditioned by the power of the human mind and by the extent of the sphere in which objects evoke human sensations. Perhaps there are in the universe things that our senses cannot perceive and relations that our minds cannot comprehend. There may also exist outside of the orbit we call the universe other systems of things about which we cannot learn anything because, for the time being, no traces of their existence penetrate into our sphere in a way that can modify our sensations. It may also be that the regularity in the conjunction of natural phenomena we are observing is not eternal but only passing, that it prevails only in the present stage (which may last millions of years) of the history of the universe and may one day be replaced by another arrangement.

Such and similar thoughts may induce in a conscientious scientist the utmost caution in formulating the results of his studies. It behooves the philosopher to be still more restrained in dealing with the apriori categories of causality and the regularity in the sequence of natural phenomena.

The apriori forms and categories of human thinking and reasoning cannot be traced back to something of which they would appear as the logically necessary conclusion. It is contradictory to expect that logic could be of any service in demonstrating the correctness or validity of the fundamental logical principles. All that can be said about them is that to deny their correctness or validity appears to the human mind nonsensical and that thinking, guided by them, has led to modes of successful acting.

Hume's skepticism was the reaction to a postulate of absolute certainty that is forever unattainable to man. Those divines who saw that nothing but revelation could provide man with perfect certainty were right. Human scientific inquiry cannot proceed beyond the limits drawn by the insufficiency of man's senses and the narrowness of his mind. There is no deductive demonstration possible of the principle of causality and of the ampliative inference of imperfect induction; there is only recourse to the no less indemonstrable statement that there is a strict regularity in the conjunction of all natural phenomena. If we were not to refer to this uniformity, all the statements of the natural sciences would appear to be hasty generalizations.

6. *Regularity and Choosing*

The main fact about human action is that in regard to it there is no such regularity in the conjunction of phenomena. It is not a shortcoming of the sciences of human action that they have not succeeded in discovering determinate stimulus-response patterns. What does not exist cannot be discovered.

If there were no regularity in nature, it would be

impossible to assert anything with regard to the behavior of classes of objects. One would have to study the individual cases and to combine what one has learned about them into a historical account.

Let us, for the sake of argument, assume that all those physical quantities that we call constants are in fact continually changing and that the inadequacy of our methods of inquiry alone prevents us from becoming aware of these slow changes. We do not take account of them because they have no perceptible influence upon our conditions and do not noticeably affect the outcome of our actions. Therefore one could say that these quantities established by the experimental natural sciences may fairly be looked upon as constants since they remain unchanged during a period of time that by far exceeds the ages for which we may plan to provide.

But it is not permissible to argue in an analogous way with regard to the quantities we observe in the field of human action. These quantities are manifestly variable. Changes occurring in them plainly affect the result of our actions. Every quantity that we can observe is a historical event, a fact which cannot be fully described without specifying the time and geographical point.

The econometrician is unable to disprove this fact, which cuts the ground from under his reasoning. He cannot help admitting that there are no "behavior constants." Nonetheless he wants to introduce some numbers, arbitrarily chosen on the basis of a historical fact, as "unknown *behavior constants*." The sole excuse he advances is that his hypotheses are "saying only that these unknown numbers remain reasonably constant through a period of years." [1] Now whether such a period of supposed constancy of a definite number is still lasting or whether a change in the number has already occurred can only be established later on. In retrospect it may be possible, although in rare cases only, to declare that over a (probably rather short) period an approximately stable ratio—which the econometrician chooses to call a "reasonably" constant ratio —prevailed between the numerical values of two factors. But this is something fundamentally different from the constants of physics. It is the assertion of a historical fact, not of a constant that can be resorted to in attempts to predict future events.

Leaving aside for the present any reference to the problem of the human will or free will, we may say: Nonhuman entities react according to regular patterns; man chooses. Man chooses first ultimate ends and then the means to attain them. These acts of choosing are determined by thoughts and ideas about which, at least for the time being, the natural sciences do not know how to give us any information.

In the mathematical treatment of physics the distinction between constants and variables makes sense; it is essential in every instance of technological computation. In economics there are no constant relations between various magnitudes. Consequently all ascertainable data are variables, or what amounts to the same

1. See the Cowles Commission for Research in Economics, *Report for Period, January 1, 1948–June 30, 1949* (University of Chicago), p. 7.

thing, *historical* data. The mathematical economists
reiterate that the plight of mathematical economics
consists in the fact that there are a great number of
variables. The truth is that there are only variables
and no constants. It is pointless to talk of variables
where there are no invariables.

7. *Means and Ends*

To choose is to pick one out of two or more possible
modes of conduct and to set aside the alternatives.
Whenever a human being is in a situation in which
various modes of behavior, precluding one another, are
open to him, he chooses. Thus life implies an endless
sequence of acts of choosing. Action is conduct directed
by choices.

The mental acts that determine the content of a
choice refer either to ultimate ends or to the means to
attain ultimate ends. The former are called judgments
of value. The latter are technical decisions derived from
factual propositions.

In the strict sense of the term, acting man aims only
at one ultimate end, at the attainment of a state of
affairs that suits him better than the alternatives.
Philosophers and economists describe this undeniable
fact by declaring that man prefers what makes him
happier to what makes him less happy, that he aims at
happiness.[1] Happiness—in the purely formal sense in

1. There is no need to refute anew the arguments advanced for
more than two thousand years against the principles of eudaemonism,
hedonism, and utilitarianism. For an exposition of the formal and sub-

which ethical theory applies the term—is the only ultimate end, and all other things and states of affairs sought are merely means to the realization of the supreme ultimate end. It is customary, however, to employ a less precise mode of expression, frequently assigning the name of ultimate ends to all those means that are fit to produce satisfaction directly and immediately.

The characteristic mark of ultimate ends is that they depend entirely on each individual's personal and subjective judgment, which cannot be examined, measured, still less corrected by any other person. Each individual is the only and final arbiter in matters concerning his own satisfaction and happiness.

As this fundamental cognition is often considered to be incompatible with the Christian doctrine, it may be proper to illustrate its truth by examples drawn from the early history of the Christian creed. The martyrs rejected what others considered supreme delights, in order to win salvation and eternal bliss. They did not heed their well-meaning fellows who exhorted them to save their lives by bowing to the statue of the divine emperor, but chose to die for their cause rather than to preserve their lives by forfeiting everlasting happiness in heaven. What arguments could a man bring for-

---

jectivistic character of the concepts "pleasure" and "pain" as employed in the context of these doctrines, see Mises, *Human Action* (New Haven, Yale University Press, 1949, pp. 14–15), and Ludwig Feuerbach, *Eudämonismus,* in Sämmtliche Werke, ed. Bolin and Jodl (Stuttgart, 1907), *10,* 230–93. Of course, those who recognize no "happiness" but that given by the orgasm, alcohol, and so forth continue to repeat the old errors and distortions.

ward who wanted to dissuade his fellow from martyrdom? He could try to undermine the spiritual foundations of his faith in the message of the Gospels and their interpretation by the Church. This would have been an attempt to shake the Christian's confidence in the efficacy of his religion as a means to attain salvation and bliss. If this failed, further argument could avail nothing, for what remained was the decision between two ultimate ends, the choice between eternal bliss and eternal damnation. Then martyrdom appeared the means to attain an end which in the martyr's opinion warranted supreme and everlasting happiness.

As soon as people venture to question and to examine an end, they no longer look upon it as an end but deal with it as a means to attain a still higher end. The ultimate end is beyond any rational examination. All other ends are but provisional. They turn into means as soon as they are weighed against other ends or means.

Means are judged and appreciated according to their ability to produce definite effects. While judgments of value are personal, subjective, and final, judgments about means are essentially inferences drawn from factual propositions concerning the power of the means in question to produce definite effects. About the power of a means to produce a definite effect there can be dissension and dispute between men. For the evaluation of ultimate ends there is no interpersonal standard available.

Choosing means is a technical problem, as it were,

the term "technique" being taken in its broadest sense. Choosing ultimate ends is a personal, subjective, individual affair. Choosing means is a matter of reason, choosing ultimate ends a matter of the soul and the will.

PART ONE. VALUE

Chapter 1. Judgments of Value

1. Judgments of Value and Propositions of Existence

PROPOSITIONS asserting existence (affirmative existential propositions) or nonexistence (negative existential propositions) are descriptive. They assert something about the state of the whole universe or of parts of the universe. With regard to them questions of truth and falsity are significant. They must not be confounded with judgments of value.

Judgments of value are voluntaristic. They express feelings, tastes, or preferences of the individual who utters them. With regard to them there cannot be any question of truth and falsity. They are ultimate and not subject to any proof or evidence.

Judgments of value are mental acts of the individual concerned. As such they must be sharply distinguished from the sentences by means of which an individual tries to inform other people about the content of his judgments of value. A man may have some reason to lie about his valuations. We may describe this state of affairs in the following way: Every judgment of value is in itself also a fact of the actual state of the universe and as such may be the topic of existential propositions. The sentence "I prefer Beethoven to Lehar" refers to a judgment of value. If looked upon as an existential proposition, it is true if I really prefer Beethoven and

19

act accordingly and false if I in fact prefer Lehar and
for some reasons lie about my real feelings, taste, or
preferences. In an analogous way the existential proposition "Paul prefers Beethoven to Lehar" may be true
or false. In declaring that with regard to a judgment of
value there cannot be any question of truth or falsity,
we refer to the judgment as such and not to the sentences communicating the content of such a judgment
of value to other people.

2. *Valuation and Action*

A judgment of value is purely academic if it does not
impel the man who utters it to any action. There are
judgments which must remain academic because it is
beyond the power of the individual to embark upon
any action directed by them. A man may prefer a starry
sky to the starless sky, but he cannot attempt to substitute the former state which he likes better for the latter
he likes less.

The significance of value judgments consists precisely in the fact that they are the springs of human
action. Guided by his valuations, man is intent upon
substituting conditions that please him better for conditions which he deems less satisfactory. He employs
means in order to attain ends sought.

Hence the history of human affairs has to deal with
the judgments of value that impelled men to act and
directed their conduct. What happened in history cannot be discovered and narrated without referring to
the various valuations of the acting individuals. It is

not the task of the historian qua historian to pass judgments of value on the individuals whose conduct is the theme of his inquiries. As a branch of knowledge history utters existential propositions only. But these existential propositions often refer to the presence or absence of definite judgments of value in the minds of the acting individuals. It is one of the tasks of the specific understanding of the historical sciences to establish what content the value judgments of the acting individuals had.

It is a task of history, for example, to trace back the origin of India's caste system to the values which prompted the conduct of the generations who developed, perfected, and preserved it. It is its further task to discover what the consequences of this system were and how these effects influenced the value judgments of later generations. But it is not the business of the historian to pass judgments of value on the system as such, to praise or to condemn it. He has to deal with its relevance for the course of affairs, he has to compare it with the designs and intentions of its authors and supporters and to depict its effects and consequences. He has to ask whether or not the means employed were fit to attain the ends the acting individuals sought.

It is a fact that hardly any historian has fully avoided passing judgments of value. But such judgments are always merely incidental to the genuine tasks of history. In uttering them the author speaks as an individual judging from the point of view of his personal valuations, not as a historian.

3. *The Subjectivity of Valuation*

All judgments of value are personal and subjective. There are no judgments of value other than those asserting *I* prefer, *I* like better, *I* wish.

It cannot be denied by anybody that various individuals disagree widely with regard to their feelings, tastes, and preferences and that even the same individuals at various instants of their lives value the same things in a different way. In view of this fact it is useless to talk about absolute and eternal values.

This does not mean that every individual draws his valuations from his own mind. The immense majority of people take their valuations from the social environment into which they were born, in which they grew up, that moulded their personality and educated them. Few men have the power to deviate from the traditional set of values and to establish their own scale of what appears to be better and what appears to be worse.

What the theorem of the subjectivity of valuation means is that there is no standard available which would enable us to reject any ultimate judgment of value as wrong, false, or erroneous in the way we can reject an existential proposition as manifestly false. It is vain to argue about ultimate judgments of value as we argue about the truth or falsity of an existential proposition. As soon as we start to refute by arguments an ultimate judgment of value, we look upon it as a means to attain definite ends. But then we merely shift the discussion to another plane. We no longer view the principle concerned as an ultimate value but as a means to attain an ultimate value, and we are again faced with the same problem. We may, for instance, try to show a Buddhist that to act in conformity with the teachings of his creed results in effects which we consider disastrous. But we are silenced if he replies that these effects are in his opinion lesser evils or no evils at all compared to what would result from nonobservance of his rules of conduct. His ideas about the supreme good, happiness, and eternal bliss are different from ours. He does not care for those values his critics are concerned with, and seeks for satisfaction in other things than they do.

4. The Logical and Syntactical Structure of Judgments of Value

A judgment of value looks upon things from the point of view of the man who utters it. It does not assert anything about things as they are. It manifests a man's affective response to definite conditions of the universe as compared with other definite conditions.

Value is not intrinsic. It is not in things and conditions but in the valuing subject. It is impossible to ascribe value to one thing or state of affairs only. Valuation invariably compares one thing or condition with another thing or condition. It grades various states of the external world. It contrasts one thing or state, whether real or imagined, with another thing or state, whether real or imagined, and arranges both in a scale of what the author of the judgment likes better and what less.

It may happen that the judging individual considers both things or conditions envisaged as equal. He is not concerned whether there is *A* or *B*. Then his judgment of value expresses indifference. No action can result from such a neutral disposition.

Sometimes the utterance of a judgment of value is elliptical and makes sense only if appropriately completed by the hearer. "I don't like measles" means "I prefer the absence of measles to its presence." Such incompleteness is the mark of all references to freedom. Freedom invariably means freedom from (absence of) something referred to expressly or implicitly. The grammatical form of such judgments may be qualified as negative. But it is vain to deduce from this idiomatic attire of a class of judgments of value any statements about their content and to blame them for an alleged negativism. Every judgment of value allows of a formulation in which the more highly valued thing or state is logically expressed in both a positive and a negative way, although sometimes a language may not have developed the appropriate term. Freedom of the press implies the rejection or negation of censorship. But, stated explicitly, it means a state of affairs in which the author alone determines the content of his publication as distinct from a state in which the police has a right to interfere in the matter.

Action necessarily involves the renunciation of something to which a lower value is assigned in order to attain or to preserve something to which a higher value is assigned. Thus, for instance, a definite amount of leisure is renounced in order to reap the product of a definite amount of labor. The renunciation of leisure is the means to attain a more highly valued thing or state.

There are men whose nerves are so sensitive that they cannot endure an unvarnished account of many facts about the physiological nature of the human body and the praxeological character of human action. Such people take offense at the statement that man must choose between the most sublime things, the loftiest human ideals, on the one hand, and the wants of his body on the other. They feel that such statements detract from the nobility of the higher things. They refuse to notice the fact that there arise in the life of man situations in which he is forced to choose between fidelity to lofty ideals and such animal urges as feeding.

Whenever man is faced with the necessity of choosing between two things or states, his decision is a judgment of value no matter whether or not it is uttered in the grammatical form commonly employed in expressing such judgments.

Chapter 2. Knowledge and Value

1. *The Bias Doctrine*

THE ACCUSATION of bias has been leveled against economists long before Marx integrated it into his doctrines. Today it is fairly generally endorsed by writers and politicians who, although they are in many respects influenced by Marxian ideas, cannot simply be considered Marxians. We must attach to their reproach a meaning that differs from that which it has in the context of dialectical materialism. We must therefore distinguish two varieties of the bias doctrine: the Marxian and the non-Marxian. The former will be dealt with in later parts of this essay in a critical analysis of Marxian materialism. The latter alone is treated in this chapter.

Upholders of both varieties of the bias doctrine recognize that their position would be extremely weak if they were merely to blame economics for an alleged bias without charging all other branches of science with the same fault. Hence they generalize the bias doctrine —but this generalized doctrine we need not examine here. We may concentrate upon its core, the assertion that economics is necessarily not *wertfrei* but is tainted by prepossessions and prejudices rooted in value judgments. For all arguments advanced to support the doctrine of general bias are also resorted to in the endeavors to prove the special bias doctrine that refers to economics, while some of the arguments brought forward in favor of the special bias doctrine are manifestly inapplicable to the general doctrine.

Some contemporary defenders of the bias doctrine have tried to link it with Freudian ideas. They contend that the bias they see in the economists is not conscious bias. The writers in question are not aware of their prejudgments and do not intentionally seek results that will justify their foregone conclusions. From the deep recesses of the subconscious, suppressed wishes, unknown to the thinkers themselves, exert a disturbing influence on their reasoning and direct their cogitations toward results that agree with their repressed desires and urges.

However, it does not matter which variety of the bias doctrine one endorses. Each of them is open to the same objections.

For the reference to bias, whether intentional or subconscious, is out of place if the accuser is not in a position to demonstrate clearly in what the deficiency of the doctrine concerned consists. All that counts is whether a doctrine is sound or unsound. This is to be established by discursive reasoning. It does not in the least detract from the soundness and correctness of a theory if the psychological forces that prompted its author are disclosed. The motives that guided the thinker are immaterial to appreciating his achievement. Biographers are busy today explaining the work of the genius as a product of his complexes and libidinous impulses and a sublimation of his sexual desires. Their studies may be valuable contributions to psychology, or rather to thymology (see below p. 265), but they do not affect in any way the evaluation of the biographee's exploits. The most sophisticated psychoanalytical examination of Pascal's life tells us nothing about the scientific soundness or unsoundness of his mathematical and philosophical doctrines.

If the failures and errors of a doctrine are unmasked by discursive reasoning, historians and biographers may try to explain them by tracing them back to their author's bias. But if no tenable objections can be raised against a theory, it is immaterial what kind of motives inspired its author. Granted that he was biased. But then we must realize that his alleged bias produced theorems which successfully withstood all objections.

Reference to a thinker's bias is no substitute for a refutation of his doctrines by tenable arguments. Those who charge the economists with bias merely show that they are at a loss to refute their teachings by critical analysis.

2. *Common Weal versus Special Interests*

Economic policies are directed toward the attainment of definite ends. In dealing with them economics does not question the value attached to these ends by acting men. It merely investigates two points: First, whether or not the policies concerned are fit to attain the ends which those recommending and applying them want to attain. Secondly, whether these policies do not perhaps produce effects which, from the point of view

of those recommending and applying them, are undesirable.

It is true that the terms in which many economists,
especially those of the older generations, expressed the
result of their inquiries could easily be misinterpreted.
In dealing with a definite policy they adopted a manner
of speech which would have been adequate from the
point of view of those who considered resorting to it in
order to attain definite ends. Precisely because the
economists were not biased and did not venture to
question the acting men's choice of ends, they presented the result of their deliberation in a mode of expression which took the valuations of the actors for
granted. People aim at definite ends when resorting to
a tariff or decreeing minimum wage rates. When the
economists thought such policies would attain the ends
sought by their supporters, they called them good—just
as a physician calls a certain therapy good because he
takes the end—curing his patient—for granted.

One of the most famous of the theorems developed
by the Classical economists, Ricardo's theory of com-
parative costs, is safe against all criticism, if we may
judge by the fact that hundreds of passionate adversaries over a period of a hundred and forty years have
failed to advance any tenable argument against it. It is
much more than merely a theory dealing with the effects of free trade and protection. It is a proposition
about the fundamental principles of human cooperation under the division of labor and specialization and
the integration of vocational groups, about the origin

and further intensification of social bonds between men, and should as such be called the law of association. It is indispensable for understanding the origin of civilization and the course of history. Contrary to popular conceptions, it does not say that free trade is good and protection bad. It merely demonstrates that protection is not a means to increase the supply of goods produced. Thus it says nothing about protection's suitability or unsuitability to attain other ends, for instance to improve a nation's chance of defending its independence in war.

Those charging the economists with bias refer to their alleged eagerness to serve "the interests." In the context of their accusation this refers to selfish pursuit of the well-being of special groups to the prejudice of the common weal. Now it must be remembered that the idea of the common weal in the sense of a harmony of the interests of all members of society is a modern idea and that it owes its origin precisely to the teachings of the Classical economists. Older generations believed that there is an irreconcilable conflict of interests among men and among groups of men. The gain of one is invariably the damage of others; no man profits but by the loss of others. We may call this tenet the Montaigne dogma because in modern times it was first expounded by Montaigne. It was the essence of the teachings of Mercantilism and the main target of the Classical economists' critique of Mercantilism, to which they opposed their doctrine of the harmony of the rightly understood or long-run interests of all members of a market society. The socialists and interventionists reject the doctrine of the harmony of interests. The socialists declare that there is irreconcilable conflict among the interests of the various social classes of a nation; while the interests of the proletarians demand the substitution of socialism for capitalism, those of the exploiters demand the preservation of capitalism. The nationalists declare that the interests of the various nations are irreconcilably in conflict.

It is obvious that the antagonism of such incompatible doctrines can be resolved only by logical reasoning. But the opponents of the harmony doctrine are not prepared to submit their views to such examination. As soon as somebody criticizes their arguments and tries to prove the harmony doctrine they cry out bias. The mere fact that only they and not their adversaries, the supporters of the harmony doctrine, raise this reproach of bias shows clearly that they are unable to reject their opponents' statements by ratiocination. They engage in the examination of the problems concerned with the prepossession that only biased apologists of sinister interests can possibly contest the correctness of their socialist or interventionist dogmas. In their eyes the mere fact that a man disagrees with their ideas is the proof of his bias.

When carried to its ultimate logical consequences this attitude implies the doctrine of polylogism. Polylogism denies the uniformity of the logical structure of the human mind. Every social class, every nation, race, or period of history is equipped with a logic that differs from the logic of other classes, nations, races, or ages. Hence bourgeois economics differs from proletarian economics, German physics from the physics of other nations, Aryan mathematics from Semitic mathematics. There is no need to examine here the essentials of the various brands of polylogism.[1] For polylogism never went beyond the simple declaration that a diversity of the mind's logical structure exists. It never pointed out in what these differences consist, for instance *how* the logic of the proletarians differs from that of the bourgeois. All the champions of polylogism did was to reject definite statements by referring to unspecified peculiarities of their author's logic.

3. Economics and Value

The main argument of the Classical harmony doctrine starts from the distinction between interests in the short run and those in the long run, the latter being referred to as the rightly understood interests. Let us examine the bearing of this distinction upon the problem of privileges.

One group of men certainly gains by a privilege granted to them. A group of producers protected by a tariff, a subsidy, or any other modern protectionist method against the competition of more efficient rivals gains at the expense of the consumers. But will the rest of the nation, taxpayers and buyers of the protected article, tolerate the privilege of a minority? They will only acquiesce in it if they themselves are benefited by an analogous privilege. Then everybody loses as much in his capacity as consumer as he wins in his capacity

1. See Mises, *Human Action*, pp. 74–89.

as producer. Moreover all are harmed by the substitution of less efficient for more efficient methods of production.

If one deals with economic policies from the point of view of this distinction between long- and short-run interests, there is no ground for charging the economist with bias. He does not condemn featherbedding of the railroadmen because it benefits the railroadmen at the expense of other groups whom he likes better. He shows that the railroadmen cannot prevent featherbedding from becoming a general practice and that then, that is, in the long run, it hurts them no less than other people.

Of course, the objections the economists advanced to the plans of the socialists and interventionists carry no weight with those who do not approve of the ends which the peoples of Western civilization take for granted. Those who prefer penury and slavery to material well-being and all that can only develop where there is material well-being may deem all these objections irrelevant. But the economists have repeatedly emphasized that they deal with socialism and interventionism from the point of view of the generally accepted values of Western civilization. The socialists and interventionists not only have not—at least not openly—denied these values but have emphatically declared that the realization of their own program will achieve them much better than will capitalism.

It is true that most socialists and many interventionists attach value to equalizing the standard of living of all individuals. But the economists did not question the value judgment implied. All they did was to point out the inevitable consequences of equalization. They did not say: The end you are aiming at is bad; they said: Realization of this end will bring effects which you yourselves deem more undesirable than inequality.

4. *Bias and Intolerance*

It is obvious that there are many people who let their reasoning be influenced by judgments of value, and that bias often corrupts the thinking of men. What is to be rejected is the popular doctrine that it is impossible to deal with economic problems without bias and that mere reference to bias, without unmasking fallacies in the chain of reasoning, is sufficient to explode a theory.

The emergence of the bias doctrine implies in fact categorical acknowledgment of the impregnability of the teachings of economics against which the reproach of bias has been leveled. It was the first stage in the return to intolerance and persecution of dissenters which is one of the main features of our age. As dissenters are guilty of bias, it is right to "liquidate" them.

Chapter 3. The Quest for Absolute Values

1. The Issue

IN DEALING with judgments of value we refer to facts, that is, to the way in which people really choose ultimate ends. While the value judgments of many people are identical, while it is permissible to speak of certain almost universally accepted valuations, it would be manifestly contrary to fact to deny that there is diversity in passing judgments of value.

From time immemorial an immense majority of men have agreed in preferring the effects produced by peaceful cooperation—at least among a limited number of people—to the effects of a hypothetical isolation of each individual and a hypothetical war of all against all. To the state of nature they have preferred the state of civilization, for they sought the closest possible attainment of certain ends—the preservation of life and health—which, as they rightly thought, require social cooperation. But it is a fact that there have been and are also men who have rejected these values and consequently preferred the solitary life of an anchorite to life within society.

It is thus obvious that any scientific treatment of the problems of value judgments must take into full account the fact that these judgments are subjective and changing. Science seeks to know what is, and to formulate

35

existential propositions describing the universe as it is. With regard to judgments of value it cannot assert more than that they are uttered by some people, and inquire what the effects of action guided by them must be. Any step beyond these limits is tantamount to substituting a personal judgment of value for knowledge of reality. Science and our organized body of knowledge teach only what is, not what ought to be.

This distinction between a field of science dealing exclusively with existential propositions and a field of judgments of value has been rejected by the doctrines that maintain there are eternal absolute values which it is just as much the task of scientific or philosophical inquiry to discover as to discover the laws of physics. The supporters of these doctrines contend that there is an absolute hierarchy of values. They tried to define the supreme good. They said it is permissible and necessary to distinguish in the same way between true and false, correct and incorrect judgments of value as between true and false, correct and incorrect existential propositions.[1] Science is not restricted to the description of what is. There is, in their opinion, another fully legitimate branch of science, the normative science of ethics, whose task it is to show the true absolute values and to set up norms for the correct conduct of men.

The plight of our age, according to the supporters of this philosophy, is that people no longer acknowledge these eternal values and do not let their actions be guided by them. Conditions were much better in the

1. Franz Brentano, *Vom Ursprung sittlicher Erkenntnis,* 2d ed. Leipzig, 1921.

past, when the peoples of Western civilization were unanimous in endorsing the values of Christian ethics.

In what follows, we will deal with the issues raised by this philosophy.

2. Conflicts within Society

Having discussed the fact that men disagree with regard to their judgments of value and their choice of ultimate ends, we must stress that many conflicts which are commonly considered valuational are actually caused by disagreement concerning the choice of the best means to attain ends about which the conflicting parties agree. The problem of the suitability or unsuitability of definite means is to be solved by existential propositions, not by judgments of value. Its treatment is the main topic of applied science.

It is thus necessary to be aware in dealing with controversies concerning human conduct whether the disagreement refers to the choice of ends or to that of means. This is often a difficult task. For the same things are ends to some people, means to others.

With the exception of the small, almost negligible number of consistent anchorites, all people agree in considering some kind of social cooperation between men the foremost means to attain any ends they may aim at. This undeniable fact provides a common ground on which political discussions between men become possible. The spiritual and intellectual unity of all specimens of *homo sapiens* manifests itself in the fact that the immense majority of men consider the same thing

—social cooperation—the best means of satisfying the biological urge, present in every living being, to preserve the life and health of the individual and to propagate the species.

It is permissible to call this almost universal acceptance of social cooperation a natural phenomenon. In resorting to this mode of expression and asserting that conscious association is in conformity with human nature, one implies that man is characterized as man by reason, is thus enabled to become aware of the great principle of cosmic becoming and evolution, viz., differentiation and integration, and to make intentional use of this principle to improve his condition. But one must not consider cooperation among the individuals of a biological species a universal natural phenomenon. The means of sustenance are scarce for every species of living beings. Hence biological competition prevails among the members of all species, an irreconcilable conflict of vital "interests." Only a part of those who come into existence can survive. Some perish because others of their own species have snatched away from them the means of sustenance. An implacable struggle for existence goes on among the members of each species precisely because they are of the same species and compete with other members of it for the same scarce opportunities of survival and reproduction. Man alone by dint of his reason substituted social cooperation for biological competition. What made social cooperation possible is, of course, a natural phenomenon, the higher productivity of labor accomplished under the principle of the division of labor and specialization of tasks. But it was necessary to discover this principle, to comprehend its bearing upon human affairs, and to employ it consciously as a means in the struggle for existence.

The fundamental facts about social cooperation have been misinterpreted by the school of social Darwinism as well as by many of its critics. The former maintained that war among men is an inevitable phenomenon and that all attempts to bring about lasting peace among nations are contrary to nature. The latter retorted that the struggle for existence is not among members of the same animal species but among the members of various species. As a rule tigers do not attack other tigers but, taking the line of least resistance, weaker animals. Hence, they concluded, war among men, who are specimens of the same species, is unnatural.[1]

Both schools misunderstood the Darwinian concept of the struggle for survival. It does not refer merely to combat and blows. It means metaphorically the tenacious impulse of beings to keep alive in spite of all factors detrimental to them. As the means of sustenance are scarce, biological competition prevails among all individuals—whether of the same or different species—which feed on the same stuff. It is immaterial whether or not tigers fight one another. What makes every specimen of an animal species a deadly foe of every other specimen is the mere fact of their life-and-death rivalry in their endeavors to snatch a sufficient amount of food. This inexorable rivalry is present also among animals gregariously roaming in droves and flocks, among ants

1. On this controversy see Paul Barth, *Die Philosophie der Geschichte als Soziologie* (4th ed. Leipzig, 1922), pp. 289–92.

of the same hill and bees of the same swarm, among
the brood hatched by common parents and among the
seeds ripened by the same plant. Only man has the
power to escape to some extent from the rule of this
law by intentional cooperation. So long as there is social
cooperation and population has not increased beyond
the optimum size, biological competition is suspended.
It is therefore inappropriate to refer to animals and
plants in dealing with the social problems of man.

Yet man's almost universal acknowledgment of the
principle of social cooperation did not result in agreement regarding all interhuman relations. While almost
all men agree in looking upon social cooperation as the
foremost means for realizing all human ends, whatever
they may be, they disagree as to the extent to which
peaceful social cooperation is a suitable means for attaining their ends and how far it should be resorted to.

Those whom we may call the harmonists base their
argument on Ricardo's law of association and on
Malthus' principle of population. They do not, as some
of their critics believe, assume that all men are biologically equal. They take fully into account the fact
that there are innate biological differences among various groups of men as well as among individuals belonging to the same group. Ricardo's law has shown that
cooperation under the principle of the division of labor
is favorable to all participants. It is an advantage for
every man to cooperate with other men, even if these
others are in every respect—mental and bodily capacities and skills, diligence and moral worth—inferior.
From Malthus' principle one can deduce that there is,

in any given state of the supply of capital goods and knowledge of how to make the best use of natural resources, an optimum size of population. So long as population has not increased beyond this size, the addition of newcomers improves rather than impairs the conditions of those already cooperating.

In the philosophy of the antiharmonists, the various schools of nationalism and racism, two different lines of reasoning must be distinguished. One is the doctrine of the irreconcilable antagonism prevailing among various groups, such as nations or races. As the antiharmonists see it, community of interests exists only within the group among its members. The interests of each group and of each of its members are implacably opposed to those of all other groups and of each of their members. So it is "natural" there should be perpetual war among various groups. This natural state of war of each group against every other group may sometimes be interrupted by periods of armistice, falsely labeled periods of peace. It may also happen that sometimes in warfare a group cooperates in alliances with other groups. Such alliances are temporary makeshifts of politics. They do not in the long run affect the inexorable natural conflict of interests. Having, in cooperation with some allied groups, defeated several of the hostile groups, the leading group in the coalition turns against its previous allies in order to annihilate them too and to establish its own world supremacy.

The second dogma of the nationalist and racist philosophies is considered by its supporters a logical conclusion derived from their first dogma. As they see it, human conditions involve forever irreconcilable conflicts, first among the various groups fighting one another, later, after the final victory of the master group, between the latter and the enslaved rest of mankind. Hence this supreme elite group must always be ready to fight, first to crush the rival groups, then to quell rebellions of the slaves. The state of perpetual preparedness for war enjoins upon it the necessity of organizing society after the pattern of an army. The army is not an instrument destined to serve a body politic; it is rather the very essence of social cooperation, to which all other social institutions are subservient. The individuals are not citizens of a commonwealth; they are soldiers of a fighting force and as such bound to obey unconditionally the orders issued by the supreme commander. They have no civil rights, merely military duties.

Thus even the fact that the immense majority of men look upon social cooperation as the foremost means to attain all desired ends does not provide a basis for a wide-reaching agreement concerning either ends or means.

3. A Remark on the Alleged Medieval Unanimity

In examining the doctrines of eternal absolute values we must also ask whether it is true or not that there was a period of history in which all peoples of the West were united in their acceptance of a uniform system of ethical norms.

Until the beginning of the fourth century the Christian creed was spread by voluntary conversions. There were also later voluntary conversions of individuals and of whole peoples. But from the days of Theodosius I on, the sword began to play a prominent role in the dissemination of Christianity. Pagans and heretics were compelled by force of arms to submit to the Christian teachings. For many centuries religious problems were decided by the outcome of battles and wars. Military campaigns determined the religious allegiance of nations. Christians of the East were forced to accept the creed of Mohammed, and pagans in Europe and America were forced to accept the Christian faith. Secular power was instrumental in the struggle between the Reformation and the Counter Reformation.

There was religious uniformity in Europe of the Middle Ages as both paganism and heresies were eradicated with fire and sword. All of Western and Central Europe recognized the Pope as the Vicar of Christ. But this did not mean that all people agreed in their judgments of value and in the principles directing their conduct. There were few people in medieval Europe who lived according to the precepts of the Gospels. Much has been said and written about the truly Christian spirit of the code of chivalry and about the religious idealism that guided the conduct of the knights. Yet anything less compatible with Luke 6:27-9 than the rules of chivalry can hardly be conceived. The gallant knights certainly did not love their enemies, they did not bless those who cursed them, and they did not offer the left cheek to him who smote them on the right cheek. The Catholic Church had the power to prevent

scholars and writers from challenging the dogmas as
defined by the Pope and the Councils and to force the
secular rulers to yield to some of its political claims.
But it could preserve its position only by condoning
conduct on the part of the laity which defied most, if
not all, of the principles of the Gospels. The values that
determined the actions of the ruling classes were entirely different from those that the Church preached.
Neither did the peasants comply with Matthew 6:25-8.
And there were courts and judges in defiance of Matthew 7:1: "Judge not, that you be not judged."

4. *The Idea of Natural Law*

The most momentous attempt to find an absolute and
eternal standard of value is presented by the doctrine
of natural law.

The term "natural law" has been claimed by various
schools of philosophy and jurisprudence. Many doctrines have appealed to nature in order to provide a
justification for their postulates. Many manifestly spurious theses have been advanced under the label of natural law. It was not difficult to explode the fallacies common to most of these lines of thought. And it is no
wonder that many thinkers become suspicious as soon
as natural law is referred to.

Yet it would be a serious blunder to ignore the fact
that all the varieties of the doctrine contained a sound
idea which could neither be compromised by connection with untenable vagaries nor discredited by any
criticism. Long before the Classical economists discov-

ered that a regularity in the sequence of phenomena prevails in the field of human action, the champions of natural law were dimly aware of this inescapable fact. From the bewildering diversity of doctrines presented under the rubric of natural law there finally emerged a set of theorems which no caviling can ever invalidate. There is first the idea that a nature-given order of things exists to which man must adjust his actions if he wants to succeed. Second: the only means available to man for the cognizance of this order is thinking and reasoning, and no existing social institution is exempt from being examined and appraised by discursive reasoning. Third: there is no standard available for appraising any mode of acting either of individuals or of groups of individuals but that of the effects produced by such action. Carried to its ultimate logical consequences, the idea of natural law led eventually to rationalism and utilitarianism.

The march of social philosophy toward this inescapable conclusion was slowed down by many obstacles which could not be removed easily. There were numerous pitfalls on the way, and many inhibitions hampered the philosophers. To deal with the vicissitudes of the evolution of these doctrines is a task of the history of philosophy. In the context of our investigation it is enough to mention only two of these problems.

There was the antagonism between the teachings of reason and the dogmas of the Church. Some philosophers were prepared to ascribe unconditional supremacy to the latter. Truth and certainty, they declared, are to be found only in revelation. Man's reason can err, and man can never be sure that his speculations were not led astray by Satan. Other thinkers did not accept this solution of the antagonism. To reject reason beforehand was in their opinion preposterous. Reason too stems from God, who endowed man with it, so there can be no genuine contradiction between dogma and the correct teachings of reason. It is the task of philosophy to show that ultimately both agree. The central problem of Scholastic philosophy was to demonstrate that human reason, unaided by revelation and Holy Writ, taking recourse only to its proper methods of ratiocination, is capable of proving the apodictic truth of the revealed dogmas.[1] A genuine conflict of faith and reason does not exist. Natural law and divine law do not disagree.

However, this way of dealing with the matter does not remove the antagonism; it merely shifts it to another field. The conflict is no longer a conflict between faith and reason but between Thomist philosophy and other modes of philosophizing. We may leave aside the genuine dogmas such as Creation, Incarnation, the Trinity, as they have no direct bearing on the problems of interhuman relations. But many issues remain with regard to which most, if not all, Christian churches and denominations are not prepared to yield to secular reasoning and an evaluation from the point of view of social utility. Thus the recognition of natural law on the part of Christian theology was only conditional. It referred to a definite type of natural law, not opposed

1. Louis Rougier, *La Scholastique et le Thomisme* (Paris, 1925), pp. 102–5, 116–17, 460–562.

to the teachings of Christ as each of these churches and denominations interpreted them. It did not acknowledge the supremacy of reason. It was incompatible with the principles of utilitarian philosophy.

A second factor that obstructed the evolution of natural law toward a consistent and comprehensive system of human action was the erroneous theory of the biological equality of all men. In repudiating arguments advanced in favor of legal discrimination among men and of a status society, many advocates of equality before the law overstepped the mark. To hold that "at birth human infants, regardless of their heredity, are as equal as Fords" [2] is to deny facts so obvious that it brought the whole philosophy of natural law into disrepute. In insisting on biological equality the natural law doctrine pushed aside all the sound arguments advanced in favor of the principle of equality before the law. It thus opened the way for the spread of theories advocating all sorts of legal discrimination against individuals and groups of individuals. It supplanted the teachings of liberal social philosophy. Stirring up hatred and violence, foreign wars and domestic revolutions, it prepared mankind for the acceptance of aggressive nationalism and racism.

The chief accomplishment of the natural law idea was its rejection of the doctrine (sometimes called legal positivism) according to which the ultimate source of statute law is to be seen in the superior military power of the legislator who is in a position to beat into sub-

2. Horace M. Kallen, "Behaviorism," *Encyclopaedia of the Social Sciences* (Macmillan, 1930–35), 3, 498.

mission all those defying his ordinances. Natural law taught that statutory laws can be bad laws, and it contrasted with the bad laws the good laws to which it ascribed divine or natural origin. But it was an illusion to deny that the best system of laws cannot be put into practice unless supported and enforced by military supremacy. The philosophers shut their eyes to manifest historical facts. They refused to admit that the causes they considered just made progress only because their partisans defeated the defenders of the bad causes. The Christian faith owes it success to a long series of victorious battles and campaigns, from various battles between rival Roman imperators and caesars down to the campaigns that opened the Orient to the activities of missionaries. The cause of American independence triumphed because the British forces were defeated by the insurgents and the French. It is a sad truth that Mars is for the big battalions, not for the good causes. To maintain the opposite opinion implies the belief that the outcome of an armed conflict is an ordeal by combat in which God always grants victory to the champions of the just cause. But such an assumption would annul all the essentials of the doctrine of natural law, whose basic idea was to contrast to the positive laws, promulgated and enforced by those in power, a "higher" law grounded in the innermost nature of man.

Yet all these deficiencies and contradictions of the doctrine of natural law must not prevent us from recognizing its sound nucleus. Hidden in a heap of illusions and quite arbitrary prepossessions was the idea that

every valid law of a country was open to critical examination by reason. About the standard to be applied
in such an examination the older representatives of the
school had only vague notions. They referred to nature
and were reluctant to admit that the ultimate standard
of good and bad must be found in the effects produced
by a law. Utilitarianism finally completed the intellectual evolution inaugurated by the Greek Sophists.

But neither utilitarianism nor any of the varieties of
the doctrine of natural law could or did find a way to
eliminate the conflict of antagonistic judgments of
value. It is useless to emphasize that nature is the ultimate arbiter of what is right and what is wrong. Nature
does not clearly reveal its plans and intentions to man.
Thus the appeal to natural law does not settle the dispute. It merely substitutes dissent concerning the interpretation of natural law for dissenting judgments of
value. Utilitarianism, on the other hand, does not deal
at all with ultimate ends and judgments of value. It
invariably refers only to means.

5. Revelation

Revealed religion derives its authority and authenticity from the communication to man of the Supreme
Being's will. It gives the faithful indisputable certainty.

However, people disagree widely about the content
of revealed truth as well as about its correct—orthodox
—interpretation. For all the grandeur, majesty, and sub-
limity of religious feeling, irreconcilable conflict exists
among various faiths and creeds. Even if unanimity

could be attained in matters of the historical authenticity and reliability of revelation, the problem of the veracity of various exegetic interpretations would still remain.

Every faith claims to possess absolute certainty. But no religious faction knows of any peaceful means that will invariably induce dissenters to divest themselves voluntarily of their error and to adopt the true creed.

If people of different faiths meet for peaceful discussion of their differences, they can find no common basis for their colloquy but the statement: by their fruits ye shall know them. Yet this utilitarian device is of no use so long as men disagree about the standard to be applied in judging the effects.

The religious appeal to absolute eternal values did not do away with conflicting judgments of value. It merely resulted in religious wars.

6. *Atheistic Intuition*

Other attempts to discover an absolute standard of values were made without reference to a divine reality. Emphatically rejecting all traditional religions and claiming for their teachings the epithet "scientific," various writers tried to substitute a new faith for the old ones. They claimed to know precisely what the mysterious power that directs all cosmic becoming has in store for mankind. They proclaimed an absolute standard of values. Good is what works along the lines that this power wants mankind to follow; everything else is bad. In their vocabulary "progressive" is a synonym of good and "reactionary" a synonym of bad. Inevitably progress will triumph over reaction because it is impossible for men to divert the course of history from the direction prescribed by the plan of the mysterious prime mover. Such is the metaphysics of Karl Marx, the faith of contemporary self-styled progressivism.

Marxism is a revolutionary doctrine. It expressly declares that the design of the prime mover will be accomplished by civil war. It implies that ultimately in the battles of these campaigns the just cause, that is, the cause of progress, must conquer. Then all conflicts concerning judgments of value will disappear. The liquidation of all dissenters will establish the undisputed supremacy of the absolute eternal values.

This formula for the solution of conflicts of value judgments is certainly not new. It is a device known and practiced from time immemorial. Kill the infidels! Burn the heretics! What is new is merely the fact that today it is sold to the public under the label of "science."

7. *The Idea of Justice*

One of the motives that impel men to search for an absolute and immutable standard of value is the presumption that peaceful cooperation is possible only among people guided by the same judgments of value.

It is obvious that social cooperation would not have evolved and could not be preserved if the immense majority were not to consider it as the means for the attainment of all their ends. Striving after the preserva-

tion of his own life and health and after the best possible removal of felt uneasiness, the individual looks
upon society as a means, not as an end. There is no
perfect unanimity even with regard to this point. But
we may neglect the dissent of the ascetics and the anchorites, not because they are few, but because their
plans are not affected if other people, in the pursuit of
their plans, cooperate in society.

There prevails among the members of society disagreement with regard to the best method for its
organization. But this is a dissent concerning means,
not ultimate ends. The problems involved can be discussed without any reference to judgments of value.

Of course, almost all people, guided by the traditional manner of dealing with ethical precepts, peremptorily repudiate such an explanation of the issue. Social
institutions, they assert, must be just. It is base to judge
them merely according to their fitness to attain definite
ends, however desirable these ends may be from any
other point of view. What matters first is justice. The
extreme formulation of this idea is to be found in the
famous phrase: *fiat justitia, pereat mundus*. Let justice
be done, even if it destroys the world. Most supporters
of the postulate of justice will reject this maxim as extravagant, absurd, and paradoxical. But it is not more
absurd, merely more shocking, than any other reference
to an arbitrary notion of absolute justice. It clearly
shows the fallacies of the methods applied in the discipline of intuitive ethics.

The procedure of this normative quasi science is to
derive certain precepts from intuition and to deal with

them as if their adoption as a guide to action would not affect the attainment of any other ends considered desirable. The moralists do not bother about the necessary consequences of the realization of their postulates. We need not discuss the attitudes of people for whom the appeal to justice is manifestly a pretext, consciously or subconsciously chosen, to disguise their short-run interests, nor expose the hypocrisy of such makeshift notions of justice as those involved in the popular concepts of just prices and fair wages.[1] The philosophers who in their treatises of ethics assigned supreme value to justice and applied the yardstick of justice to all social institutions were not guilty of such deceit. They did not support selfish group concerns by declaring them alone just, fair, and good, and smear all dissenters by depicting them as the apologists of unfair causes. They were Platonists who believed that a perennial idea of absolute justice exists and that it is the duty of man to organize all human institutions in conformity with this ideal. Cognition of justice is imparted to man by an inner voice, i.e., by intuition. The champions of this doctrine did not ask what the consequences of realizing the schemes they called just would be. They silently assumed either that these consequences will be beneficial or that mankind is bound to put up even with very painful consequences of justice. Still less did these teachers of morality pay attention to the fact that people can and really do disagree with regard to the interpretation of the inner voice and that no method of peacefully settling such disagreements can be found.

1. See Mises, *Human Action*, pp. 719–25.

All these ethical doctrines have failed to comprehend that there is, outside of social bonds and preceding, temporally or logically, the existence of society, nothing to which the epithet "just" can be given. A hypothetical isolated individual must under the pressure of biological competition look upon all other people as deadly foes. His only concern is to preserve his own life and health; he does not need to heed the consequences which his own survival has for other men; he has no use for justice. His only solicitudes are hygiene and defense. But in social cooperation with other men the individual is forced to abstain from conduct incompatible with life in society. Only then does the distinction between what is just and what is unjust emerge. It invariably refers to interhuman social relations. What is beneficial to the individual without affecting his fellows, such as the observance of certain rules in the use of some drugs, remains hygiene.

The ultimate yardstick of justice is conduciveness to the preservation of social cooperation. Conduct suited to preserve social cooperation is just, conduct detrimental to the preservation of society is unjust. There cannot be any question of organizing society according to the postulates of an arbitrary preconceived idea of justice. The problem is to organize society for the best possible realization of those ends which men want to attain by social cooperation. Social utility is the only standard of justice. It is the sole guide of legislation.

Thus there are no irreconcilable conflicts between selfishness and altruism, between economics and ethics, between the concerns of the individual and those of society. Utilitarian philosophy and its finest product, economics, reduced these apparent antagonisms to the opposition of short-run and long-run interests. Society could not have come into existence or been preserved without a harmony of the rightly understood interests of all its members.

There is only one way of dealing with all problems of social organization and the conduct of the members of society, viz., the method applied by praxeology and economics. No other method can contribute anything to the elucidation of these matters.

The concept of justice as employed by jurisprudence refers to legality, that is, to legitimacy from the point of view of the valid statutes of a country. It means justice *de lege lata*. The science of law has nothing to say *de lege ferenda*, i.e., about the laws as they ought to be. To enact new laws and to repeal old laws is the task of the legislature, whose sole criterion is social utility. The assistance the legislator can expect from lawyers refers only to matters of legal technique, not to the gist of the statutes and decrees.

There is no such thing as a normative science, a science of what ought to be.

8. *The Utilitarian Doctrine Restated*

The essential teachings of utilitarian philosophy as applied to the problems of society can be restated as follows:

Human effort exerted under the principle of the division of labor in social cooperation achieves, other things remaining equal, a greater output per unit of input than the isolated efforts of solitary individuals. Man's reason is capable of recognizing this fact and of adapting his conduct accordingly. Thus social cooperation becomes for almost every man the great means for the attainment of all ends. An eminently human common interest, the preservation and intensification of social bonds, is substituted for pitiless biological competition, the significant mark of animal and plant life. Man becomes a social being. He is no longer forced by the inevitable laws of nature to look upon all other specimens of his animal species as deadly foes. Other people become his fellows. For animals the generation of every new member of the species means the appearance of a new rival in the struggle for life. For man, until the optimum size of population is reached, it means rather an improvement than a deterioration in his quest for material well-being.

Notwithstanding all his social achievements man remains in biological structure a mammal. His most urgent needs are nourishment, warmth, and shelter. Only when these wants are satisfied can he concern himself with other needs, peculiar to the human species and therefore called specifically human or higher needs. Also the satisfaction of these depends as a rule, at least to some extent, on the availability of various material tangible things.

As social cooperation is for acting man a means and not an end, no unanimity with regard to value judgments is required to make it work. It is a fact that almost all men agree in aiming at certain ends, at those pleasures which ivory-tower moralists disdain as base and shabby. But it is no less a fact that even the most sublime ends cannot be sought by people who have not first satisfied the wants of their animal body. The loftiest exploits of philosophy, art, and literature would never have been performed by men living outside of society.

Moralists praise the nobility of people who seek a thing for its own sake. "Deutsch sein heisst eine Sache um ihrer selbst willen tun," declared Richard Wagner,[1] and the Nazis, of all people, adopted the dictum as a fundamental principle of their creed. Now what is sought as an ultimate end is valued according to the immediate satisfaction to be derived from its attainment. There is no harm in declaring elliptically that it is sought for its own sake. Then Wagner's phrase is reduced to the truism: Ultimate ends are ends and not means for the attainment of other ends.

Moralists furthermore level against utilitarianism the charge of (ethical) materialism. Here too they misconstrue the utilitarian doctrine. Its gist is the cognition that action pursues definite chosen ends and that consequently there can be no other standard for appraising conduct but the desirability or undesirability of its effects. The precepts of ethics are designed to preserve, not to destroy, the "world." They may call upon people to put up with undesirable short-run effects in order to avoid producing still more undesirable long-run effects. But they must never recommend actions whose effects they themselves deem undesirable for the sole

1. In *Deutsche Kunst und Deutsche Politik*, Sämtliche Werke (6th ed. Leipzig, Breitkopf and Härtel), 8, 96.

purpose of not defying an arbitrary rule derived from
intuition. The formula *fiat justitia, pereat mundus* is
exploded as sheer nonsense. An ethical doctrine that
does not take into full account the effects of action is
mere fancy.

Utilitarianism does not teach that people should
strive only after sensuous pleasure (though it recog-
nizes that most or at least many people behave in this
way). Neither does it indulge in judgments of value. By
its recognition that social cooperation is for the immense majority a means for attaining all their ends, it
dispels the notion that society, the state, the nation, or
any other social entity is an ultimate end and that individual men are the slaves of that entity. It rejects the
philosophies of universalism, collectivism, and totalitarianism. In this sense it is meaningful to call utilitarianism a philosophy of individualism.

The collectivist doctrine fails to recognize that social
cooperation is for man a means for the attainment of all
his ends. It assumes that irreconcilable conflict prevails
between the interests of the collective and those of individuals, and in this conflict it sides unconditionally
with the collective entity. The collective alone has real
existence; the individuals' existence is conditioned by
that of the collective. The collective is perfect and can
do no wrong. Individuals are wretched and refractory;
their obstinacy must be curbed by the authority to
which God or nature has entrusted the conduct of
society's affairs. The powers that be, says the Apostle
Paul, are ordained of God.[2] They are ordained by nature

2. Epistle to the Romans 13:1.

or by the superhuman factor that directs the course of all cosmic events, says the atheist collectivist.

Two questions immediately arise. First: If it were true that the interests of the collective and those of individuals are implacably opposed to one another, how could society function? One may assume that the individuals would be prevented by force of arms from resorting to open rebellion. But it cannot be assumed that their active cooperation could be secured by mere compulsion. A system of production in which the only incentive to work is the fear of punishment cannot last. It was this fact that made slavery disappear as a system of managing production.

Second: If the collective is not a means by which individuals may achieve their ends, if the collective's flowering requires sacrifices by the individuals which are not outweighed by advantages derived from social cooperation, what prompts the advocate of collectivism to assign to the concerns of the collective precedence over the personal wishes of the individuals? Can any argument be advanced for such exaltation of the collective but personal judgments of value?

Of course, everybody's judgments of value are personal. If a man assigns a higher value to the concerns of a collective than to his other concerns, and acts accordingly, that is his affair. So long as the collectivist philosophers proceed in this way, no objection can be raised. But they argue differently. They elevate their personal judgments of value to the dignity of an absolute standard of value. They urge other people to stop valuing according to their own will and to adopt unconditionally the precepts to which collectivism has assigned absolute eternal validity.

The futility and arbitrariness of the collectivist point of view become still more evident when one recalls that various collectivist parties compete for the exclusive allegiance of the individuals. Even if they employ the same word for their collectivist ideal, various writers and leaders disagree on the essential features of the thing they have in mind. The state which Ferdinand Lassalle called god and to which he assigned paramountcy was not precisely the collectivist idol of Hegel and Stahl, the state of the Hohenzollern. Is mankind as a whole the sole legitimate collective or is each of the various nations? Is the collective to which the German-speaking Swiss owe exclusive allegiance the Swiss Confederacy or the *Volksgemeinschaft* comprising all German-speaking men? All major social entities such as nations, linguistic groups, religious communities, party organizations have been elevated to the dignity of the supreme collective that overshadows all other collectives and claims the submission of the whole personality of all right-thinking men. But an individual can renounce autonomous action and unconditionally surrender his self only in favor of *one* collective. Which collective this ought to be can be determined only by a quite arbitrary decision. The collective creed is by necessity exclusive and totalitarian. It craves the whole man and does not want to share him with any other collective. It seeks to establish the exclusive supreme validity of only one system of values.

There is, of course, but one way to make one's own

judgments of value supreme. One must beat into sub-mission all those dissenting. This is what all representa-tives of the various collectivist doctrines are striving for. They ultimately recommend the use of violence and pitiless annihilation of all those whom they condemn as heretics. Collectivism is a doctrine of war, intolerance, and persecution. If any of the collectivist creeds should succeed in its endeavors, all people but the great dicta-tor would be deprived of their essential human quality. They would become mere soulless pawns in the hands of a monster.

The characteristic feature of a free society is that it can function in spite of the fact that its members dis-agree in many judgments of value. In the market economy business serves not only the majority but also various minorities, provided they are not too small in respect of the economic goods which satisfying their special wishes would require. Philosophical treatises are published—though few people read them, and the masses prefer other books or none—if enough readers are foreseen to recover the costs.

9. *On Aesthetic Values*

The quest for absolute standards of value was not limited to the field of ethics. It concerned aesthetic values as well.

In ethics a common ground for the choice of rules of conduct is given so far as people agree in considering the preservation of social cooperation the foremost means for attaining all their ends. Thus virtually any controversy concerning the rules of conduct refers to means and not to ends. It is consequently possible to appraise these rules from the point of view of their adequacy for the peaceful functioning of society. Even rigid supporters of an intuitionist ethics could not help eventually resorting to an appraisal of conduct from the point of view of its effects upon human happiness.[1]

It is different with aesthetic judgments of value. In this field there is no such agreement as prevails with regard to the insight that social cooperation is the foremost means for the attainment of all ends. All disagreement here invariably concerns judgments of value, none the choice of means for the realization of an end agreed upon. There is no way to reconcile conflicting judgments. There is no standard by which a verdict of "it pleases me" or "it does not please me" can be rectified.

The unfortunate propensity to hypostatize various aspects of human thinking and acting has led to attempts to provide a definition of beauty and then to apply this arbitrary concept as a measure. However there is no acceptable definition of beauty but "that which pleases." There are no norms of beauty, and there is no such thing as a normative discipline of aesthetics. All that a professional critic of art and literature can say apart from historical and technical observations is that he likes or dislikes a work. The work may stir him to profound commentaries and disquisitions. But his judgments of value remain personal and subjective and do

1. Even Kant. See *Kritik der praktischen Vernunft*, Pt. I, Bk. II, Sec. I (Insel-Ausgabe, 5, 240–1). Compare Friedrich Jodl, *Geschichte der Ethik* (2d ed. Stuttgart, 1912), 2, 35–8.

not necessarily affect the judgments of other people. A discerning person will note with interest what a thoughtful writer says about the impression a work of art made upon him. But it depends upon a man's own discretion whether or not he will let his own judgment be influenced by that of other men, however excellent they may be.

The enjoyment of art and literature presupposes a certain disposition and susceptibility on the part of the public. Taste is inborn to only a few. Others must cultivate their aptitude for enjoyment. There are many things a man must learn and experience in order to become a connoisseur. But however a man may shine as a well-informed expert, his judgments of value remain personal and subjective. The most eminent critics and, for that matter, also the most noted writers, poets and artists widely disagreed in their appreciation of the most famous masterpieces.

Only stilted pedants can conceive the idea that there are absolute norms to tell what is beautiful and what is not. They try to derive from the works of the past a code of rules with which, as they fancy, the writers and artists of the future should comply. But the genius does not cooperate with the pundit.

10. *The Historical Significance of the Quest for Absolute Values*

The value controversy is not a scholastic quarrel of interest only to hair-splitting dons. It touches upon the vital issues of human life.

The world view that was displaced by modern rationalism did not tolerate dissenting judgments of value. The mere fact of dissent was considered an insolent provocation, a mortal outrage to one's own feelings. Protracted religious wars resulted.

Although some intolerance, bigotry, and lust for persecution is still left in religious matters, it is unlikely that religious passion will kindle wars in the near future. The aggressive spirit of our age stems from another source, from endeavors to make the state totalitarian and to deprive the individual of autonomy.

It is true that the supporters of socialist and interventionist programs recommend them only as means to attain ends which they have in common with all other members of society. They hold that a society organized according to their principles will best supply people with those material goods they toil to acquire. What more desirable societal state of affairs can be thought of than that "higher phase of communist society" in which, as Marx told us, society will give "to each according to his needs"?

However, the socialists failed entirely in attempts to prove their case. Marx was at a loss to refute the well-founded objections that were raised even in his time about the minor difficulties of the socialist schemes. It was his helplessness in this regard that prompted him to develop the three fundamental doctrines of his dogmatism.[1] When economics later demonstrated why a socialist order, necessarily lacking any method of eco-

1. Mises, *Socialism* (new ed., New Haven, Yale University Press, 1951), pp. 15–16.

nomic calculation, could never function as an economic system, all arguments advanced in favor of the great reform collapsed. From that time on socialists no longer based their hopes upon the power of their arguments but upon the resentment, envy, and hatred of the masses. Today even the adepts of "scientific" socialism rely exclusively upon these emotional factors. The basis of contemporary socialism and interventionism is judgments of value. Socialism is praised as the only fair variety of society's economic organization. All socialists, Marxians as well as non-Marxians, advocate socialism as the only system consonant with a scale of arbitrarily established absolute values. These values, they claim, are the only values that are valid for all decent people, foremost among them the workers, the majority in a modern industrial society. They are considered absolute because they are supported by the majority—and the majority is always right.

A rather superficial and shallow view of the problems of government saw the distinction between freedom and despotism in an outward feature of the system of rule and administration, viz., in the number of people exercising direct control of the social apparatus of coercion and compulsion. Such a numerical standard is the basis of Aristotle's famous classification of the various forms of government. The concepts of monarchy, oligarchy, and democracy still preserve this way of dealing with the matter. Yet its inadequacy is so obvious that no philosopher could avoid referring to facts which did not agree with it and therefore were considered paradoxical. There was for instance the fact, already well recognized by Greek authors, that tyranny was often, or even regularly, supported by the masses and was in this sense popular government. Modern writers have employed the term "Caesarism" for this type of government and have continued to look upon it as an exceptional case conditioned by peculiar circumstances; but they have been at a loss to explain satisfactorily what made the conditions exceptional. Yet, fascinated by the traditional classification, people acquiesced in this superficial interpretation as long as it seemed that it had to explain only one case in modern European history, that of the second French Empire. The final collapse of the Aristotelian doctrine came only when it had to face the "dictatorship of the proletariat" and the autocracy of Hitler, Mussolini, Peron, and other modern successors of the Greek tyrants.

The way toward a realistic distinction between freedom and bondage was opened, two hundred years ago, by David Hume's immortal essay, *On the First Principles of Government.* Government, taught Hume, is always government of the many by the few. Power is therefore always ultimately on the side of the governed, and the governors have nothing to support them but opinion. This cognition, logically followed to its conclusion, completely changed the discussion concerning liberty. The mechanical and arithmetical point of view was abandoned. If public opinion is ultimately responsible for the structure of government, it is also the agency that determines whether there is freedom or bondage. There is virtually only one factor that has the power to make people unfree—tyrannical public opinion. The struggle for freedom is ultimately not resistance to autocrats or oligarchs but resistance to the despotism of public opinion. It is not the struggle of the many against the few but of minorities—sometimes of a minority of but one man—against the majority. The worst and most dangerous form of absolutist rule is that of an intolerant majority. Such is the conclusion arrived at by Tocqueville and John Stuart Mill.

In his essay on Bentham, Mill pointed out why this eminent philosopher failed to see the real issue and why his doctrine found acceptance with some of the noblest spirits. Bentham, he says, lived "in a time of reaction against the aristocratic governments of modern Europe." The reformers of his age "have been accustomed to see the numerical majority everywhere unjustly depressed, everywhere trampled upon, or at the best overlooked, by governments." In such an age one could easily forget that "all countries which have long continued progressive, or been durably great, have been so because there has been an organized opposition to the ruling power, of whatever kind that power was. . . . Almost all the greatest men who ever lived have formed part of such an opposition. Wherever some such quarrel has not been going on—wherever it has been terminated by the complete victory of one of the contending principles, and no new contest has taken the place of the old— society has either hardened into Chinese stationariness, or fallen into dissolution." [2]

Much of what was sound in Bentham's political doctrines was slighted by his contemporaries, was denied by

2. John Stuart Mill on Bentham, ed. by F. R. Leavis under the title *Mill on Bentham and Coleridge* (New York, Stewart, 1950), pp. 85–7.

later generations, and had little practical influence. But his failure to distinguish correctly between despotism and liberty was accepted without qualms by most nineteenth-century writers. In their eyes true liberty meant the unbridled despotism of the majority.

Lacking the power to think logically, and ignorant of history as well as of theory, the much admired "progressive" writers gave up the essential idea of the Enlightenment: freedom of thought, speech, and communication. Not all of them were so outspoken as Comte and Lenin; but they all, in declaring that freedom means only the right to say the correct things, not also the right to say the wrong things, virtually converted the ideas of freedom of thought and conscience into their opposite. It was not the Syllabus of Pope Pius IX that paved the way for the return of intolerance and the persecution of dissenters. It was the writings of the socialists. After a short-lived triumph of the idea of freedom, bondage made a comeback disguised as a consummation and completion of the philosophy of freedom, as the finishing of the unfinished revolution, as the final emancipation of the individual.

The concept of absolute and eternal values is an indispensable element in this totalitarian ideology. A new notion of truth was established. Truth is what those in power declare to be true. The dissenting minority is undemocratic because it refuses to accept as true the opinion of the majority. All means to "liquidate" such rebellious scoundrels are "democratic" and therefore morally good.

Chapter 4. The Negation of Valuation

IN DEALING with judgments of value we have looked upon them as ultimate data not liable to any reduction to other data. We do not contend that judgments of value as they are uttered by men and used as guides to action are primary facts independent of all the other conditions of the universe. Such an assumption would be preposterous. Man is a part of the universe, he is the product of the forces operating in it, and all his thoughts and actions are, like the stars, the atoms, and the animals, elements of nature. They are embedded in the inexorable concatenation of all phenomena and events.

Saying that judgments of value are ultimately given facts means that the human mind is unable to trace them back to those facts and happenings with which the natural sciences deal. We do not know why and how definite conditions of the external world arouse in a human mind a definite reaction. We do not know why different people and the same people at various instants of their lives react differently to the same external stimuli. We cannot discover the necessary connection between an external event and the ideas it produces within the human mind.

To clarify this issue we must now analyze the doctrines supporting the contrary opinion. We must deal with all varieties of materialism.

PART TWO. DETERMINISM AND MATERIALISM

Chapter 5. Determinism and Its Critics

1. Determinism

WHATEVER the true nature of the universe and of reality may be, man can learn about it only what the logical structure of his mind makes comprehensible to him. Reason, the sole instrument of human science and philosophy, does not convey absolute knowledge and final wisdom. It is vain to speculate about ultimate things. What appears to man's inquiry as an ultimate given, defying further analysis and reduction to something more fundamental, may or may not appear such to a more perfect intellect. We do not know.

Man cannot grasp either the concept of absolute nothingness or that of the genesis of something out of nothing. The very idea of creation transcends his comprehension. The God of Abraham, Isaac, and Jacob, whom Pascal in his Mémorial opposed to that of the "philosophes et savants," is a living image and has a clear and definite meaning for the faithful believer. But the philosophers in their endeavors to construct a concept of God, his attributes, and his conduct of world affairs, became involved in insoluble contradictions and paradoxes. A God whose essence and ways of acting mortal man could neatly circumscribe and define would not resemble the God of the prophets, the saints, and the mystics.

The logical structure of his mind enjoins upon man determinism and the category of causality. As man sees it, whatever happens in the universe is the necessary evolution of forces, powers, and qualities which were already present in the initial stage of the X out of which all things stem. All things in the universe are interconnected, and all changes are the effects of powers inherent in things. No change occurs that would not be the necessary consequence of the preceding state. All facts are dependent upon and conditioned by their causes. No deviation from the necessary course of affairs is possible. Eternal law regulates everything.

In this sense determinism is the epistemological basis of the human search for knowledge[1] Man cannot even conceive the image of an undetermined universe. In such a world there could not be any awareness of material things and their changes. It would appear a senseless chaos. Nothing could be identified and distinguished from anything else. Nothing could be expected and predicted. In the midst of such an environment man would be as helpless as if spoken to in an unknown language. No action could be designed, still less put into execution. Man is what he is because he lives in a world of regularity and has the mental power to conceive the relation of cause and effect.

Any epistemological speculation must lead toward determinism. But the acceptance of determinism raises some theoretical difficulties that have seemed to be in-

1. "La science est déterministe; elle l'est a priori; elle postule le déterminisme, parce que sans lui elle ne pourrait être." Henri Poincaré, Dernières pensées (Paris, Flammarion, 1913), p. 244.

soluble. While no philosophy has disproved determinism, there are some ideas that people have not been able to bring into agreement with it. Passionate attacks have been directed against it because people believed that it must ultimately result in absurdity.

2. *The Negation of Ideological Factors*

Many authors have assumed that determinism, fully implying consistent materialism, strictly denies that mental acts play any role in the course of events. Causation, in the context of the doctrine so understood, means mechanical causation. All changes are brought about by material entities, processes, and events. Ideas are just intermediary stages in the process through which a material factor produces a definite material effect. They have no autonomous existence. They merely mirror the state of the material entities that begot them. There is no history of ideas and of actions directed by them, only a history of the evolution of the real factors that engender ideas.

From the point of view of this integral materialism, the only consistent materialist doctrine, the customary methods of historians and biographers are to be rejected as idealistic nonsense. It is vain to search for the development of certain ideas out of other previously held ideas. For example, it is "unscientific" to describe how the philosophical ideas of the seventeenth and eighteenth centuries evolved out of those of the sixteenth century. "Scientific" history would have to describe how out of the real—physical and biological—conditions of each age its philosophical tenets necessarily spring. It is "unscientific" to describe as a mental process the evolution of Saint Augustine's ideas that led him from Cicero to Manichaeus and from Manichaeism to Catholicism. The "scientific" biographer would have to reveal the physiological processes that necessarily resulted in the corresponding philosophical doctrines.

The examination of materialism is a task to be left to the following chapters. At this point it is enough to establish the fact that determinism in itself does not imply any concessions to the materialist standpoint. It does not negate the obvious truth that ideas have an existence of their own, contribute to the emergence of other ideas, and influence one another. It does not deny mental causation and does not reject history as a metaphysical and idealistic illusion.

3. *The Free-Will Controversy*

Man chooses between modes of action incompatible with one another. Such decisions, says the free-will doctrine, are basically undetermined and uncaused; they are not the inevitable outcome of antecedent conditions. They are rather the display of man's inmost disposition, the manifestation of his indelible moral freedom. This moral liberty is the essential characteristic of man, raising him to a unique position in the universe.

Determinists reject this doctrine as illusory. Man, they say, deceives himself in believing that he chooses. Something unknown to the individual directs his will. He thinks that he weighs in his mind the pros and cons of the alternatives left to his choice and then makes a decision. He fails to realize that the antecedent state of things enjoins on him a definite line of conduct and that there is no means to elude this pressure. Man does not act, he is acted upon.

Both doctrines neglect to pay due attention to the role of ideas. The choices a man makes are determined by the ideas that he adopts.

The determinists are right in asserting that everything that happens is the necessary sequel of the preceding state of things. What a man does at any instant of his life is entirely dependent on his past, that is, on his physiological inheritance as well as of all he went through in his previous days. Yet the significance of this thesis is considerably weakened by the fact that nothing is known about the way in which ideas arise. Determinism is untenable if based upon or connected with the materialist dogma.[1] If advanced without the support of materialism, it says little indeed and certainly does not sustain the determinists' rejection of the methods of history.

The free-will doctrine is correct in pointing out the fundamental difference between human action and animal behavior. While the animal cannot help yielding to the physiological impulse which prevails at the moment, man chooses between alternative modes of conduct. Man has the power to choose even between yielding to the most imperative instinct, that of self-preservation, and the aiming at other ends. All the sarcasms and sneers of the positivists cannot annul the fact that ideas

1. See below, pp. 94–9.

have a real existence and are genuine factors in shaping the course of events.

The offshoots of human mental efforts, the ideas and the judgments of value that direct the individuals' actions, cannot be traced back to their causes, and are in this sense ultimate data. In dealing with them we refer to the concept of individuality. But in resorting to this notion we by no means imply that ideas and judgments of value spring out of nothing by a sort of spontaneous generation and are in no way connected and related to what was already in the universe before their appearance. We merely establish the fact that we do not know anything about the mental process which produces within a human being the thoughts that respond to the state of his physical and ideological environment.

This cognition is the grain of truth in the free-will doctrine. However, the passionate attempts to refute determinism and to salvage the notion of free will did not concern the problem of individuality. They were prompted by the practical consequences to which, as people believed, determinism inevitably leads: fatalist quietism and absolution from moral responsibility.

4. Foreordination and Fatalism

As theologians teach, God in his omniscience knows in advance all the things that will happen in the universe for all time to come. His foresight is unlimited and is not merely the result of his knowledge of the laws of becoming that determine all events. Even in a universe in which there is free will, whatever this may be, his precognition is perfect. He anticipates fully and correctly all the arbitrary decisions any individual will ever make.

Laplace proudly declared that his system does not need to resort to the hypothesis of God's existence. But he constructed his own image of a quasi God and called it superhuman intelligence. This hypothetical mind knows all things and events beforehand, but only because it is familiar with all the immutable and eternal laws regulating all occurrences, mental as well as physical.

The idea of God's omniscience has been popularly pictured as a book in which all future things are recorded. No deviation from the lines described in this register is possible. All things will turn out precisely as written in it. What must happen will happen no matter what mortal man may undertake to bring about a different result. Hence, consistent fatalism concluded, it is useless for man to act. Why bother if everything must finally come to a preordained end?

Fatalism is so contrary to human nature that few people were prepared to draw all the conclusions to which it leads and to adjust their conduct accordingly. It is a fable that the victories of the Arabian conquerors in the first centuries of Islam were due to the fatalist teachings of Mohammed. The leaders of the Moslem armies which within an unbelievably short time conquered a great part of the Mediterranean area did not put a fatalistic confidence in Allah. Rather they believed that their God was for the big, well-equipped, and skillfully led battalions. Other reasons than blind trust in fate account for the courage of the Saracen warriors; and the Christians in the forces of Charles Martel and Leo the Isaurian who stopped their advance were no less courageous than the Moslems although fatalism had no hold on their minds. Nor was the lethargy which spread later among the Islamitic peoples caused by the fatalism of their religion. It was despotism that paralyzed the initiative of the subjects. The harsh tyrants who oppressed the masses were certainly not lethargic and apathetic. They were indefatigable in their quest for power, riches, and pleasures.

Soothsayers have claimed to have reliable knowledge of some pages at least of the great book in which all coming events are recorded. But none of these prophets was consistent enough to reject activism and to advise his disciples to wait quietly for the day of fulfillment.

The best illustration is provided by Marxism. It teaches perfect foreordination, yet still aims to inflame people with revolutionary spirit. What is the use of revolutionary action if events must inevitably turn out according to a preordained plan, whatever men may do? Why are the Marxians so busy organizing socialist parties and sabotaging the operation of the market economy if socialism is bound to come anyway "with the inexorability of a law of nature"? It is a lame excuse indeed to declare that the task of a socialist party is not to bring about socialism but merely to provide obstetrical assistance at its birth. The obstetrician too diverts the course of events from the way they would run without his intervention. Otherwise expectant mothers would not request his aid. Yet the essential teaching of

Marxian dialectic materialism precludes the assumption that any political or ideological fact could influence the course of historical events, since the latter are substantially determined by the evolution of the material productive forces. What brings about socialism is the "operation of the immanent laws of capitalistic production itself." [1] Ideas, political parties, and revolutionary actions are merely superstructural; they can neither delay nor accelerate the march of history. Socialism will come when the material conditions for its appearance have matured in the womb of capitalist society, neither sooner nor later.[2] If Marx had been consistent, he would not have embarked upon any political activity.[3] He would have quietly waited for the day on which the "knell of private capitalist property sounds." [4]

In dealing with fatalism we may ignore the claims of soothsayers. Determinism has nothing at all to do with the art of fortune tellers, crystal gazers, and astrologers or with the more pretentious effusions of the authors of "philosophies of history." It does not predict future events. It asserts that there is regularity in the universe in the concatenation of all phenomena.

Those theologians who thought that in order to refute fatalism they must adopt the free-will doctrine were

1. Marx, *Das Kapital* (7th ed. Hamburg, 1914), *1*, 728.
2. Cf. below pp. 107 and 128.
3. Neither would he have written the often quoted eleventh aphorism on Feuerbach: "The philosophers have only provided different interpretations of the world, but what matters is to change it." According to the teachings of dialectical materialism only the evolution of the material productive forces, not the philosophers, can change the world.
4. Marx, *Das Kapital,* as quoted above.

badly mistaken. They had a very defective image of God's omniscience. Their God would know only what is in perfect textbooks of the natural sciences; he would not know what is going on in human minds. He would not anticipate that some people might endorse the doctrine of fatalism and, sitting with clasped hands, indolently await the events which God, erroneously assuming that they would not indulge in inactivity, had meted out to them.

5. Determinism and Penology

A factor that often entered the controversies concerning determinism was misapprehension as to its practical consequences.

All nonutilitarian systems of ethics look upon the moral law as something outside the nexus of means and ends. The moral code has no reference to human well-being and happiness, to expediency, and to the mundane striving after ends. It is heteronomous, i.e., enjoined upon man by an agency that does not depend on human ideas and does not bother about human concerns. Some believe that this agency is God, others that it is the wisdom of the forefathers, some that it is a mystical inner voice alive in every decent man's conscience. He who violates the precepts of this code commits a sin, and his guilt makes him liable to punishment. Punishment does not serve human ends. In punishing offenders, the secular or theocratic authorities acquit themselves of a duty entrusted to them by the moral code and its author. They are bound to punish sin and guilt whatever the consequences of their action may be.

Now these metaphysical notions of guilt, sin, and retribution are incompatible with the doctrine of determinism. If all human actions are the inevitable effect of their causes, if the individual cannot help acting in the way antecedent conditions make him act, there can no longer be any question of guilt. What a haughty presumption to punish a man who simply did what the eternal laws of the universe had determined!

The philosophers and lawyers who attacked determinism on these grounds failed to see that the doctrine of an almighty and omniscient God led to the same conclusions that moved them to reject philosophical determinism. If God is almighty, nothing can happen that he does not want to happen. If he is omniscient, he knows in advance all things that will happen. In either case, man cannot be considered answerable.[1] The young Benjamin Franklin argued "from the supposed attributes of God" in this manner: "That in erecting and governing the world, as he was infinitely wise, he knew what would be best; infinitely good, he must be disposed; and infinitely powerful, he must be able to execute it. Consequently all is right."[2] In fact, all attempts

1. See Fritz Mauthner, *Wörterbuch der Philosophie* (2d ed. Leipzig, 1923), *1*, 462–7.

2. Benjamin Franklin, *Autobiography* (New York, A. L. Burt, n.d.), pp. 73–4. Franklin very soon gave up this reasoning. He declared: "The great uncertainty I found in metaphysical reasonings disgusted me, and I quitted that kind of reading and study for others more satisfactory." In the posthumous papers of Franz Brentano a rather unconvincing refutation of Franklin's flash of thought was found. It was published by Oskar Kraus in his edition of Brentano's *Vom Ursprung sittlicher Erkenntnis* (Leipzig, 1921), pp. 91–5.

to justify, on metaphysical and theological grounds, society's right to punish those whose actions jeopardize peaceful social cooperation are open to the same criticism that is leveled against philosophical determinism.

Utilitarian ethics approaches the problem of punishment from a different angle. The offender is not punished because he is bad and deserves chastisement but so that neither he nor other people will repeat the offense. Punishment is not inflicted as retribution and retaliation but as a means to prevent future crimes. Legislators and judges are not the mandataries of a metaphysical retributive justice. They are committed to the task of safeguarding the smooth operation of society against encroachments on the part of antisocial individuals. Hence it is possible to deal with the problem of determinism without being troubled by inane considerations of practical consequences concerning the penal code.

6. Determinism and Statistics

In the nineteenth century some thinkers maintained that statistics have irrefutably demolished the doctrine of free will. It was argued that statistics show a regularity in the occurrence of certain human acts, e.g., crimes and suicides; and this alleged regularity was interpreted by Adolphe Quetelet and by Thomas Henry Buckle as an empirical demonstration of the correctness of rigid determinism.

However, what the statistics of human actions really show is not regularity but irregularity. The number of crimes, suicides, and acts of forgetfulness—which play such a conspicuous role in Buckle's deductions—varies from year to year. These yearly changes are as a rule small, and over a period of years they often—but not always—show a definite trend toward either increase or decrease. These statistics are indicative of historical change, not of regularity in the sense which is attached to this term in the natural sciences.

The specific understanding of history can try to interpret the why of such changes effected in the past and to anticipate changes likely to happen in the future. In doing this it deals with judgments of value determining the choice of ultimate ends, with reasoning and knowledge determining the choice of means, and with thymological traits of individuals.[1] It must, sooner or later, but inevitably, reach a point at which it can only refer to individuality. From beginning to end the treatment of the problems involved is bound to follow the lines of every scrutiny of human affairs; it must be teleological and as such radically different from the methods of the natural sciences.

But Buckle, blinded by the positivist bigotry of his environment, was quick to formulate his law: "In a given state of society a certain number of persons must put an end to their own life. This is the general law; and the special question as to who shall commit the crime depends of course upon special laws; which, however, in their total action must obey the large social law to which they are all subordinate. And the power of the larger law is so irresistible that neither the love of

1. On thymology see pp. 264 ff.

life nor the fear of another world can avail anything towards even checking its operation." [2] Buckle's law seems to be very definite and unambiguous in its formulation. But in fact it defeats itself entirely by including the phrase "a given state of society," which even an enthusiastic admirer of Buckle termed "viciously vague." [3] As Buckle does not provide us with criteria for determining changes in the state of society, his formulation can be neither verified nor disproved by experience and thus lacks the distinctive mark of a law of the natural sciences.

Many years after Buckle, eminent physicists began to assume that certain or even all laws of mechanics may be "only" statistical in character. This doctrine was considered incompatible with determinism and causality. When later on quantum mechanics considerably enlarged the scope of "merely" statistical physics, many writers cast away all the epistemological principles that had guided the natural sciences for centuries. On the macroscopic scale, they say, we observe certain regularities which older generations erroneously interpreted as a manifestation of natural law. In fact, these regularities are the result of the statistical compensation of contingent events. The apparent causal arrangement on a large scale is to be explained by the law of large numbers. [4]

2. Buckle, *Introduction to the History of Civilization in England*, J. M. Robertson, ed. (London, G. Routledge; New York, E. P. Dutton, n.d.), ch. 1 in *1*, 15–16.

3. J. M. Robertson, *Buckle and His Critics* (London, 1895), p. 288.

4. John von Neumann, *Mathematische Grundlagen der Quantenmechanik* (New York, 1943), pp. 172 ff.

Now the law of large numbers and statistical compensation is operative only in fields in which there prevail large-scale regularity and homogeneity of such a character that they offset any irregularity and heterogeneity that may seem to exist on the small-scale level. If one assumes that seemingly contingent events always compensate one another in such a way that a regularity appears in the repeated observation of large numbers of these events, one implies that these events follow a definite pattern and can therefore no longer be considered as contingent. What we mean in speaking of natural law is that there is a regularity in the concatenation and sequence of phenomena. If a set of events on the microscopic scale always produces a definite event on the macroscopic scale, such a regularity is present. If there were no regularity in the microscopic scale, no regularity could emerge on the macroscopic scale either.

Quantum mechanics deals with the fact that we do not know how an atom will behave in an individual instance. But we know what patterns of behavior can possibly occur and the proportion in which these patterns really occur. While the perfect form of a causal law is: A "produces" B, there is also a less perfect form: A "produces" C in $n\%$ of all cases, D in $m\%$ of all cases, and so on. Perhaps it will at a later day be possible to dissolve this A of the less perfect form into a number of disparate elements to each of which a definite "effect" will be assigned according to the perfect form. But whether this will happen or not is of no relevance for the problem of determinism. The imperfect law too is a causal law, although it discloses shortcomings in our knowledge. And because it is a display of a peculiar type both of knowledge and of ignorance, it opens a field for the employment of the calculus of probability. We know, with regard to a definite problem, all about the behavior of the whole class of events, we know that class A will produce definite effects in a known proportion; but all we know about the individual A's is that they are members of the A class. The mathematical formulation of this mixture of knowledge and ignorance is: We know the probability of the various effects that can possibly be "produced" by an individual A.

What the neo-indeterminist school of physics fails to see is that the proposition: A produces B in $n\%$ of the cases and C in the rest of the cases is, epistemologically, not different from the proposition: A always produces B. The former proposition differs from the latter only in combining in its notion of A two elements, X and Y, which the perfect form of a causal law would have to distinguish. But no question of contingency is raised. Quantum mechanics does not say: The individual atoms behave like customers choosing dishes in a restaurant or voters casting their ballots. It says: The atoms invariably follow a definite pattern. This is also manifested in the fact that what it predicates about atoms contains no reference either to a definite period of time or to a definite location within the universe. One could not deal with the behavior of atoms in general, that is, without reference to time and space, if the individual atom were not inevitably and fully ruled by natural law. We are free to use the term "individual" atom, but we must never ascribe to an "individual" atom individuality in the sense in which this term is applied to men and to historical events.

In the field of human action the determinist philosophers referred to statistics in order to refute the doctrine of free will and to prove determinism in the acts of man. In the field of physics the neo-indeterminist philosophers refer to statistics in order to refute the doctrine of determinism and to prove indeterminism in nature. The error of both sides arises from confusion as to the meaning of statistics.

In the field of human action statistics is a method of historical research. It is a description in numerical terms of historical events that happened in a definite period of time with definite groups of people in a definite geographical area. Its meaning consists precisely in the fact that it describes changes, not something unchanging.

In the field of nature statistics is a method of inductive research. Its epistemological justification and its meaning lie in the firm belief that there are regularity and perfect determinism in nature. The laws of nature are considered perennial. They are fully operative in each instance. What happens in one case must also happen in all other like cases. Therefore the information conveyed by statistical material has general validity with regard to the classes of phenomena to which it refers; it does not concern only definite periods of history and definite geographical sites.

Unfortunately the two entirely different categories of statistics have been confused. And the matter has been still further tangled by jumbling it together with the notion of probability.

To unravel this imbroglio of errors, misunderstanding, and contradictions let us emphasize some truisms.

It is impossible, as has been pointed out above, for the human mind to think of any event as uncaused. The concepts of chance and contingency, if properly analyzed, do not refer ultimately to the course of events in the universe. They refer to human knowledge, prevision, and action. They have a praxeological, not an ontological connotation.

Calling an event contingent is not to deny that it is the necessary outcome of the preceding state of affairs. It means that we mortal men do not know whether or not it will happen.

Our notion of nature refers to an ascertainable, permanent regularity in the concatenation and sequence of phenomena. Whatever happens in nature and can be conceived by the natural sciences is the outcome of the operation, repeated and repeated again, of the same laws. Natural science means the cognition of these laws. The historical sciences of human action, on the other hand, deal with events which our mental faculties cannot interpret as a manifestation of a general law. They deal with individual men and individual events even in dealing with the affairs of masses, peoples, races, and the whole of mankind. They deal with individuality and with an irreversible flux of events. If the natural sciences scrutinize an event that happened but once, such as a geological change or the biological evolution of a species, they look upon it as an instance of the operation of general laws. But history is not in a position to trace events back to the operation of perennial laws. Therefore in dealing with an event it is primarily interested not in the features such an event may have in common with other events but in its individual characteristics. In dealing with the assassination of Caesar history does not study murder but the murder of the man Caesar.

The very notion of a natural law whose validity is restricted to a definite period of time is self-contradictory. Experience, whether that of mundane observation as made in daily life or that of deliberately prearranged experiments, refers to individual historical cases. But the natural sciences, guided by their indispensable aprioristic determinism, assume that the law must manifest itself in every individual case, and generalize by what is called inductive inference.

The present epistemological situation in the field of quantum mechanics would be correctly described by the statement: We know the various patterns according to which atoms behave and we know the proportion in which each of these patterns becomes actual. This would describe the state of our knowledge as an instance of class probability: We know all about the behavior of the whole class; about the behavior of the individual members of the class we know only that they are members.[5] It is inexpedient and misleading to apply to the problems concerned terms used in dealing with human action. Bertrand Russell resorts to such figurative speech: the atom "will do" something, there is "a

5. On the distinction between class probability and case probability, see Mises, *Human Action*, pp. 107–13.

definite set of alternatives open to it, and it chooses sometimes one, sometimes another." [6] The reason Lord Russell chooses such inappropriate terms becomes obvious if we take into account the tendency of his book and of all his other writings. He wants to obliterate the difference between acting man and human action on the one hand and nonhuman events on the other hand. In his eyes "the difference between us and a stone is only one of degree"; for "we react to stimuli, and so do stones, though the stimuli to which they react are fewer." [7] Lord Russell omits to mention the fundamental difference in the way stones and men "react." Stones react according to a perennial pattern, which we call a law of nature. Men do not react in such a uniform way; they behave, as both praxeologists and historians say, in an individual way. Nobody has ever succeeded in assigning various men to classes each member of which behaves according to the same pattern.

7. *The Autonomy of the Sciences of Human Action*

The phraseology employed in the old antagonism of determinism and indeterminism is inappropriate. It does not correctly describe the substance of the controversy.

The search for knowledge is always concerned with the concatenation of events and the cognition of the factors producing change. In this sense both the natural sciences and the sciences of human action are committed to the category of causality and to determinism.

6. Bertrand Russell, *Religion and Science,* Home University Library (London, Oxford University Press, 1936), pp. 152–8.
7. Ibid., p. 131.

No action can ever succeed if not guided by a true—in the sense of pragmatism—insight into what is commonly called a relation of cause and effect. The fundamental category of action, viz., means and ends, presupposes the category of cause and effect.

What the sciences of human action must reject is not determinism but the positivistic and panphysicalistic distortion of determinism. They stress the fact that ideas determine human action and that at least in the present state of human science it is impossible to reduce the emergence and the transformation of ideas to physical, chemical, or biological factors. It is this impossibility that constitutes the autonomy of the sciences of human action. Perhaps natural science will one day be in a position to describe the physical, chemical, and biological events which in the body of the man Newton necessarily and inevitably produced the theory of gravitation. In the meantime, we must be content with the study of the history of ideas as a part of the sciences of human action.

The sciences of human action by no means reject determinism. The objective of history is to bring out in full relief the factors that were operative in producing a definite event. History is entirely guided by the category of cause and effect. In retrospect, there is no question of contingency. The notion of contingency as employed in dealing with human action always refers to man's uncertainty about the future and the limitations of the specific historical understanding of future events. It refers to a limitation of the human search for knowledge, not to a condition of the universe or of some of its parts.

Chapter 6. Materialism

1. *Two Varieties of Materialism*

THE TERM "materialism" as applied in contemporary speech has two entirely different connotations.

The first connotation refers to values. It characterizes the mentality of people who desire only material wealth, bodily satisfactions, and sensuous pleasures.

The second connotation is ontological. It signifies the doctrine that all human thoughts, ideas, judgments of value, and volitions are the product of physical, chemical, and physiological processes going on in the human body. Consequently materialism in this sense denies the meaningfulness of thymology and the sciences of human action, of praxeology as well as of history; the natural sciences alone are scientific. We shall deal in this chapter only with this second connotation.

The materialist thesis has never yet been proved or particularized. The materialists have brought forward no more than analogies and metaphors. They have compared the working of the human mind with the operation of a machine or with physiological processes. Both analogies are insignificant and do not explain anything.

A machine is a device made by man. It is the realization of a design and it runs precisely according to the plan of its authors. What produces the product of its operation is not something within it but the purpose the constructor wanted to realize by means of its construction. It is the constructor and the operator who create the product, not the machine. To ascribe to a machine any activity is anthropomorphism and animism. The machine has no control over its running. It does not move; it is put into motion and kept in motion by men. It is a dead tool which is employed by men and comes to a standstill as soon as the effects of the operator's impulse cease. What the materialist who resorts to the machine metaphor would have to explain first of all is: Who constructed this human machine and who operates it? In whose hands does it serve as a tool? It is difficult to see how any other answer could be given to this question than: It is the Creator.

It is customary to call an automatic contrivance self-acting. This idiom too is a metaphor. It is not the calculating machine that calculates, but the operator by means of a tool ingeniously devised by an inventor. The machine has no intelligence; it neither thinks nor chooses ends nor resorts to means for the realization of the ends sought. This is always done by men.

The physiological analogy is more sensible than the mechanistic analogy. Thinking is inseparably tied up with a physiological process. As far as the physiological thesis merely stresses this fact, it is not metaphorical; but it says very little. For the problem is precisely this, that we do not know anything about the physiological phenomena constituting the process that produces poems, theories, and plans. Pathology provides abundant information about the impairment or total annihilation of mental faculties resulting from injuries of the brain. Anatomy provides no less abundant information about the chemical structure of the brain cells and their physiological behavior. But notwithstanding the advance in physiological knowledge, we do not know more about the mind-body problem than the old philosophers who first began to ponder it. None of the doctrines they advanced has been either proved or disproved by newly won physiological knowledge.

Thoughts and ideas are not phantoms. They are real things. Although intangible and immaterial, they are factors in bringing about changes in the realm of tangible and material things. They are generated by some unknown process going on in a human being's body and can be perceived only by the same kind of process going on in the body of their author or in other human beings' bodies. They can be called creative and original insofar as the impulse they give and the changes they bring about depend on their emergence. We can ascertain what we wish to about the life of an idea and the effects of its existence. About its birth we know only that it was engendered by an individual. We cannot trace its history further back. The emergence of an idea is an innovation, a new fact added to the world. It is, because of the deficiency of our knowledge, *for human minds* the origin of something new that did not exist before.

What a satisfactory materialist doctrine would have to describe is the sequence of events going on in matter that produces a definite idea. It would have to explain why people agree or disagree with regard to definite problems. It would have to explain why one man succeeded in solving a problem which other people failed to solve. But no materialistic doctrine has up to now tried to do this.

The champions of materialism are intent upon pointing out the untenability of all other doctrines that have been advanced for the solution of the mind-body problem. They are especially zealous in fighting the theological interpretation. Yet the refutation of a doctrine does not prove the soundness of any other doctrine at variance with it.

Perhaps it is too bold a venture for the human mind to speculate about its own nature and origin. It may be true, as agnosticism maintains, that knowledge about these problems is forever denied to mortal men. But even if this is so, it does not justify the logical positivists' condemning the questions implied as meaningless and nonsensical. A question is not nonsensical merely because it cannot be answered satisfactorily by the human mind.

2. *The Secretion Analogy*

A notorious formulation of the materialist thesis states that thoughts stand in about the same relation to the brain as the gall to the liver or urine to the kidneys.[1] As a rule materialist authors are more cautious in their utterances. But essentially all they say is tantamount to this challenging dictum.

Physiology distinguishes between urine of a chem-

1. C. Vogt, *Köhlerglaube und Wissenschaft* (2d ed. Giessen, 1855), p. 32.

ically normal composition and other types of urine. Deviation from the normal composition is accounted for by certain deviations in the body's physique or in the functioning of the body's organs from what is considered normal and healthy. These deviations too follow a regular pattern. A definite abnormal or pathological state of the body is reflected in a corresponding alteration of the urine's chemical composition. The assimilation of certain foodstuffs, beverages, and drugs brings about related phenomena in the urine's composition. With hale people, those commonly called normal, urine is, within certain narrow margins, of the same chemical nature.

It is different with thoughts and ideas. With them there is no question of normalcy or of deviations from normalcy following a definite pattern. Certain bodily injuries or the assimilation of certain drugs and beverages obstruct and trouble the mind's faculty to think. But even these derangements are not uniform with various people. Different people have different ideas, and no materialist ever succeeded in tracing back these differences to factors that could be described in terms of physics, chemistry, or physiology. Any reference to the natural sciences and to material factors they are dealing with is vain when we ask why some people vote the Republican and others the Democratic ticket.

Up to now at least the natural sciences have not succeeded in discovering any bodily or material traits to whose presence or absence the content of ideas and thoughts can be imputed. In fact, the problem of the diversity of the content of ideas and thoughts does not even arise in the natural sciences. They can deal only with objects that affect or modify sensuous intuition. But ideas and thoughts do not directly affect sensation. What characterizes them is meaning—and for the cognition of meaning the methods of the natural sciences are inappropriate.

Ideas influence one another, they provide stimulation for the emergence of new ideas, they supersede or transform other ideas. All that materialism could offer for the treatment of these phenomena is a metaphorical reference to the notion of contagion. The comparison is superficial and does not explain anything. Diseases are communicated from body to body through the migrations of germs and viruses. Nobody knows anything about the migration of a factor that would transmit thoughts from man to man.

3. *The Political Implications of Materialism*

Materialism originated as a reaction against a primeval dualistic interpretation of man's being and essential nature. In the light of these beliefs, living man was a compound of two separable parts: a mortal body and an immortal soul. Death severed these two parts. The soul moved out of sight of the living and continued a shadow-like existence beyond the reach of earthly powers in the realm of the deceased. In exceptional cases it was permitted to a soul to reappear for a while in the sensible world of the living or for a still living man to pay a short visit to the fields of the dead.

These rather crude representations have been sublimated by religious doctrines and by idealistic philosophy. While the primitive descriptions of a realm of souls and the activities of its inhabitants cannot bear critical examination and can easily be exposed to ridicule, it is impossible both for aprioristic reasoning and for the natural sciences to refute cogently the refined tenets of religious creeds. History can explode many of the historical narrations of theological literature. But higher criticism does not affect the core of the faith. Reason can neither prove nor disprove the essential religious doctrines.

But materialism as it had developed in eighteenth-century France was not merely a scientific doctrine. It was also a part of the vocabulary of the reformers who fought the abuses of the ancien régime. The prelates of the Church in royal France were with few exceptions members of the aristocracy. Most of them were more interested in court intrigues than in the performance of their ecclesiastical duties. Their well-deserved unpopularity made antireligious tendencies popular.

The debates on materialism would have subsided about the middle of the nineteenth century if no political issues had been involved. People would have realized that contemporary science has not contributed anything to the elucidation or analysis of the physiological processes that generate definite ideas and that it is doubtful whether future scientists will succeed better in this task. The materialist dogma would have been regarded as a conjecture about a problem whose satisfactory solution seemed, at least for the time being, beyond the reach of man's search for knowledge. Its supporters would no longer have been in a position to consider it an irrefutable scientific truth and would not have been permitted to accuse its critics of obscurantism, ignorance, and superstition. Agnosticism would have replaced materialism.

But in most of the European and Latin American countries Christian churches cooperated, at least to some extent, with the forces that opposed representative government and all institutions making for freedom. In these countries one could hardly avoid attacking religion if one aimed at the realization of a program that by and large corresponded with the ideals of Jefferson and of Lincoln. The political implications of the materialism controversy prevented its fading away. Prompted not by epistemological, philosophical, or scientific considerations but by purely political reasons, a desperate attempt was made to salvage the politically very convenient slogan "materialism." While the type of materialism that flourished until the middle of the nineteenth century receded into the background, gave way to agnosticism, and could not be regenerated by such rather crude and naïve writings as those of Haeckel, a new type was developed by Karl Marx under the name of dialectical materialism.

Chapter 7. Dialectical Materialism

1. Dialectics and Marxism

DIALECTICAL MATERIALISM as taught by Karl Marx and Frederick Engels is the most popular metaphysical doctrine of our age. It is today the official philosophy of the Soviet empire and of all the schools of Marxism outside of this empire. It dominates the ideas of many people who do not consider themselves Marxians and even of many authors and parties who believe they are anti-Marxians and anti-communists. It is this doctrine which most of our contemporaries have in mind when they refer to materialism and determinism.

When Marx was a young man, two metaphysical doctrines whose teachings were incompatible with one another dominated German thought. One was Hegelian spiritualism, the official doctrine of the Prussian state and of the Prussian universities. The other was materialism, the doctrine of the opposition bent upon a revolutionary overthrow of the political system of Metternich and of Christian orthodoxy as well as of private property. Marx tried to blend the two into a compound in order to prove that socialism is bound to come "with the inexorability of a law of nature."

In the philosophy of Hegel logic, metaphysics, and ontology are essentially identical. The process of real

102

becoming is an aspect of the logical process of thinking. In grasping the laws of logic by aprioristic thinking, the mind acquires correct knowledge of reality. There is no road to truth but that provided by the study of logic.

The peculiar principle of Hegel's logic is the dialectic method. Thinking takes a triadic way. It proceeds from thesis to antithesis, i.e., the negation of the thesis, and from antithesis to synthesis, i.e., the negation of the negation. The same trinal principle of thesis, antithesis, and synthesis manifests itself in real becoming. For the only real thing in the universe is *Geist* (mind or spirit). Matter has its substance not in itself. Natural things are not for themselves (*für sich selber*). But Geist is for itself. What—apart from reason and divine action—is called reality is, viewed in the light of philosophy, something rotten or inert (*ein Faules*) which may seem but is not in itself real.[1]

No compromise is possible between this Hegelian idealism and any kind of materialism. Yet, fascinated by the prestige Hegelianism enjoyed in the Germany of the 1840's, Marx and Engels were afraid to deviate too radically from the only philosophical system with which they and their contemporary countrymen were familiar. They were not audacious enough to discard Hegelianism entirely as was done a few years later even in Prussia. They preferred to appear as continuators and reformers of Hegel, not as iconoclastic dissenters. They boasted of having transformed and improved Hegelian dialectics, of having turned it upside down, or rather,

1. See Hegel, *Vorlesungen über die Philosophie der Weltgeschichte,* ed. Lasson (Leipzig, 1917), pp. 31–4, 55.

of having put it on its feet.[2] They did not realize that
it was nonsensical to uproot dialectics from its idealistic
ground and transplant it to a system that was labeled
materialistic and empirical. Hegel was consistent in
assuming that the logical process is faithfully reflected
in the processes going on in what is commonly called
reality. He did not contradict himself in applying the
logical apriori to the interpretation of the universe. But
it is different with a doctrine that indulges in a naïve
realism, materialism, and empiricism. Such a doctrine
ought to have no use for a scheme of interpretation that
is derived not from experience but from apriori reasoning. Engels declared that dialectics is the science of the
general laws of motion, of the external world as well as
of human thinking; two series of laws which are substantially identical but in their manifestation different
insofar as the human mind can apply them consciously,
while in nature, and hitherto also to a great extent in
human history, they assert themselves in an unconscious way as external necessity in the midst of an infinite series of apparently contingent events.[3] He himself, says Engels, had never had any doubts about this.
His intensive preoccupation with mathematics and the
natural sciences, to which he confesses to have devoted
the greater part of eight years, was, he declares, obviously prompted only by the desire to test the validity
of the laws of dialectics in detail in specific instances.[4]

2. Engels, *Ludwig Feuerbach und der Ausgang der klassischen
deutschen Philosophie* (5th ed. Stuttgart, 1910), pp. 36–9.

3. Ibid., p. 38.

4. Preface, Engels, *Herrn Eugen Dührings Umwälzung der Wissenschaft* (7th ed. Stuttgart, 1910), pp. xiv and xv.

These studies led Engels to startling discoveries. Thus he found that "the whole of geology is a series of negated negations." Butterflies "come into existence from the egg through negation of the egg . . . they are negated again as they die," and so on. The normal life of barley is this: "The barleycorn . . . is negated and is supplanted by the barley plant, the negation of the corn. . . . The plant grows . . . is fructified and produces again barleycorns and as soon as these are ripe, the ear withers away, is negated. As a result of this negation of the negation we have again the original barleycorn, however not plainly single but in a quantity ten, twenty, or thirty times larger." [5]

It did not occur to Engels that he was merely playing with words. It is a gratuitous pastime to apply the terminology of logic to the phenomena of reality. Propositions about phenomena, events, and facts can be affirmed or negated, but not the phenomena, events, and facts themselves. But if one is committed to such inappropriate and logically vicious metaphorical language, it is not less sensible to call the butterfly the affirmation of the egg than to call it its negation. Is not the emergence of the butterfly the self-assertion of the egg, the maturing of its inherent purpose, the perfection of its merely passing existence, the fulfillment of all its potentialities? Engels' method consisted in substituting the term "negation" for the term "change." There is, however, no need to dwell longer upon the fallacy of integrating Hegelian dialectics into a philosophy that does not endorse Hegel's fundamental principle, the

5. Ibid., pp. 138–9.

identity of logic and ontology, and does not radically reject the idea that anything could be learned from experience. For in fact dialectics plays a merely ornamental part in the constructions of Marx and Engels without substantially influencing the course of reasoning.[6]

2. *The Material Productive Forces*

The essential concept of Marxian materialism is "the material productive forces of society." These forces are the driving power producing all historical facts and changes. In the social production of their subsistence, men enter into certain relations—production relations —which are necessary and independent of their will and correspond to the prevailing stage of development of the material productive forces. The totality of these production relations forms "the economic structure of society, the real basis upon which there arises a juridical and political superstructure and to which definite forms of social consciousness correspond." The mode of production of material life conditions the social, political, and spiritual (intellectual) life process in general (in each of its manifestations). It is not the consciousness (the ideas and thoughts) of men that determines their being (existence) but, on the contrary, their social being that determines their consciousness. At a certain stage of their development the material productive forces of society come into contradiction with the exist-

6. E. Hammacher, *Das philosophisch-ökonomische System des Marxismus* (Leipzig, 1909), pp. 506–11.

ing production relations, or, what is merely a juridical expression for them, with the property relations (the social system of property laws) within the frame of which they have hitherto operated. From having been forms of development of the productive forces these relations turn into fetters of them. Then comes an epoch of social revolution. With the change in the economic foundation the whole immense superstructure slowly or rapidly transforms [1] itself. In reviewing such a transformation,[1] one must always distinguish between the material transformation [1] of the economic conditions of production, which can be precisely ascertained with the methods of the natural sciences, and the juridical, political, religious, artistic,[2] or philosophical, in short ideological, forms in which men become conscious (aware) of this conflict and fight it out. Such an epoch of transformation can no more be judged according to its own consciousness than an individual can be judged according to what he imagines himself to be; one must rather explain this consciousness out of the contradictions of the material life, out of the existing conflict between social productive forces and production relations. No social formation ever disappears before all the productive forces have been developed for which its frame is broad enough, and new, higher production relations never appear before the material conditions of their existence have been hatched out in the womb of the old society.

1. The term used by Marx, *umwälzen, Umwälzung*, is the German-language equivalent of "revolution."
2. The German term *Kunst* includes all branches of poetry, fiction, and playwriting.

Hence mankind never sets itself tasks other than those it can solve, for closer observation will always discover that the task itself only emerges where the material conditions of its solution are already present or at least in the process of becoming.[3]

The most remarkable fact about this doctrine is that it does not provide a definition of its basic concept, material productive forces. Marx never told us what he had in mind in referring to the material productive forces. We have to deduce it from occasional historical exemplifications of his doctrine. The most outspoken of these incidental examples is to be found in his book, *The Poverty of Philosophy*, published in 1847 in French. It reads: The hand mill gives you feudal society, the steam mill industrial capitalism.[4] This means that the state of practical technological knowledge or the technological quality of the tools and machines used in production is to be considered the essential feature of the material productive forces, which uniquely determine the production relations and thereby the whole "superstructure." The production technique is the real thing, the material being that ultimately determines the social, political, and intellectual manifestations of human life. This interpretation is fully confirmed by all other examples provided by Marx and Engels and by the response every new technological advance roused in their minds. They welcomed it enthusiastically because they

3. K. Marx, *Zur Kritik der politischen Oekonomie,* ed. Kautsky (Stuttgart, 1897), Preface, pp. x–xii.
4. "Le moulin à bras vous donnera la société avec le souzerain; le moulin à vapeur, la société avec le capitaliste industriel." Marx, *La Misère de la philosophie* (Paris and Brussels, 1847), p. 100.

were convinced that each such new invention brought them a step nearer the realization of their hopes, the coming of socialism.[5]

There have been, before Marx and after Marx, many historians and philosophers who emphasized the prominent role the improvement of technological methods of production has played in the history of civilization. A glance into the popular textbooks of history published in the last one hundred and fifty years shows that their authors duly stressed the importance of new inventions and of the changes they brought about. They never contested the truism that material well-being is the indispensable condition of a nation's moral, intellectual, and artistic achievement.

But what Marx says is entirely different. In his doctrine the tools and machines are the ultimate thing, a material thing, viz., the material productive forces. Everything else is the necessary superstructure of this material basis. This fundamental thesis is open to three irrefutable objections.

First, a technological invention is not something material. It is the product of a mental process, of reasoning and conceiving new ideas. The tools and machines may be called material, but the operation of the mind which created them is certainly spiritual. Marxian materialism does not trace back "superstructural" and

5. Marx and some of his followers at times also included natural resources in the notion of material productive forces. But these remarks were made only incidentally and were never elaborated, obviously because this would have led them into the doctrine that explains history as determined by the structure of the people's geographical environment.

"ideological" phenomena to "material" roots. It explains these phenomena as caused by an essentially mental process, viz., invention. It assigns to this mental process, which it falsely labels an original, nature-given, material fact, the exclusive power to beget all other social and intellectual phenomena. But it does not attempt to explain how inventions come to pass.

Second, mere invention and designing of technologically new implements are not sufficient to produce them. What is required, in addition to technological knowledge and planning, is capital previously accumulated out of saving. Every step forward on the road toward technological improvement presupposes the requisite capital. The nations today called underdeveloped know what is needed to improve their backward apparatus of production. Plans for the construction of all the machines they want to acquire are ready or could be completed in a very short time. Only lack of capital holds them up. But saving and capital accumulation presuppose a social structure in which it is possible to save and to invest. The production relations are thus not the product of the material productive forces but, on the contrary, the indispensable condition of their coming into existence.

Marx, of course, cannot help admitting that capital accumulation is "one of the most indispensable conditions for the evolution of industrial production." [6] Part of his most voluminous treatise, *Das Kapital*, provides

6. Marx, *La Misère de la philosophie*, English trans., *The Poverty of Philosophy* (New York, International Publishers, n.d.), p. 115.

a history—wholly distorted—of capital accumulation. But as soon as he comes to his doctrine of materialism, he forgets all he said about this subject. Then the tools and machines are created by spontaneous generation, as it were.

Furthermore it must be remembered that the utilization of machines presupposes social cooperation under the division of labor. No machine can be constructed and put into use under conditions in which there is no division of labor at all or only a rudimentary stage of it. Division of labor means social cooperation, i.e., social bonds between men, society. How then is it possible to explain the existence of society by tracing it back to the material productive forces which themselves can only appear in the frame of a previously existing social nexus? Marx could not comprehend this problem. He accused Proudhon, who had described the use of machines as a consequence of the division of labor, of ignorance of history. It is a distortion of fact, he shouted, to start with the division of labor and to deal with machines only later. For the machines are "a productive force," not a "social production relation," not an "economic category." [7] Here we are faced with a stubborn dogmatism that does not shrink from any absurdity.

We may summarize the Marxian doctrine in this way: In the beginning there are the "material productive forces," i.e., the technological equipment of human productive efforts, the tools and machines. No question concerning their origin is permitted; they are, that is

7. Ibid., pp. 112–13.

all; we must assume that they are dropped from heaven. These material productive forces compel men to enter into definite production relations which are independent of their wills. These production relations farther on determine society's juridical and political superstructure as well as all religious, artistic, and philosophical ideas.

3. *The Class Struggle*

As will be pointed out below, any philosophy of history must demonstrate the mechanism by means of which the supreme agency that directs the course of all human affairs induces individuals to walk in precisely the ways which are bound to lead mankind toward the goal set. In Marx's system the doctrine of the class struggle is designed to answer this question.

The inherent weakness of this doctrine is that it deals with classes and not with individuals. What has to be shown is how the individuals are induced to act in such a way that mankind finally reaches the point the productive forces want it to attain. Marx answers that consciousness of the interests of their class determines the conduct of the individuals. It still remains to be explained why the individuals give the interests of their class preference over their own interests. We may for the moment refrain from asking how the individual learns what the genuine interests of his class are. But even Marx cannot help admitting that a conflict exists between the interests of an individual and those of the class to which he belongs.[1] He distinguishes between those proletarians who are class conscious, i.e., place the concerns of their class before their individual concerns, and those who are not. He considers it one of the objectives of a socialist party to awake to class consciousness those proletarians who are not spontaneously class conscious.

Marx obfuscated the problem by confusing the notions of caste and class. Where status and caste differences prevail, all members of every caste but the most privileged have one interest in common, viz., to wipe out the legal disabilities of their own caste. All slaves, for instance, are united in having a stake in the abolition of slavery. But no such conflicts are present in a society in which all citizens are equal before the law. No logical objection can be advanced against distinguishing various classes among the members of such a society. Any classification is logically permissible, however arbitrarily the mark of distinction may be chosen. But it is nonsensical to classify the members of a capitalistic society according to their position in the framework of the social division of labor and then to identify these classes with the castes of a status society.

In a status society the individual inherits his caste membership from his parents, he remains through all his life in his caste, and his children are born as members

1. Thus we read in the Communist Manifesto: "The organization of the proletarians into a class, and consequently into a political party, is at every instant again shattered by the competition between the workers themselves."

of it. Only in exceptional cases can good luck raise a
man into a higher caste. For the immense majority birth
unalterably determines their station in life. The classes
which Marx distinguishes in a capitalistic society are
different. Their membership is fluctuating. Class affiliation is not hereditary. It is assigned to each individual
by a daily repeated plebiscite, as it were, of all the
people. The public in spending and buying determines
who should own and run the plants, who should play
the parts in the theater performances, who should work
in the factories and mines. Rich men become poor, and
poor men rich. The heirs as well as those who themselves have acquired wealth must try to hold their own
by defending their assets against the competition of
already established firms and of ambitious newcomers.
In the unhampered market economy there are no privileges, no protection of vested interests, no barriers pre-
venting anybody from striving after any prize. Access
to any of the Marxian classes is free to everybody. The
members of each class compete with one another; they
are not united by a common class interest and not opposed to the members of other classes by being allied
either in the defense of a common privilege which those
wronged by it want to see abolished or in the attempt
to abolish an institutional disability which those deriv-
ing advantage from it want to preserve.

The laissez-faire liberals asserted: If the old laws establishing status privileges and disabilities are repealed
and no new practices of the same character—such as
tariffs, subsidies, discriminatory taxation, indulgence
granted for nongovernmental agencies like churches,

unions, and so on to use coercion and intimidation—are introduced, there is equality of all citizens before the law. Nobody is hampered in his aspirations and ambitions by any legal obstacles. Everybody is free to compete for any social position or function for which his personal abilities qualify him.

The communists denied that this is the way capitalistic society as organized under the liberal system of equality before the law, is operating. In their eyes private ownership of the means of production conveys to the owners—the bourgeois or capitalists in Marx's terminology—a privilege virtually not different from those once accorded to the feudal lords. The "bourgeois revolution" has not abolished privilege and discrimination against the masses; it has, says the Marxian, merely supplanted the old ruling and exploiting class of noblemen by a new ruling and exploiting class, the bourgeoisie. The exploited class, the proletarians, did not profit from this reform. They have changed masters but they have remained oppressed and exploited. What is needed is a new and final revolution, which in abolishing private ownership of the means of production will establish the classless society.

This socialist or communist doctrine fails entirely to take into account the essential difference between the conditions of a status or caste society and those of a capitalistic society. Feudal property came into existence either by conquest or by donation on the part of a conqueror. It came to an end either by revocation of the donation or by conquest on the part of a more powerful conqueror. It was property by "the grace of God," because it was ultimately derived from military victory which the humility or conceit of the princes ascribed to special intervention of the Lord. The owners of feudal property did not depend on the market, they did not serve the consumers; within the range of their property rights they were real lords. But it is quite different with the capitalists and entrepreneurs of a market economy. They acquire and enlarge their property through the services they have rendered to the consumers, and they can retain it only by serving daily again in the best possible way. This difference is not eradicated by metaphorically calling a successful manufacturer of spaghetti "the spaghetti king."

Marx never embarked on the hopeless task of refuting the economists' description of the working of the market economy. Instead he was eager to show that capitalism must in the future lead to very unsatisfactory conditions. He undertook to demonstrate that the operation of capitalism must inevitably result in the concentration of wealth in the possession of an ever diminishing number of capitalists on the one hand and in the progressive impoverishment of the immense majority on the other hand. In the execution of this task he started from the spurious iron law of wages according to which the average wage rate is that quantum of the means of subsistence which is absolutely required to enable the laborer to barely survive and to rear progeny.[2] This alleged law has long since been entirely dis-

---

2. Of course, Marx did not like the German term "das eherne Lohngesetz" because it had been devised by his rival Ferdinand Lassalle.

credited, and even the most bigoted Marxians have dropped it. But even if one were prepared for the sake of argument to call the law correct, it is obvious that it can by no means serve as the basis of a demonstration that the evolution of capitalism leads to progressive impoverishment of the wage earners. If wage rates under capitalism are always so low that for physiological reasons they cannot drop any further without wiping out the whole class of wage earners, it is impossible to maintain the thesis of the Communist Manifesto that the laborer "sinks deeper and deeper" with the progress of industry. Like all Marx's other arguments this demonstration is contradictory and self-defeating. Marx boasted of having discovered the immanent laws of capitalist evolution. The most important of these laws he considered the law of progressive impoverishment of the wage-earning masses. It is the operation of this law that brings about the final collapse of capitalism and the emergence of socialism.[3] When this law is seen to be spurious, the foundation is pulled from under both Marx's system of economics and his theory of capitalist evolution.

Incidentally we have to establish the fact that in capitalistic countries the standard of living of the wage earners has improved in an unprecedented and undreamt-of way since the publication of the *Communist Manifesto* and the first volume of *Das Kapital*. Marx misrepresented the operation of the capitalist system in every respect.

The corollary of the alleged progressive impoverish-

3. Marx, *Das Kapital, 1,* 728.

ment of the wage earners is the concentration of all riches in the hands of a class of capitalist exploiters whose membership is continually shrinking. In dealing with this issue Marx failed to take into account the fact that the evolution of big business units does not necessarily involve the concentration of wealth in a few hands. The big business enterprises are almost without exception corporations, precisely because they are too big for single individuals to own them entirely. The growth of business units has far outstripped the growth of individual fortunes. The assets of a corporation are not identical with the wealth of its shareholders. A considerable part of these assets, the equivalent of preferred stock and bonds issued and of loans raised, belong virtually, if not in the sense of the legal concept of ownership, to other people, viz., to owners of bonds and preferred stock and to creditors. Where these securities are held by savings banks and insurance companies and these loans were granted by such banks and companies, the virtual owners are the people who have claims against them. Also the common stock of a corporation is as a rule not concentrated in the hands of one man. The bigger the corporation, as a rule, the more widely its shares are distributed.

Capitalism is essentially mass production to fill the needs of the masses. But Marx always labored under the deceptive conception that the workers are toiling for the sole benefit of an upper class of idle parasites. He did not see that the workers themselves consume by far the greater part of all the consumers' goods turned out. The millionaires consume an almost negligible part of what is called the national product. All branches of big business cater directly or indirectly to the needs of the common man. The luxury industries never develop beyond small-scale or medium-size units. The evolution of big business is in itself proof of the fact that the masses and not the nabobs are the main consumers. Those who deal with the phenomenon of big business under the rubric "concentration of economic power" fail to realize that economic power is vested in the buying public on whose patronage the prosperity of the factories depends. In his capacity as buyer, the wage earner is the customer who is "always right." But Marx declares that the bourgeoisie "is incompetent to assure an existence to its slave within his slavery."

Marx deduced the excellence of socialism from the fact that the driving force of historical evolution, the material productive forces, is bound to bring about socialism. As he was engrossed in the Hegelian brand of optimism, there was to his mind no further need to demonstrate the merits of socialism. It was obvious to him that socialism, being a later stage of history than capitalism, was also a better stage.[4] It was sheer blasphemy to doubt its merits.

What was still left to show was the mechanism by means of which nature brings about the transition from capitalism to socialism. Nature's instrument is the class struggle. As the workers sink deeper and deeper with the progress of capitalism, as their misery, oppression, slavery, and degradation increase, they are driven to revolt, and their rebellion establishes socialism.

4. On the fallacy implied in this reasoning, see below pp. 175 ff.

The whole chain of this reasoning is exploded by the establishment of the fact that the progress of capitalism does not pauperize the wage earners increasingly but on the contrary improves their standard of living. Why should the masses be inevitably driven to revolt when they get more and better food, housing and clothing, cars and refrigerators, radio and television sets, nylon and other synthetic products? Even if, for the sake of argument, we were to admit that the workers are driven to rebellion, why should their revolutionary upheaval aim just at the establishment of socialism? The only motive which could induce them to ask for socialism would be the conviction that they themselves would fare better under socialism than under capitalism. But Marxists, anxious to avoid dealing with the economic problems of a socialist commonwealth, did nothing to demonstrate the superiority of socialism over capitalism apart from the circular reasoning that runs: Socialism is bound to come as the next stage of historical evolution. Being a later stage of history than capitalism, it is necessarily higher and better than capitalism. Why is it bound to come? Because the laborers, doomed to progressive impoverishment under capitalism, will rebel and establish socialism. But what other motive could impel them to aim at the establishment of socialism than the conviction that socialism is better than capitalism? And this pre-eminence of socialism is deduced by Marx from the fact that the coming of socialism is inevitable. The circle is closed.

In the context of the Marxian doctrine the superiority of socialism is proved by the fact that the proletarians are aiming at socialism. What the philosophers, the utopians, think does not count. What matters is the ideas of the proletarians, the class that history has entrusted with the task of shaping the future.

The truth is that the concept of socialism did not originate from the "proletarian mind." No proletarian or son of a proletarian contributed any substantial idea to the socialist ideology. The intellectual fathers of socialism were members of the intelligentsia, scions of the "bourgeoisie." Marx himself was the son of a well-to-do lawyer. He attended a German *Gymnasium*, the school all Marxians and other socialists denounce as the main offshoot of the bourgeois system of education, and his family supported him through all the years of his studies; he did not work his way through the university. He married the daughter of a member of the German nobility; his brother-in-law was Prussian minister of the interior and as such head of the Prussian police. In his household served a maid, Helene Demuth, who never married and who followed the Marx ménage in all its shifts of residence, the perfect model of the exploited slavey whose frustration and stunted sex life have been repeatedly depicted in the German "social" novel. Friedrich Engels was the son of a wealthy manufacturer and himself a manufacturer; he refused to marry his mistress Mary because she was uneducated and of "low" descent; [5] he enjoyed the amusements of the British gentry such as riding to hounds.

The workers were never enthusiastic about socialism.

5. After the death of Mary, Engels took her sister Lizzy as mistress. He married her on her deathbed "in order to provide her a last pleasure." Gustav Mayer, *Frederick Engels* (The Hague, Martinus Nijhoff, 1934), 2, 329.

They supported the union movement whose striving after higher wages Marx despised as useless.[6] They asked for all those measures of government interference with business which Marx branded petty-bourgeois nonsense. They opposed technological improvement, in earlier days by destroying new machines, later by union pressure and compulsion in favor of feather-bedding. Syndicalism—appropriation of the enterprises by the workers employed in them—is a program that the workers developed spontaneously. But socialism was brought to the masses by intellectuals of bourgeois background. Dining and wining together in the luxurious London homes and country seats of late Victorian "society," ladies and gentlemen in fashionable evening clothes concocted schemes for converting the British proletarians to the socialist creed.

4. The Ideological Impregnation of Thought

From the supposed irreconcilable conflict of class interests Marx deduces his doctrine of the ideological impregnation of thought. In a class society man is inherently unfit to conceive theories which are a substantially true description of reality. As his class affiliation, his social being, determines his thoughts, the products of his intellectual effort are ideologically tainted and distorted. They are not truth, but ideologies. An ideology in the Marxian sense of the term is a false doctrine which, however, precisely on account of its falsity,

6. Marx, *Value, Price and Profit,* ed. E. Marx Aveling (Chicago, Charles H. Kerr & Co. Cooperative), pp. 125–6. See below p. 137.

serves the interests of the class from which its author stems.

We may omit here dealing with many aspects of this ideology doctrine. We need not disprove anew the doctrine of polylogism, according to which the logical structure of mind differs in the members of various classes.[1] We may furthermore admit that the main concern of a thinker is exclusively to promote the interests of his class even if these clash with his interests as an individual. We may finally abstain from questioning the dogma that there is no such thing as the disinterested search for truth and knowledge and that all human inquiry is exclusively guided by the practical purpose of providing mental tools for successful action. The ideology doctrine would remain untenable even if all the irrefutable objections that can be raised from the point of view of these three aspects could be rejected.

Whatever one may think of the adequacy of the pragmatist definition of truth, it is obvious that at least one of the characteristic marks of a true theory is that action based on it succeeds it attaining the expected result. In this sense truth works, while untruth does not work. Precisely if we assume, in agreement with the Marxians, that the end of theorizing is always success in action, the question must be raised why and how an ideological (that is, in the Marxian sense, a false) theory should be more useful to a class than a correct theory? There is no doubt that the study of mechanics was motivated, at least to some extent, by practical considerations. People wanted to make use of the theorems of mechanics to

1. Mises, *Human Action*, pp. 72–91.

solve various problems of engineering. It was precisely the pursuit of these practical results that impelled them to search for a correct, not for a merely ideological (false) science of mechanics. No matter how one looks at it, there is no way in which a false theory can serve a man or a class or the whole of mankind better than a correct theory. How did Marx come to teach such a doctrine?

To answer this question we must remember the motive that impelled Marx to all his literary ventures. He was driven by one passion—to fight for the adoption of socialism. But he was fully aware of his inability to oppose any tenable objection to the economists' devastating criticism of all socialist plans. He was convinced that the system of economic doctrine developed by the Classical economists was impregnable, and remained unaware of the serious doubts which essential theorems of this system had already raised in some minds. Like his contemporary John Stuart Mill he believed "there is nothing in the laws of value which remains for the present or any future writer to clear up; the theory of the subject is complete." [2] When in 1871 the writings of Carl Menger and William Stanley Jevons inaugurated a new epoch of economic studies, Marx's career as a writer on economic problems had already come to a virtual end. The first volume of *Das Kapital* had been published in 1867; the manuscript of the following volumes was well along. There is no indication that Marx ever grasped the meaning of the new theory. Marx's economic teachings are essentially a garbled rehash of

2. Mill, *Principles of Political Economy*, Bk. III, ch. 1, § 1.

the theories of Adam Smith and, first of all, of Ricardo. Smith and Ricardo had not had any opportunity to refute socialist doctrines, as these were advanced only after their death. So Marx let them alone. But he vented his full indignation upon their successors who had tried to analyze the socialist schemes critically. He ridiculed them, calling them "vulgar economists" and "sycophants of the bourgeoisie." And as it was imperative for him to defame them, he contrived his ideology scheme.

These "vulgar economists" are, because of their bourgeois background, constitutionally unfit to discover truth. What their reasoning produces can only be ideological, that is, as Marx employed the term "ideology," a distortion of truth serving the class interests of the bourgeoisie. There is no need to refute their chains of argument by discursive reasoning and critical analysis. It is enough to unmask their bourgeois background and thereby the necessarily "ideological" character of their doctrines. They are wrong because they are bourgeois. No proletarian must attach any importance to their speculations.

To conceal the fact that this scheme was invented expressly to discredit the economists, it was necessary to elevate it to the dignity of a general epistemological law valid for all ages and for all branches of knowledge. Thus the ideology doctrine became the nucleus of Marxian epistemology. Marx and all his disciples concentrated their efforts upon the justification and exemplification of this makeshift. They did not shrink from any absurdity. They interpreted all philosophical systems, physical and biological theories, all literature, music, and art from the "ideological" point of view. But, of course, they were not consistent enough to assign to their own doctrines merely ideological character. The Marxian tenets, they implied, are not ideologies. They are a foretaste of the knowledge of the future classless society which, freed from the fetters of class conflicts, will be in a position to conceive pure knowledge, untainted by ideological blemishes.

Thus we can understand the thymological motives that led Marx to his ideology doctrine. Yet this does not answer the question why an ideological distortion of truth should be more advantageous to the interests of a class than a correct doctrine. Marx never ventured to explain this, probably aware that any attempt to would entangle him in an inextricable jumble of absurdities and contradictions.

There is no need to emphasize the ridiculousness of contending that an ideological physical, chemical, or therapeutical doctrine could be more advantageous for any class or individual than a correct one. One may pass over in silence the declarations of the Marxians concerning the ideological character of the theories developed by the bourgeois Mendel, Hertz, Planck, Heisenberg, and Einstein. It is sufficient to scrutinize the alleged ideological character of bourgeois economics.

As Marx saw it, their bourgeois background impelled the Classical economists to develop a system from which a justification of the unfair claims of the capitalist exploiters must logically follow. (In this he contradicts himself, as he drew from the same system just the opposite conclusions.) These theorems of the Classical economists from which the apparent justification of capitalism could be deduced were the theorems which Marx attacked most furiously: that the scarcity of the material factors of production on which man's well-being depends is an inevitable, nature-given condition of human existence; that no system of society's economic organization could create a state of abundance in which to everybody could be given according to his needs; that the recurrence of periods of economic depressions is not inherent in the very operation of an unhampered market economy but, on the contrary, the necessary outcome of government's interfering with business with the spurious aim of lowering the rate of interest and making business boom by inflation and credit expansion. But, we must ask, of what use, from the very Marxian point of view, could such a justification of capitalism be for the capitalists? They themselves did not need any justification for a system which —according to Marx—while wronging the workers was beneficial to themselves. They did not need to quiet their own consciences since, again according to Marx, every class is remorseless in the pursuit of its own selfish class interests.

Neither is it, from the point of view of the Marxian doctrine, permissible to assume that the service which the ideological theory, originating from a "false consciousness" and therefore distorting the true state of affairs, rendered to the exploiting class was to beguile the exploited class and to make it pliable and subservient, and thereby to preserve or at least to prolong the unfair system of exploitation. For, according to Marx, the duration of a definite system of production relations does not depend on any spiritual factors. It is exclusively determined by the state of the material productive forces. If the material productive forces change, the production relations (i.e., the property relations) and the whole ideological superstructure must change too. This transformation cannot be accelerated by any human effort. For as Marx said, "no social formation ever disappears before all the productive forces are developed for which it is broad enough, and new higher production relations never appear before the material conditions of their existence have been hatched out in the womb of the old society." [3]

This is by no means merely an incidental observation of Marx. It is one of the essential points of his doctrine. It is the theorem on which he based his claim to call his own doctrine scientific socialism as distinguished from the merely utopian socialism of his predecessors. The characteristic mark of the utopian socialists, as he saw it, was that they believed that the realization of socialism depends on spiritual and intellectual factors. You have to convince people that socialism is better than capitalism and then they will substitute socialism for capitalism. In Marx's eyes this utopian creed was absurd. The coming of socialism in no way depends on the thoughts and wills of men; it is an outgrowth of the development of the material productive forces. When the time is fulfilled and capitalism has reached its maturity, socialism will come. It can appear neither earlier nor

3. Marx, *Zur Kritik der politischen Oekonomie*, p. xii (see above pp. 107 f.).

later. The bourgeois may contrive the most cleverly elaborated ideologies—in vain; they cannot delay the day of the breakdown of capitalism.

Perhaps some people, intent upon salvaging the Marxian "ideology" concept, would argue this way: The capitalists are ashamed of their role in society. They feel guilty at being "robber barons, usurers, and ex- ploiters" and pocketing profits. They need a class ide- ology in order to restore their self-assertion. But why should they blush? There is, from the point of view of the Marxian doctrine, nothing in their conduct to be ashamed of. Capitalism, in the Marxian view, is an in- dispensable stage in the historical evolution of mankind. It is a necessary link in the succession of events which finally results in the bliss of socialism. The capitalists, in being capitalists, are merely tools of history. They execute what, according to the preordained plan for mankind's evolution, must be done. They comply with the eternal laws which are independent of the human will. They cannot help acting the way they do. They do not need any ideology, any "false consciousness," to tell them that they are right. They are right in the light of the Marxian doctrine. If Marx had been consistent, he would have exhorted the workers: Don't blame the cap- italists; in "exploiting" you they do what is best for your- selves; they are paving the way for socialism.

However one may turn the matter, one cannot dis- cover any reason why an ideological distortion of truth should be more useful to the bourgeoisie than a correct theory.

5. *The Conflict of Ideologies*

Class consciousness, says Marx, produces class ideologies. The class ideology provides the class with an interpretation of reality and at the same time teaches the members how to act in order to benefit their class. The content of the class ideology is uniquely determined by the historical stage of the development of the material productive forces and by the role the class concerned plays in this stage of history. The ideology is not an arbitrary brain child. It is the reflection of the thinker's material class condition as mirrored in his head. It is therefore not an individual phenomenon conditional upon the thinker's fancy. It is enjoined upon the mind by reality, i.e., by the class situation of the man who thinks. It is consequently identical with all members of the class. Of course, not every class comrade is an author and publishes what he has thought. But all writers belonging to the class conceive the same ideas and all other members of the class approve of them. There is no room left in Marxism for the assumption that the various members of the same class could seriously disagree in ideology. There exists for all members of the class only one ideology.

If a man expresses opinions at variance with the ideology of a definite class, that is because he does not belong to the class concerned. There is no need to refute his ideas by discursive reasoning. It is enough to unmask his background and class affiliation. This settles the matter.

But if a man whose proletarian background and membership in the workers' class cannot be contested diverges from the correct Marxian creed, he is a traitor. It is impossible to assume that he could be sincere in his rejection of Marxism. As a proletarian he must necessarily think like a proletarian. An inner voice tells him in an unmistakable way what the correct proletarian ideology is. He is dishonest in overriding this voice and publicly professing unorthodox opinions. He is a rogue, a Judas, a snake in the grass. In fighting such a betrayer all means are permissible.

Marx and Engels, two men of unquestionable bourgeois background, hatched out the class ideology of the proletarian class. They never ventured to discuss their doctrine with dissenters as scientists, for instance, discuss the pros and cons of the doctrines of Lamarck, Darwin, Mendel, and Weismann. As they saw it, their adversaries could only be either bourgeois idiots [1] or proletarian traitors. As soon as a socialist deviated an inch from the orthodox creed, Marx and Engels attacked him furiously, ridiculed and insulted him, represented him as a scoundrel and a wicked and corrupt monster. After Engels' death the office of supreme arbiter of what is and what is not correct Marxism devolved upon Karl Kautsky. In 1917 it passed into the hands of Lenin and became a function of the chief of the Soviet government. While Marx, Engels, and Kautsky had to content themselves with assassinating the character of their op-

1. E.g., "bourgeois stupidity" (about Bentham, *Das Kapital, 1,* 574), "bourgeois cretinism" (about Destutt de Tracy, ibid., 2, 465), and so on.

ponents, Lenin and Stalin could assassinate them physically. Step by step they anathematized those who once were considered by all Marxians, including Lenin and Stalin themselves, as the great champions of the proletarian cause: Kautsky, Max Adler, Otto Bauer, Plechanoff, Bukharin, Trotsky, Riasanov, Radek, Sinoviev, and many others. Those whom they could seize were imprisoned, tortured, and finally murdered. Only those who were happy enough to dwell in countries dominated by "plutodemocratic reactionaries" survived and were permitted to die in their beds.

A good case can be made, from the Marxian point of view, in favor of decision by the majority. If a doubt concerning the correct content of the proletarian ideology arises, the ideas held by the majority of the proletarians are to be considered those which truthfully reflect the genuine proletarian ideology. As Marxism supposes that the immense majority of people are proletarians, this would be tantamount to assigning the competence to make the ultimate decisions in conflicts of opinion to parliaments elected under adult franchise. But although to refuse to do this is to explode the whole ideology doctrine, neither Marx nor his successors were ever prepared to submit their opinions to majority vote. Throughout his career Marx mistrusted the people and was highly suspicious of parliamentary procedures and decisions by the ballot. He was enthusiastic about the Paris revolution of June 1848, in which a small minority of Parisians rebelled against the government supported by a parliament elected under universal manhood suffrage. The Paris Commune of the spring of 1871, in which again Parisian socialists fought against the regime duly established by the overwhelming majority of the French people's representatives, was still more to his liking. Here he found his ideal of the dictatorship of the proletariat, the dictatorship of a self-appointed band of leaders, realized. He tried to persuade the Marxian parties of all countries of Western and Central Europe to base their hopes not upon election campaigns but upon revolutionary methods. In this regard the Russian communists were his faithful disciples. The Russian parliament elected in 1917 under the auspices of the Lenin government by all adult citizens had, in spite of the violence offered to the voters by the ruling party, less than 25 per cent communist members. Three-quarters of the people had voted against the communists. But Lenin dispersed the parliament by force of arms and firmly established the dictatorial rule of a minority. The head of the Soviet power became the supreme pontiff of the Marxian sect. His title to this office is derived from the fact that he had defeated his rivals in a bloody civil war.

As the Marxians do not admit that differences of opinion can be settled by discussion and persuasion or decided by majority vote, no solution is open but civil war. The mark of the good ideology, i.e., the ideology adequate to the genuine class interests of the proletarians, is the fact that its supporters succeeded in conquering and liquidating their opponents.

6. *Ideas and Interests*

Marx assumes tacitly that the social condition of a class uniquely determines its interests and that there can be no doubt what kind of policy best serves these interests. The class does not have to choose between various policies. The historical situation enjoins upon it a definite policy. There is no alternative. It follows that the class does not act, since acting implies choosing among various possible ways of procedure. The material productive forces act through the medium of the class members.

But Marx, Engels, and all other Marxians ignored this fundamental dogma of their creed as soon as they stepped beyond the borders of epistemology and began commenting upon historical and political issues. Then they not only charged the nonproletarian classes with hostility to the proletarians but criticized their policies as not conducive to promoting the true interests of their own classes.

The most important of Marx's political pamphlets is the *Address on the Civil War in France* (1871). It furiously attacks the French government which, backed by the immense majority of the nation, was intent upon quelling the rebellion of the Paris Commune. It recklessly calumniates all the leading members of that government, calling them swindlers, forgers, and embezzlers. Jules Favre, it charges, was "living in concubinage with the wife of a dipsomaniac," and General de Gallifet profited from the alleged prostitution of his wife. In short, the pamphlet set the pattern for the defamation tactics of the socialist press which the Marxians indignantly chastised as one of the worst excrescences of capitalism when the tabloid press adopted it. Yet all these slanderous lies, however reprehensible, may be interpreted as partisan strategems in the implacable war against bourgeois civilization. They are at least not incompatible with Marxian epistemological principles. But it is another thing to question the expediency of the bourgeois policy from the standpoint of the class interests of the bourgeoisie. The *Address* maintains that the policy of the French bourgeoisie has unmasked the essential teachings of its own ideology, the only purpose of which is "to delay the class struggle"; henceforth it will no longer be possible for the class rule of the bourgeoisie "to hide in a nationalist uniform." Henceforth there will no longer be any question of peace or armistice between the workers and their exploiters. The battle will be resumed again and again and there can be no doubt about the final victory of the workingmen.[1]

It must be noted that these observations were made with regard to a situation in which the majority of the French people had only to choose between unconditional surrender to a small minority of revolutionaries or fighting them. Neither Marx nor anybody else had ever expected that the majority of a nation would yield without resistance to armed aggression on the part of a minority.

Still more important is the fact that Marx in these observations ascribes to the policies adopted by the French bourgeoisie a decisive influence upon the course of events. In this he contradicts all his other writings. In the *Communist Manifesto* he had announced the implacable and relentless class struggle without any re-

1. Marx, *Der Bürgerkrieg in Frankreich,* ed. Pfemfert (Berlin, 1919), p. 7.

gard to the defense tactics the bourgeois may resort to. He had deduced the inevitability of this struggle from the class situation of the exploiters and that of the exploited. There is no room in the Marxian system for the assumption that the policies adopted by the bourgeoisie could in any way affect the emergence of the class struggle and its outcome.

If it is true that one class, the French bourgeoisie of 1871, was in a position to choose between alternative policies and through its decision to influence the course of events, the same must be true also of other classes in other historical situations. Then all the dogmas of Marxian materialism are exploded. Then it is not true that the class situation teaches a class what its genuine class interests are and what kind of policy best serves these interests. It is not true that only such ideas as are conducive to the real interests of a class meet with approval on the part of those who direct the policies of the class. It may happen that different ideas direct those policies and thus get an influence upon the course of events. But then it is not true that what counts in history are only interests, and that ideas are merely an ideological superstructure, uniquely determined by these interests. It becomes imperative to scrutinize ideas in order to sift those which are really beneficial to the interests of the class concerned from those which are not. It becomes necessary to discuss conflicting ideas with the methods of logical reasoning. The makeshift by means of which Marx wanted to outlaw such dispassionate weighing of the pros and cons of definite ideas breaks down. The way toward an examination of the merits and demerits of socialism which Marx wanted to prohibit as "unscientific" is reopened.

Another important address of Marx was his paper of 1865, *Value, Price and Profit*. In this document Marx criticizes the traditional policies of the labor unions. They should abandon their "*conservative* motto, *A fair day's wages for a fair day's work!* and ought to inscribe on their banner the *revolutionary* watchword, *Abolition of the wages system!*" [2] This is obviously a controversy about which kind of policy best serves the class interests of the workers. Marx in this case deviates from his usual procedure of branding all his proletarian opponents traitors. He implicitly admits that there can prevail dissent even among honest and sincere champions of the class interests of the workers and that such differences must be settled by debating the issue. Perhaps on second thought he himself discovered that the way he had dealt with the problem involved was incompatible with all his dogmas, for he did not have printed this paper which he had read on June 26, 1865, in the General Council of the International Workingmen's Association. It was first published in 1898 by one of his daughters.

But the theme we are scrutinizing is not Marx's failure to cling consistently to his own doctrine and his lapses into ways of thinking incompatible with it. We have to examine the tenability of the Marxian doctrine and must therefore turn to the peculiar connotation the term "interests" has in the context of this doctrine.

Every individual, and for that matter every group of

2. Marx, *Value, Price and Profit*, pp. 126–7.

individuals, aims in acting at the substitution of a state of affairs that suits him better for a state of affairs that he considers less satisfactory. Without any regard to the qualification of these two states of affairs from any other point of view, we may say in this sense that he pursues his own interests. But the question of what is more desirable and what is less is decided by the acting individual. It is the outcome of choosing among various possible solutions. It is a judgment of value. It is determined by the individual's ideas about the effects these various states may have upon his own well-being. But it ultimately depends upon the value he attaches to these anticipated effects.

If we keep this in mind, it is not sensible to declare that ideas are a product of interests. Ideas tell a man what his interests are. At a later date, looking upon his past actions, the individual may form the opinion that he has erred and that another mode of acting would have served his own interests better. But this does not mean that at the critical instant in which he acted he did not act according to his interests. He acted according to what he, at that time, considered would serve his interests best.

If an unaffected observer looks upon another man's action, he may think: This fellow errs; what he does will not serve what he considers to be his interest; another way of acting would be more suitable for attaining the ends he aims at. In this sense a historian can say today or a judicious contemporary could say in 1939: In invading Poland Hitler and the Nazis made a mistake; the invasion harmed what they considered to be their interests. Such criticism is sensible so long as it deals only with the means and not with the ultimate ends of an action. The choice of ultimate ends is a judgment of value solely dependent on the judging individual's valuation. All that another man can say about it is: I would have made a different choice. If a Roman had said to a Christian doomed to be lacerated by wild beasts in the circus: You will best serve your interests by bowing down and worshiping the statue of our divine Emperor, the Christian would have answered: My prime interest is to comply with the precepts of my creed.

But Marxism, as a philosophy of history claiming to know the ends which men are bound to aim at, employs the term "interests" with a different connotation. The interests it refers to are not those chosen by men on the ground of judgments of value. They are the ends the material productive forces are aiming at. These forces aim at the establishment of socialism. They use the proletarians as a means for the realization of this end. The superhuman material productive forces pursue their own interests, independently of the will of mortal men. The proletarian class is merely a tool in their hands. The actions of the class are not its own actions but those which the material productive forces perform in using the class as an instrument without a will of its own. The class interests to which Marx refers are in fact the interests of the material productive forces which want to be freed from "the fetters upon their development."

Interests of this kind, of course, do not depend upon the ideas of ordinary men. They are determined exclusively by the ideas of the man Marx, who generated both the phantom of the material productive forces and the anthropomorphic image of their interests.

In the world of reality, life, and human action there is no such thing as interests independent of ideas, preceding them temporally and logically. What a man considers his interest is the result of his ideas.

If there is any sense in the proposition that the interests of the proletarians would be best served by socialism, it is this: the ends which the individual proletarians are aiming at will be best achieved by socialism. Such a proposition requires proof. It is vain to substitute for such a proof the recourse to an arbitrarily contrived system of philosophy of history.

All this could never occur to Marx because he was engrossed by the idea that human interests are uniquely and entirely determined by the biological nature of the human body. Man, as he saw it, is exclusively interested in the procurement of the largest quantity of tangible goods. There is no qualitative, only a quantitative, problem in the supply of goods and services. Wants do not depend on ideas but solely on physiological conditions. Blinded by this preconception, Marx ignored the fact that one of the problems of production is to decide what kind of goods are to be produced.

With animals and with primitive men on the verge of starvation it is certainly true that nothing counts but the quantity of edible things they can secure. There is no need to point out that conditions are entirely different for men, even for those in the earliest stages of civilization. Civilized man is faced with the problem of choosing among the satisfactions of various needs and among various modes of satisfying the same need. His interests are diversified and are determined by the ideas that influence his choosing. One does not serve the interests of a man who wants a new coat by giving him a pair of shoes or those of a man who wants to hear a Beethoven symphony by giving him admission to a boxing match. It is ideas that are responsible for the fact that the interests of people are disparate.

Incidentally it may be mentioned that this misconstruing of human wants and interests prevented Marx and other socialists from comprehending the distinction between freedom and slavery, between the condition of a man who himself decides how to spend his income and that of a man whom a paternal authority supplies with those things which, as the authority thinks, he needs. In the market economy the consumers choose and thereby determine the quantity and the quality of the goods produced. Under socialism the authority takes care of these matters. In the eyes of Marx and the Marxians there is no substantial difference between these two methods of want satisfaction; it is of no consequence who chooses, the "paltry" individual for himself or the authority for all its subjects. They fail to realize that the authority does not give its wards what they want to get but what, according to the opinion, of the authority, they ought to get. If a man who wants to get the Bible gets the Koran instead, he is no longer free.

But even if, for the sake of argument, we were to admit that there is uncertainty neither concerning the kind of goods people are asking for nor concerning the most expedient technological methods of producing them, there remains the conflict between interests in the short run and those in the long run. Here again the decision depends on ideas. It is judgments of value that determine the amount of time preference attached to the value of present goods as against that of future goods. Should one consume or accumulate capital? And how far should capital depletion or accumulation go?

Instead of dealing with all these problems Marx contented himself with the dogma that socialism will be an earthly paradise in which everybody will get all he needs. Of course, if one starts from this dogma, one can quietly declare that the interests of everybody, whatever they may be, will be best served under socialism. In the land of Cockaigne people will no longer need any ideas, will no longer have to resort to any judgments of value, will no longer think and act. They will only open their mouths to let the roast pigeons fly in.

In the world of reality, the conditions of which are the only object of the scientific search for truth, ideas determine what people consider to be their interests. There is no such thing as interests that could be independent of ideas. It is ideas that determine what people consider as their interests. Free men do not act in accordance with their interests. They act in accordance with what they believe furthers their interests.

7. *The Class Interests of the Bourgeoisie*

One of the starting points of the thinking of Karl Marx was the dogma that capitalism, while utterly detrimental to the working class, is favorable to the class interests of the bourgeoisie and that socialism, while thwarting only the unfair claims of the bourgeoisie, is highly beneficial to the whole of mankind. These were ideas developed by the French communists and socialists and disclosed to the German public in 1842 by Lorenz von Stein in his voluminous book *Socialism and Communism in Present-Day France*. Without any qualms Marx adopted this doctrine and all that was implied in it. It never occurred to him that its fundamental dogma might require a demonstration, and the concepts it employs a definition. He never defined the concepts of a social class and of class interests and their conflicts. He never explained why socialism serves the class interests of the proletarians and the true interests of the whole of mankind better than any other system. This attitude has been up to our time the characteristic mark of all socialists. They simply take it for granted that life under socialism will be blissful. Whoever dares to ask for reasons is by this very demand unmasked as a bribed apologist of the selfish class interests of the exploiters.

The Marxian philosophy of history teaches that what brings about the coming of socialism is the operation of the immanent laws of capitalistic production itself. With the inexorability of a law of nature, capitalistic production begets its own negation.[1] As no social formation ever disappears before all the productive forces are developed for which it has room,[2] capitalism must run its full course before the time comes for the emergence

1. Marx, *Das Kapital*, *1*, 728.
2. See above, pp. 107 and 128.

of socialism. The free evolution of capitalism, not upset by any political interference, is therefore, from the Marxian point of view, highly beneficial to the—we would have to say "rightly understood" or long-term—class interests of the proletarians. With the progress of capitalism on the way to its maturity and consequently to its collapse, says the Communist Manifesto, the laborer "sinks deeper and deeper," he "becomes a pauper." But seen *sub specie aeternitatis*, from the point of view of mankind's destination and the long-run interests of the proletariat, this "mass of misery, oppression, slavery, degradation, and exploitation" is in fact to be regarded as a step forward on the road toward eternal bliss. It appears therefore not only vain but manifestly contrary to the—rightly understood—interests of the working class to indulge in—necessarily futile—attempts to improve the wage earners' conditions through reforms within the framework of capitalism. Hence Marx rejected labor union endeavors to raise wage rates and to shorten the hours of work. The most orthodox of all Marxian parties, the German Social-Democrats, voted in the eighties in the Reichstag against all measures of Bismarck's famous *Sozialpolitik*, including its most spectacular feature, social security. Likewise in the opinion of the communists the American New Deal was just a foredoomed scheme to salvage dying capitalism by postponing its breakdown and thereby the appearance of the socialist millennium.

If employers oppose what is commonly called prolabor legislation, they are consequently not guilty of fighting what Marx considered to be the true interests of the proletarian class. On the contrary. In virtually freeing economic evolution from the fetters by means of which ignorant petty bourgeois, bureaucrats, and such utopian and humanitarian pseudo socialists as the Fabians plan to slow it down, they are serving the cause of labor and socialism. The very selfishness of the exploiters turns into a boon for the exploited and for the whole of mankind. Would not Marx, if he had been able to follow his own ideas to their ultimate logical consequences, have been tempted to say, with Mandeville, "private vices, public benefits," or, with Adam Smith, that the rich "are led by an invisible hand" in such a way that they "without intending it, without knowing it, advance the interest of the society?" [3]

However, Marx was always anxious to bring his reasoning to an end before the point beyond which its inherent contradictions would have become manifest. In this regard his followers copied their master's attitude.

The bourgeois, both capitalists and entrepreneurs, say these inconsistent disciples of Marx, are interested in the preservation of the laissez-faire system. They are opposed to all attempts to alleviate the lot of the most numerous, most useful, and most exploited class of men; they are intent upon stopping progress; they are reactionaries committed to the—of course, hopeless—task of turning history's clock back. Whatever one may think of these passionate effusions, repeated daily by newspapers, politicians, and governments, one cannot deny that they are incompatible with the essential tenets of

3. Adam Smith, *The Theory of Moral Sentiments,* Pt. IV, ch. 1 (Edinburgh, 1813), *1,* 419 ff.

Marxism. From a consistent Marxian point of view the champions of what is called prolabor legislation are reactionary petty bourgeois, while those whom the Marxians call labor-baiters are progressive harbingers of the bliss to come.

In their ignorance of all business problems, the Marxians failed to see that the present-day bourgeois, those who are already wealthy capitalists and entrepreneurs, are in their capacity as bourgeois not selfishly interested in the preservation of laissez faire. Under laissez faire their eminent position is daily threatened anew by the ambitions of impecunious newcomers. Laws that put obstacles in the way of talented upstarts are detrimental to the interests of the consumers but they protect those who have already established their position in business against the competition of intruders. In making it more difficult for a businessman to reap profit and in taxing away the greater part of the profits made, they prevent the accumulation of capital by newcomers and thus remove the inducement that impels old firms toward the utmost exertion in serving the customers. Measures sheltering the less efficient against the competition of the more efficient and laws that aim at reducing or confiscating profits are from the Marxian point of view conservative, nay, reactionary. They tend to prevent technological improvement and economic progress and to preserve inefficiency and backwardness. If the New Deal had started in 1900 and not in 1933, the American consumer would have been deprived of many things today provided by industries which grew in the first decades of the century from insignificant beginnings to national importance and mass production.

The culmination of this misconstruction of industrial problems is the animosity displayed against big business and against the efforts of smaller concerns to become bigger. Public opinion, under the spell of Marxism, considers "bigness" one of the worst vices of business and condones every scheme devised to curb or to hurt big business by government action. There is no comprehension of the fact that it is solely bigness in business which makes it possible to supply the masses with all those products the present-day American common man does not want to do without. Luxury goods for the few can be produced in small shops. Luxury goods for the many require big business. Those politicians, professors, and union bosses who curse big business are fighting for a lower standard of living. They are certainly not furthering the interests of the proletarians. And they are, precisely also from the point of view of the Marxian doctrine, ultimately enemies of progress and of improvement of the conditions of the workers.

8. *The Critics of Marxism*

The materialism of Marx and Engels differs radically from the ideas of classical materialism. It depicts human thoughts, choices, and actions as determined by the material productive forces—tools and machines. Marx and Engels failed to see that tools and machines are themselves products of the operation of the human mind. Even if their sophisticated attempts to describe all spiritual and intellectual phenomena, which they call superstructural, as produced by the material productive forces had been successful, they would only have traced these phenomena back to something which in itself is a spiritual and intellectual phenomenon. Their reasoning moves in a circle. Their alleged materialism is in fact no materialism at all. It provides merely a verbal solution of the problems involved.

Occasionally even Marx and Engels were aware of the fundamental inadequacy of their doctrine. When Engels at the grave of Marx summed up what he considered to be the quintessence of his friend's achievements, he did not mention the material productive forces at all. Said Engels: "As Darwin discovered the law of evolution of organic nature, Marx discovered the law of mankind's historical evolution, that is the simple fact, hitherto hidden beneath ideological overgrowths, that men must first of all eat, drink, have shelter and clothing before they can pursue politics, science, art, religion, and the like, that consequently the production of the immediately required foodstuffs and therewith the stage of economic evolution attained by a people or an epoch constitute the foundation out of which the governmental institutions, the ideas about right and wrong, art, and even the religious ideas of men have been developed and by means of which they must be explained—not, as hitherto had been done, the other way round.[1] Certainly no man was more competent than Engels to provide an authoritative interpretation of dialectic materialism. But if Engels was right in this obituary, then the whole of Marxian materialism fades

---

1. Engels, *Karl Marx, Rede an seinem Grab*, many editions. Reprinted in Franz Mehring, *Karl Marx* (2d ed. Leipzig, 1919, Leipziger Buchdruckerei Aktiengesellschaft), p. 535.

away. It is reduced to a truism known to everybody from time immemorial and never contested by anybody. It says no more than the worn-out aphorism: Primum vivere, deinde philosophari.

As an eristic trick Engels' interpretation turned out very well. As soon as somebody begins to unmask the absurdities and contradictions of dialectical materialism, the Marxians retort: Do you deny that men must first of all eat? Do you deny that men are interested in improving the material conditions of their existence? Since nobody wants to contest these truisms, they conclude that all the teachings of Marxian materialism are unassailable. And hosts of pseudo philosophers fail to see through this non sequitur.

The main target of Marx's rancorous attacks was the Prussian state of the Hohenzollern dynasty. He hated this regime not because it was opposed to socialism but precisely because it was inclined to accept socialism. While his rival Lassalle toyed with the idea of realizing socialism in cooperation with the Prussian government led by Bismarck, Marx's International Workingmen's Association sought to supplant the Hohenzollern. Since in Prussia the Protestant Church was subject to the government and was administered by government officials, Marx never tired of vilifying the Christian religion too. Anti-Christianism became all the more a dogma of Marxism in that the countries whose intellectuals first were converted to Marxism were Russia and Italy. In Russia the church was even more dependent on the government than in Prussia. In the eyes of the Italians of the nineteenth century anti-Catholic bias was the mark of all who opposed the restoration of the Pope's secular rule and the disintegration of the newly won national unity.

The Christian churches and sects did not fight socialism. Step by step they accepted its essential political and social ideas. Today they are, with but few exceptions, outspoken in rejecting capitalism and advocating either socialism or interventionist policies which must inevitably result in the establishment of socialism. But, of course, no Christian church can ever acquiesce in a brand of socialism which is hostile to Christianity and aims at its suppression. The churches are implacably opposed to the anti-Christian aspects of Marxism. They try to distinguish between their own program of social reform and the Marxian program. The inherent viciousness of Marxism they consider to be its materialism and atheism.

However, in fighting Marxian materialism the apologists of religion have entirely missed the point. Many of them look upon materialism as an ethical doctrine teaching that men *ought* only to strive after satisfaction of the needs of their bodies and after a life of pleasure and revelry, and *ought* not to bother about anything else. What they advance against this ethical materialism has no reference to the Marxian doctrine and no bearing on the issue in dispute.

No more sensible are the objections raised to Marxian materialism by those who pick out definite historical events—such as the rise of the Christian creed, the crusades, the religious wars—and triumphantly assert that no materialist interpretation of them could be provided.

Every change in conditions affects the structure of demand and supply of various material things and thereby the short-run interests of some groups of people. It is therefore possible to show that there were some groups who profited in the short run and others who were prejudiced in the short run. Hence the advocates of Marxism are always in a position to point out that class interests were involved and thus to annul the objections raised. Of course, this method of demonstrating the correctness of the materialist interpretation of history is entirely wrong. The question is not whether group interests were affected; they are necessarily always affected at least in the short run. The question is whether the striving after lucre of the groups concerned was the cause of the event under discussion. For instance, were the short-run interests of the munitions industry instrumental in bringing about the bellicosity and the wars of our age? In dealing with such problems the Marxians never mention that where there are interests pro there are necessarily also interests con. They would have to explain why the latter did not prevail over the former. But the "idealist" critics of Marxism were to dull to expose any of the fallacies of dialectical materialism. They did not even notice that the Marxians resorted to their class-interest interpretation only in dealing with phenomena which were generally condemned as bad, never in dealing with phenomena of which all people approve. If one ascribes warring to the machinations of munitions capital and alcoholism to machinations of the liquor trade, it would be consistent to ascribe cleanliness to the designs of the soap manufacturers and the flowering of literature and education to the maneuvering of the publishing and printing industries. But neither the Marxians nor their critics ever thought of it.

The outstanding fact in all this is that the Marxian doctrine of historical change has never received any judicious critique. It could triumph because its adversaries never disclosed its fallacies and inherent contradictions.

How entirely people have misunderstood Marxian materialism is shown in the common practice of lumping together Marxism and Freud's psychoanalysis. Actually no sharper contrast can be thought of than that between these two doctrines. Materialism aims at reducing mental phenomena to material causes. Psychoanalysis, on the contrary, deals with mental phenomena as with an autonomous field. While traditional psychiatry and neurology tried to explain all pathological conditions with which they were concerned as caused by definite pathological conditions of some bodily organs, psychoanalysis succeeded in demonstrating that abnormal states of the body are sometimes produced by mental factors. This discovery was the achievement of Charcot and of Josef Breuer, and it was the great exploit of Sigmund Freud to build upon this foundation a comprehensive systematic discipline. Psychoanalysis is the opposite of all brands of materialism. If we look upon it not as a branch of pure knowledge but as a method of healing the sick, we would have to call it a thymological branch (*geisteswissenschaftlicher Zweig*) of medicine.

Freud was a modest man. He did not make extrava-

gant pretensions regarding the importance of his contributions. He was very cautious in touching upon problems of philosophy and branches of knowledge to the
development of which he himself had not contributed.
He did not venture to attack any of the metaphysical
propositions of materialism. He even went so far as to
admit that one day science may succeed in providing a
purely physiological explanation of the phenomena psychoanalysis deals with. Only so long as this does not
happen, psychoanalysis appeared to him scientifically
sound and practically indispensable. He was no less
cautious in criticizing Marxian materialism. He freely
confessed his incompetence in this field.[2] But all this
does not alter the fact that the psychoanalytical approach is essentially and substantially incompatible
with the epistemology of materialism.

Psychoanalysis stresses the role that the libido, the
sexual impulse, plays in human life. This role had been
neglected before by psychology as well as by all other
branches of knowledge. Psychoanalysis also explains the
reasons for this neglect. But it by no means asserts that
sex is the only human urge seeking satisfaction and
that all psychic phenomena are induced by it. Its preoccupation with sexual impulses arose from the fact that
it started as a therapeutical method and that most of
the pathological conditions it had to deal with are
caused by the repression of sexual urges.

The reason some authors linked psychoanalysis and
Marxism was that both were considered to be at vari-

2. Freud, *Neue Folge der Vorlesungen zur Einführung in die
Psychoanalyse* (Vienna, 1933), pp. 246–53.

ance with theological ideas. However, with the passing of time theological schools and groups of various denominations are adopting a different evaluation of the teachings of Freud. They are not merely dropping their radical opposition as they have already done before with regard to modern astronomical and geological achievements and the theories of phylogenetic change in the structure of organisms. They are trying to integrate psychoanalysis into the system and the practice of pastoral theology. They view the study of psychoanalysis as an important part of the training for the ministry.[3]

As conditions are today, many defenders of the authority of the church are guideless and bewildered in their attitude toward philosophical and scientific problems. They condemn what they could or even should endorse. In fighting spurious doctrines, they resort to untenable objections which in the minds of those who can discern the fallaciousness of the objections rather strengthen the tendency to believe that the attacked doctrines are sound. Being unable to discover the real flaw in false doctrines, these apologists for religion may finally end by approving them. This explains the curious fact that there are nowadays tendencies in Christian writings to adopt Marxian dialectical materialism. Thus a Presbyterian theologian, Professor Alexander Miller,

3. Of course, few theologians would be prepared to endorse the interpretation of an eminent Catholic historian of medicine, Professor Petro L. Entralgo, according to which Freud has "brought to full development some of the possibilities offered by Christianity." P. L. Entralgo, *Mind and Body*, trans. by A. M. Espinosa, Jr. (New York, P. J. Kennedy and Sons, 1956), p. 131.

believes that Christianity "can reckon with the truth in historical materialism and with the fact of class-struggle." He not only suggests, as many eminent leaders of various Christian denominations have done before him, that the church should adopt the essential principles of Marxian politics. He thinks the church ought to "accept Marxism" as "the essence of a scientific sociology." [4] How odd to reconcile with the Nicene creed a doctrine teaching that religious ideas are the superstructure of the material productive forces!

9. *Marxian Materialism and Socialism*

Like many frustrated intellectuals and like almost all contemporary Prussian noblemen, civil servants, teachers, and writers, Marx was driven by a fanatical hatred of business and businessmen. He turned toward socialism because he considered it the worst punishment that could be inflicted upon the odious bourgeois. At the same time he realized that the only hope for socialism was to prevent further discussion of its pros and cons. People must be induced to accept it emotionally without asking questions about its effects.

In order to achieve this, Marx adapted Hegel's philosophy of history, the official creed of the schools from which he had graduated. Hegel had arrogated to himself the faculty of revealing the Lord's hidden plans to the public. There was no reason why Doctor Marx should stand back and withhold from the people the

4. Alexander Miller, *The Christian Significance of Karl Marx* (New York, Macmillan, 1947), pp. 80–1.

good tidings that an inner voice had communicated to him. Socialism, this voice announced, is bound to come because this is the course that destiny is steering. There is no use indulging in debate about the blessings or ills to be expected from a socialist or communist mode of production. Such debates would be reasonable only if men were free to choose between socialism and some alternative. Besides, being later in the succession of stages of historical evolution, socialism is also necessarily a higher and better stage, and all doubts about the benefits to be derived from it are futile.[1]

The scheme of philosophy of history that describes human history as culminating and ending in socialism is the essence of Marxism, is Karl Marx's main contribution to the prosocialist ideology. Like all similar schemes including that of Hegel, it was begot by intuition. Marx called it science, *Wissenschaft,* because in his day no other epithet could give a doctrine higher prestige. In pre-Marxian ages it was not customary to call philosophies of history scientific. Nobody ever applied the term "science" to the prophecies of Daniel, the Revelation of St. John, or the writings of Joachim of Flora.

For the same reasons Marx called his doctrine materialistic. In the environment of left-wing Hegelianism in which Marx lived before he settled in London, materialism was the accepted philosophy. It was taken for granted that philosophy and science admit of no treatment of the mind-body problem but that taught by materialism. Authors who did not want to be anathematized by their set had to avoid being suspected of any

1. See below, pp. 175 ff.

concession to "idealism." Thus Marx was anxious to call his philosophy materialistic. In fact, as has been pointed out above, his doctrine does not deal at all with the mind-body problem. It does not raise the question of how the "material productive forces" come into existence and how and why they change. Marx's doctrine is not a materialist but a technological interpretation of history. But, from a political point of view, Marx did well in calling his doctrine scientific and materialistic. These predicates lent it a reputation it would never have acquired without them.

Incidentally it must be noted that Marx and Engels made no effort to establish the validity of their technological interpretation of history. In the earlier days of their careers as authors they enunciated their dogmas in clear-cut, challenging formulations such as the above-quoted dictum about the hand mill and the steam mill.[2] In later years they became more reserved and cautious; after the death of Marx Engels occasionally even made remarkable concessions to the "bourgeois" and "idealistic" point of view. But never did Marx or Engels or any of their numerous followers try to give any specifications about the operation of a mechanism which would out of a definite state of the material productive forces bring forth a definite juridical, political, and spiritual superstructure. Their famous philosophy never grew beyond the abrupt enunciation of a piquant aperçu.

The eristic tricks of Marxism succeeded very well and enrolled hosts of pseudo intellectuals in the ranks of revolutionary socialism. But they did not discredit what

2. See above, p. 108.

economists had asserted about the disastrous consequences of a socialist mode of production. Marx had
tabooed the analysis of the operation of a socialist system as utopian, that is, in his terminology, as unscientific, and he as well as his successors smeared all authors
who defied this taboo. Yet these tactics did not alter the
fact that all Marx contributed to the discussion on socialism was to disclose what an inner voice had told him,
namely that the end and aim of mankind's historical
evolution is expropriation of the capitalists.

From the epistemological point of view it must be
emphasized that Marxian materialism does not accomplish what a materialist philosophy claims to do. It does
not explain how definite thoughts and judgments of
value originate in the human mind.

The exposure of an untenable doctrine is not tantamount to confirmation of a doctrine conflicting with it.
There is need to state this obvious fact because many
people have forgotten it. The refutation of dialectical
materialism implies, of course, invalidation of the Marxian vindication of socialism. But it does not demonstrate
the truth of the assertions that socialism is unrealizable,
that it would destroy civilization and result in misery
for all, and that its coming is not inevitable. These propositions can be established only by economic analysis.

Marx and all those who sympathize with his doctrines
have been aware that an economic analysis of socialism
will show the fallacy of the prosocialist arguments.
The Marxists cling to historical materialism and stubbornly refuse to listen to its critics because they want
socialism for emotional reasons.

Chapter 8. Philosophy of History

1. The Theme of History

HISTORY deals with human action, that is, the actions performed by individuals and groups of individuals. It describes the conditions under which people lived and the way they reacted to these conditions. Its subject are human judgments of value and the ends men aimed at guided by these judgments, the means men resorted to in order to attain the ends sought, and the outcome of their actions. History deals with man's conscious reaction to the state of his environment, both the natural environment and the social environment as determined by the actions of preceding generations as well as by those of his contemporaries.

Every individual is born into a definite social and natural milieu. An individual is not simply man in general, whom history can regard in the abstract. An individual is at any instant of his life the product of all the experiences to which his ancestors were exposed plus those to which he himself has so far been exposed. An actual man lives as a member of his family, his race, his people, and his age; as a citizen of his country; as a member of a definite social group; as a practitioner of a certain vocation. He is imbued with definite religious, philosophical, metaphysical, and political ideas, which he sometimes enlarges or modifies by his own thinking.

His actions are guided by ideologies that he has acquired through his environment.

However, these ideologies are not immutable. They are products of the human mind and they change when new thoughts are added to the old stock of ideas or are substituted for discarded ideas. In searching for the origin of new ideas history cannot go beyond establishing that they were produced by a man's thinking. The ultimate data of history beyond which no historical research can go are human ideas and actions. The historian can trace ideas back to other, previously developed ideas. He can describe the environmental conditions to which actions were designed to react. But he can never say more about a new idea and a new mode of acting than that they originated at a definite point of space and time in the mind of a man and were accepted by other men.

Attempts have been made to explain the birth of ideas out of "natural" factors. Ideas were described as the necessary product of the geographical environment, the physical structure of people's habitat. This doctrine manifestly contradicts the data available. Many ideas are the response elicited by the stimulus of a man's physical environment. But the content of these ideas is not determined by the environment. To the same physical environment various individuals and groups of individuals respond in a different way.

Others have tried to explain the diversity of ideas and actions by biological factors. The species man is subdivided into racial groups with distinctive hereditary biological traits. Historical experience does not preclude the assumption that the members of some racial groups are better gifted for conceiving sound ideas than those of other races. However, what is to be explained is why a man's ideas differ from those of people of the same race. Why do brothers differ from one another?

It is moreover questionable whether cultural backwardness conclusively indicates a racial group's permanent inferiority. The evolutionary process that transformed the animal-like ancestors of man into modern men extended over many hundreds of thousands of years. Viewed in the perspective of this period, the fact that some races have not yet reached a cultural level other races passed several thousand years ago does not seem to matter very much. There are individuals whose physical and mental development proceeds more slowly than the average who yet in later life far excel most normally developing persons. It is not impossible that the same phenomenon may occur with whole races.

There is for history nothing beyond people's ideas and the ends they were aiming at motivated by these ideas. If the historian refers to the meaning of a fact, he always refers either to the interpretation acting men gave to the situation in which they had to live and to act, and to the outcome of their ensuing actions, or to the interpretation which other people gave to the result of these actions. The final causes to which history refers are always the ends individuals and groups of individuals are aiming at. History does not recognize in the course of events any other meaning and sense than those attributed to them by acting men, judging from the point of view of their own human concerns.

2. *The Theme of the Philosophy of History*

Philosophy of history looks upon mankind's history from a different point of view. It assumes that God or nature or some other superhuman entity providentially directs the course of events toward a definite goal different from the ends which acting men are aiming at. There is a meaning in the sequence of events which supersedes the intentions of men. The ways of Providence are not those of mortal men. The shortsighted individual deludes himself in believing that he chooses and acts according to his own concerns. In fact he unknowingly must act in such a way that finally the providential plan will be realized. The historical process has a definite purpose set by Providence without any regard to the human will. It is a progress toward a preordained end. The task of the philosophy of history is to judge every phase of history from the point of view of this purpose.

If the historian speaks of progress and retrogression, he refers to one of the ends men are consciously aiming at in their actions. In his terminology progress means the attainment of a state of affairs which acting men considered or consider more satisfactory than preceding states. In the terminology of a philosophy of history progress means advance on the way that leads to the ultimate goal set by Providence.

Every variety of the philosophy of history must answer two questions. First: What is the final end aimed at and the route by which it is to be reached? Second:

By what means are people induced or forced to pursue this course? Only if both questions are fully answered is the system complete.

In answering the first question the philosopher refers to intuition. In order to corroborate his surmise, he may quote the opinions of older authors, that is, the intuitive speculations of other people. The ultimate source of the philosopher's knowledge is invariably a divination of the intentions of Providence, hitherto hidden to the non-initiated and revealed to the philosopher by dint of his intuitive power. To objections raised about the correctness of his guess the philosopher can only reply: An inner voice tells me that I am right and you are wrong.

Most philosophies of history not only indicate the final end of historical evolution but also disclose the way mankind is bound to wander in order to reach the goal. They enumerate and describe successive states or stages, intermediary stations on the way from the early beginnings to the final end. The systems of Hegel, Comte, and Marx belong to this class. Others ascribe to certain nations or races a definite mission entrusted to them by the plans of Providence. Such are the role of the Germans in the system of Fichte and the role of the Nordics and the Aryans in the constructions of modern racists.

With regard to the answer given to the second question, two classes of philosophies of history are to be distinguished.

The first group contends that Providence elects some mortal men as special instruments for the execution of its plan. In the charismatic leader superhuman powers are vested. He is the plenipotentiary of Providence whose office it is to guide the ignorant populace the right way. He may be a hereditary king, or a commoner who has spontaneously seized power and whom the blind and wicked rabble in their envy and hatred call a usurper. For the charismatic leader but one thing matters: the faithful performance of his mission no matter what the means he may be forced to resort to. He is above all laws and moral precepts. What he does is always right, and what his opponents do is always wrong. Such was the doctrine of Lenin, who in this point deviated from the doctrine of Marx.[1]

It is obvious that the philosopher does not attribute the office of charismatic leadership to every man who claims that he has been called. He distinguishes between the legitimate leader and the fiendish impostor, between the God-sent prophet and the hell-born tempter. He calls only those heroes and seers legitimate leaders who make people walk toward the goal set by Providence. As the philosophies disagree with regard to this goal, so they disagree with regard to the distinction between the legitimate leader and the devil incarnate. They disagree in their judgments about Caesar and Brutus, Innocent III and Frederick II, Charles I and Cromwell, the Bourbons and the Napoleons.

But their dissent goes even further. There are rivalries between various candidates for the supreme office which are caused only by personal ambition. No ideological convictions separated Caesar and Pompey, the house of Lancaster and that of York, Trotsky and Stalin.

1. On the doctrine of Marx see above, pp. 112 ff.

Their antagonism was due to the fact that they aimed at the same office, which of course only one man could get. Here the philosopher must choose among various pretenders. Having arrogated to himself the power to pronounce judgment in the name of Providence, the philosopher blesses one of the pretenders and condemns his rivals.

The second group suggested another solution of the problem. As they see it, Providence resorted to a cunning device. It implanted in every man's mind certain impulses the operation of which must necessarily result in the realization of its own plan. The individual thinks that he goes his own way and strives after his own ends. But unwittingly he contributes his share to the realization of the end Providence wants to attain. Such was the method of Kant.[2] It was restated by Hegel and later adopted by many Hegelians, among them by Marx. It was Hegel who coined the phrase "cunning of reason" (*List der Vernunft*).[3]

There is no use arguing with doctrines derived from intuition. Every system of the philosophy of history is an arbitrary guess which can neither be proved nor disproved. There is no rational means available for either endorsing or rejecting a doctrine suggested by an inner voice.

2. Kant, *Idee zu einer allgemeinen Geschichte in weltbürgerlicher Absicht*, Werke (Inselausgabe, Leipzig, 1921), *1*, 221–40.
3. Hegel, *Vorlesungen über die Philosophie der Weltgeschichte*, *1*, 83.

3. *The Difference between the Point of View of History and That of Philosophy of History*

Before the eighteenth century most dissertations dealing with human history in general and not merely with concrete historical experience interpreted history from the point of view of a definite philosophy of history. This philosophy was seldom clearly defined and particularized. Its tenets were taken for granted and implied in commenting on events. Only in the Age of Enlightenment did some eminent philosophers abandon the traditional methods of the philosophy of history and stop brooding about the hidden purpose of Providence directing the course of events. They inaugurated a new social philosophy, entirely different from what is called the philosophy of history. They looked upon human events from the point of view of the ends aimed at by acting men, instead of from the point of view of the plans ascribed to God or nature.

The significance of this radical change in the ideological outlook can best be illustrated by referring to Adam Smith's point of view. But in order to analyze the ideas of Smith we must first refer to Mandeville.

The older ethical systems were almost unanimous in the condemnation of self-interest. They were ready to find the self-interest of the tillers of the soil pardonable and very often tried to excuse or even to glorify the kings' lust for aggrandisement. But they were adamant in their disapprobation of other people's craving for well-being and riches. Referring to the Sermon on the Mount, they exalted self-denial and indifference with regard to the treasures which moth and rust corrupt, and branded self-interest a reprehensible vice. Bernard de Mandeville in his *Fable of the Bees* tried to discredit this doctrine. He pointed out that self-interest and the desire for material well-being, commonly stigmatized as vices, are in fact the incentives whose operation makes for welfare, prosperity, and civilization.

Adam Smith adopted this idea. It was not the object of his studies to develop a philosophy of history according to the traditional pattern. He did not claim to have guessed the goals which Providence has set for mankind and aims to realize by directing men's actions. He abstained from any assertions concerning the destiny of mankind and from any prognostication about the ineluctable end of historical change. He merely wanted to determine and to analyze the factors that had been instrumental in man's progress from the straitened conditions of older ages to the more satisfactory conditions of his own age. It was from this point of view that he stressed the fact that "every part of nature, when attentively surveyed, equally demonstrates the providential care of its Author" and that "we may admire the wisdom and goodness of God, even in the weakness and folly of men." The rich, aiming at the "gratification of their own vain and insatiable desires," are "led by an invisible hand" in such a way that they "without intending it, without knowing it, advance the interest of society, and afford means for the multiplication of the species." [1] Believing in the existence of God, Smith could not help tracing back all earthly things to him and his providential care, just as later the Catholic Bastiat spoke of God's finger.[2] But in referring in this way to God neither of them intended to make any assertion about the ends God may want to realize in historical evolution. The ends they dealt with in their writings were those aimed at by acting men, not by Providence. The pre-established harmony to which they alluded did not affect their epistemological principles and the methods of their reasoning. It was merely a means devised to reconcile the purely secular and mundane procedures they applied in their scientific efforts with their religious beliefs. They borrowed this expedient from pious astronomers, physicists, and biologists who had resorted to it without deviating in their research from the empirical methods of the natural sciences.

What made it necessary for Adam Smith to look for such a reconciliation was the fact that—like Mandeville before him—he could not free himself from the standards and the terminology of traditional ethics that condemned as vicious man's desire to improve his own material conditions. Consequently he was faced with a paradox. How can it be that actions commonly blamed as vicious generate effects commonly praised as beneficial? The utilitarian philosophers found the right answer. What results in benefits must not be rejected as morally bad. Only those actions are bad which produce

1. Adam Smith, *The Theory of Moral Sentiments*, Pt. II, Sec. III, ch. 3, and Pt. IV, ch. 1 (Edinburgh, 1813), *1*, 243, 419–20.

2. Bastiat, *Harmonies économiques* (2d ed. Paris, 1851), p. 334.

bad results. But the utilitarian point of view did not prevail. Public opinion still clings to pre-Mandevillian ideas. It does not approve of a businessman's success in supplying the customers with merchandise that best suits their wishes. It looks askance at wealth acquired in trade and industry, and finds it pardonable only if the owner atones for it by endowing charitable institutions.

For the agnostic, atheistic, and antitheistic historians and economists there is no need to refer to Smith's and Bastiat's invisible hand. The Christian historians and economists who reject capitalism as an unfair system consider it blasphemous to describe egoism as a means Providence has chosen in order to attain its ends. Thus the theological views of Smith and Bastiat no longer have any meaning for our age. But it is not impossible that the Christian churches and sects will one day discover that religious freedom can be realized only in a market economy and will stop supporting anticapitalistic tendencies. Then they will either cease to disapprove of self-interest or return to the solution suggested by these eminent thinkers.

Just as important as realizing the essential distinction between the philosophy of history and the new, purely mundane social philosophy which developed from the eighteenth century on is awareness of the difference between the stage-doctrine implied in almost every philosophy of history and the attempts of historians to divide the totality of historical events into various periods or ages.

In the context of a philosophy of history the various states or stages are, as has been mentioned already, intermediary stations on the way to a final stage which will fully realize the plan of Providence. For many Christian philosophies of history the pattern was set by the four kingdoms of the Book of Daniel. The modern philosophies of history borrowed from Daniel the notion of the final stage of human affairs, the notion of "an everlasting dominion, which shall not pass away." [3] However Hegel, Comte, and Marx may disagree with Daniel and with one another, they all accept this notion, which is an essential element in every philosophy of history. They announce either that the final stage has already been reached (Hegel), or that mankind is just entering it (Comte), or that its coming is to be expected every day (Marx).

The ages of history as distinguished by historians are of a different character. Historians do not claim to know anything about the future. They deal only with the past. Their periodization schemes aim at classifying historical phenomena without any presumption of forecasting future events. The readiness of many historians to press general history or special fields—like economic or social history or the history of warfare—into artificial subdivisions has had serious drawbacks. It has been a handicap rather than an aid to the study of history. It was often prompted by political bias. Modern historians agree in paying little attention to such period schemes. But what counts for us is merely establishing the fact that the epistemological character of the periodization of history by historians is different from the stage schemes of the philosophy of history.

3. Daniel 7:14.

4. Philosophy of History and the Idea of God

The three most popular pre-Darwinian [1] philosophies of history of the nineteenth century—those of Hegel, Comte, and Marx—were adaptations of the Enlightenment's idea of progress. And this doctrine of human progress was an adaptation of the Christian philosophy of salvation.

Christian theology discerns three stages in human history: the bliss of the age preceding the fall of man, the age of secular depravity, and finally the coming of the Kingdom of Heaven. If left alone, man would not be able to expiate the original sin and to attain salvation. But God in his mercy leads him to eternal life. In spite of all the frustrations and adversities of man's temporal pilgrimage, there is hope for a blessed future.

The Enlightenment altered this scheme in order to make it agree with its scientific outlook. God endowed man with reason that leads him on the road toward perfection. In the dark past superstition and sinister machinations of tyrants and priests restrained the exercise of this most precious gift bestowed upon man. But

1. The Marxian system of philosophy of history and dialectic materialism was completed with the Preface, dated January 1859, of *Zur Kritik der Politischen Oekonomie.* Darwin's *The Origin of Species* appeared in the same year. Marx read it in the first part of December 1860 and declared in letters to Engels and Lassalle that in spite of various shortcomings it provided a biological foundation ("naturhistorische Grundlage" or "naturwissenschaftliche Unterlage") for his doctrine of the class struggle. *Karl Marx, Chronik seines Lebens in Einzeldaten* (Moscow, Marx-Engels-Lenin Institute, 1934), pp. 206, 207.

at last reason has burst its chains and a new age has been inaugurated. Henceforth every generation will surpass its predecessors in wisdom, virtue, and success in improving earthly conditions. Progress toward perfection will continue forever. Reason, now emancipated and put in its right place, will never again be relegated to the unseemly position the dark ages assigned to it. All "reactionary" ventures of obscurantists are doomed to failure. The trend toward progress is irresistible.

Only in the doctrines of the economists did the notion of progress have a definite, unambiguous meaning. All men are striving after survival and after improvement of the material conditions of their existence. They want to live and to raise their standard of living. In employing the term "progress" the economist abstains from expressing judgments of value. He appraises things from the point of view of acting men. He calls better or worse what appears as such in their eyes. Thus capitalism means progress since it brings about progressive improvement of the material conditions of a continually increasing population. It provides people with some satisfactions which they did not get before and which gratify some of their aspirations.

But to most of the eighteenth-century champions of meliorism this "mean, materialistic" content of the economists' idea of progress was repulsive. They nurtured vague dreams of an earthly paradise. Their ideas about the conditions of man in this paradise were rather negative than affirmative. They pictured a state of affairs free of all those things which they found unsatisfactory in their environment: no tyrants, no oppression or persecution, no wars, no poverty, no crime; liberty, equality, and fraternity; all men happy, peacefully united, and cooperating in brotherly love. As they assumed that nature is bountiful and all men were good and reasonable, they could see no cause for the existence of all that they branded evil but inherent deficiencies in mankind's social and political organization. What was needed was a constitutional reform that would substitute good laws for bad laws. All who opposed this reform dictated by reason were considered hopelessly depraved individuals, enemies of the common weal, whom the good people were bound to annihilate physically.

The main defect of this doctrine was its incomprehension of the liberal program as developed by the economists and put into effect by the harbingers of capitalistic private enterprise. The disciples of Jean Jacques Rousseau who raved about nature and the blissful condition of man in the state of nature did not take notice of the fact that the means of subsistence are scarce and that the natural state of man is extreme poverty and insecurity. They disparaged as greed and predatory selfishness the businessmen's endeavors to remove need and want so far as possible. Witnesses to the inauguration of new ways of economic management that were destined to provide unprecedented improvement in the standard of living for an unprecedented increase of population, they indulged in daydreams about a return to nature or to the alleged virtuous simplicity of early republican Rome. While manufacturers were busy improving the methods of production and turning out more and better commodities for the consumption of the masses, the followers of Rousseau perorated about reason and virtue and liberty.

It is vain to talk about progress pure and simple. One must first clearly designate the goal one has chosen to attain. Only then is it permissible to call an advance on the way that leads to this goal progress. The philosophers of the Enlightenment entirely failed in this regard. They did not say anything definite about the characteristics of the goal they had in mind. They only glorified this insufficiently described goal as the state of perfection and the realization of all that is good. But they were rather hazy in employing the epithets perfect and good.

As against the pessimism of ancient and modern authors who had described the course of human history as the progressive deterioration of the perfect conditions of the fabulous golden age of the past, the Enlightenment displayed an optimistic view. As has been pointed out above, its philosophers derived their belief in the inevitability of progress toward perfection from the confidence they placed in man's reason. By dint of his reason man learns more and more from experience. Every new generation inherits a treasure of wisdom from its forbears and adds something to it. Thus the descendents necessarily surpass their ancestors.

It did not occur to the champions of this idea that man is not infallible and that reason can err in the choice both of the ultimate goal to be aimed at and of the means to be resorted to for its attainment. Their theistic faith implied faith in the goodness of almighty Providence that will guide mankind along the right path. Their philosophy had eliminated the Incarnation and all the other Christian dogmas but one: salvation. God's magnificence manifested itself in the fact that the work of his creation was necessarily committed to progressive improvement.

Hegel's philosophy of history assimilated these ideas. Reason (*Vernunft*) rules the world, and this cognition is tantamount to the insight that Providence rules it. The task of philosophy of history is to discern the plans of Providence.[2] The ultimate foundation of the optimism that Hegel displayed with regard to the course of historical events and the future of mankind was his firm faith in God's infinite goodness. God is genuine goodness. "The cognition of philosophy is that no power surpasses the might of the good, i.e., God, and could prevent God from asserting himself, that God is right at the last, that human history is nothing else than the plan of Providence. God rules the world; the content of his government, the realization of his plan, is the history of mankind." [3]

In the philosophy of Comte as well as in that of Marx there is no room left for God and his infinite goodness. In the system of Hegel it made sense to speak of a necessary progress of mankind from less to more satisfactory conditions. God had decided that every later stage of human affairs should be a higher and better stage. No other decision could be expected from the almighty and infinitely good Lord. But the atheists Comte and

2. Hegel, *Vorlesungen über die Philosophie der Weltgeschichte, 1,* 4, 17–18.
3. Ibid., p. 55.

Marx should not have simply assumed that the march
of time is necessarily a march toward ever better conditions and will eventually lead to a perfect state. It was
up to them to prove that progress and improvement are
inevitable and a relapse into unsatisfactory conditions
impossible. But they never embarked upon such a demonstration.

If for the sake of argument one were prepared to acquiesce in Marx's arbitrary prediction that society is
moving "with the inexorability of a law of nature" toward socialism, it would still be necessary to examine
the question whether socialism can be considered as a
workable system of society's economic organization and
whether it does not rather mean the disintegration of
social bonds, the return to primitive barbarism, and
poverty and starvation for all.

The purpose of Marx's philosophy of history was to
silence the critical voices of the economists by pointing
out that socialism was the next and final stage of the
historical process and *therefore* a higher and better
stage than the preceding stages; that it was even the
final state of human perfection, the ultimate goal of
human history. But this conclusion was a non sequitur
in the frame of a godless philosophy of history. The
idea of an irresistible trend toward salvation and the
establishment of a perfect state of everlasting bliss is
an eminently theological idea. In the frame of a system
of atheism it is a mere arbitrary guess, deprived of any
sense. There is no theology without God. An atheistic
system of philosophy of history must not base its opti-

mism upon confidence in the infinite goodness of God
Almighty.

5. Activistic Determinism and
Fatalistic Determinism

Every philosophy of history is an instance of the popular idea, mentioned above,[1] that all future events are
recorded in advance in the great book of fate. A special
dispensation has allowed the philosopher to read pages
of this book and to reveal their content to the unini-
tiated.

This brand of determinism inherent in a philosophy
of history must be distinguished from the type of determinism that guides man's actions and search for knowledge. The latter type—we may call it activistic determinism—is the outgrowth of the insight that every
change is the result of a cause and that there is a regularity in the concatenation of cause and effect. However
unsatisfactory the endeavors of philosophy to throw
light upon the problem of causality may have been
hitherto, it is impossible for the human mind to think of
uncaused change. Man cannot help assuming that every
change is caused by a preceding change and causes
further change. Notwithstanding all the doubts raised
by the philosophers, human conduct is entirely and in
every sphere of life—action, philosophy and science
—directed by the category of causality. The lesson
brought home to man by activistic determinism is: If

1. See above, p. 79.

you want to attain a definite end, you must resort to the appropriate means; there is no other way to success.

But in the context of a philosophy of history determinism means: This will happen however much you may try to avoid it. While activistic determinism is a call to action and the utmost exertion of a man's physical and mental capacities, this type of determinism—we may call it fatalistic determinism—paralyzes the will and engenders passivity and lethargy. As has been pointed out,[2] it is so contrary to the innate impulse toward activity that it never could really get hold of the human mind and prevent people from acting.

In depicting the history of the future the philosopher of history as a rule restricts himself to describing big-scale events and the final outcome of the historical process. He thinks that this limitation distinguishes his guesswork from the augury of common soothsayers who dwell upon details and unimportant little things. Such minor events are in his view contingent and unpredictable. He does not bother about them. His attention is exclusively directed toward the great destiny of the whole, not to the trifle which, as he thinks, does not matter.

However, the historical process is the product of all these small changes going on ceaselessly. He who claims to know the final end must necessarily know them too. He must either take them all in at a glance with all their consequences or be aware of a principle that inevitably directs their result to a preordained end. The arrogance with which a writer elaborating his system of philosophy of history looks down upon the small fry of palmists

2. See above, pp. 79 ff.

and crystal gazers is therefore hardly different from the haughtiness which in precapitalistic times wholesalers displayed toward retailers and peddlers. What he sells is essentially the same questionable wisdom.

Activistic determinism is by no means incompatible with the—rightly understood—idea of freedom of the will. It is, in fact, the correct exposition of this often misinterpreted notion. Because there is in the universe a regularity in the concatenation and sequence of phenomena, and because man is capable of acquiring knowledge about some of these regularities, human action becomes possible within a definite margin. Free will means that man can aim at definite ends because he is familiar with some of the laws determining the flux of world affairs. There is a sphere within which man can choose between alternatives. He is not, like other animals, inevitably and irremediably subject to the operation of blind fate. He can, within definite narrow limits, divert events from the course they would take if left alone. He is an acting being. In this consists his superiority to mice and microbes, plants and stones. In this sense he applies the—perhaps inexpedient and misleading—term "free will."

The emotional appeal of the cognizance of this freedom, and the idea of moral responsibility which it engenders, are as much facts as anything else called by that name. Comparing himself with all other beings, man sees his own dignity and superiority in his will. The will is unbendable and must not yield to any violence and oppression, because man is capable of choosing between life and death and of preferring death if life can be preserved only at the price of sub-mitting to unbearable conditions. Man alone can die for a cause. It was this that Dante had in mind: "Chè volontà, se non vuol, non s'ammorza." [3]

One of the fundamental conditions of man's existence and action is the fact that he does not know what will happen in the future. The exponent of a philosophy of history, arrogating to himself the omniscience of God, claims that an inner voice has revealed to him knowledge of things to come.

3. Dante, *Paradiso*, IV, 76: "The will does not die if it does not will."

PART THREE. EPISTEMOLOGICAL
PROBLEMS OF HISTORY

Chapter 9. The Concept of Historical Individuality

1. The Ultimate Given of History

THE HUMAN SEARCH for knowledge cannot go on endlessly. Inevitably, sooner or later, it will reach a point beyond which it cannot proceed. It will then be faced with an ultimate given, a datum that man's reason cannot trace back to other data. In the course of the evolution of knowledge science has succeeded in tracing back to other data some things and events which previously had been viewed as ultimate. We may expect that this will also occur in the future. But there will always remain something that is for the human mind an ultimate given, unanalyzable and irreducible. Human reason cannot even conceive a kind of knowledge that would not encounter such an insurmountable obstacle. There is for man no such thing as omniscience.

In dealing with such ultimate data history refers to individuality. The characteristics of individual men, their ideas and judgments of value as well as the actions guided by those ideas and judgments, cannot be traced back to something of which they would be the derivatives. There is no answer to the question why Frederick II invaded Silesia except: because he was Frederick II. It is customary, although not very expedient, to call the mental process by means of which a datum is traced back to other data rational. Then an ultimate datum is

183

called irrational. No historical research can be thought of that would not ultimately meet such irrational facts.

Philosophies of history claim to avoid referring to individuality and irrationality. They pretend to provide a thorough-going interpretation of all historical events. What they really do is relegate the ultimate given to two points of their scheme, to its supposed beginning and its supposed end. They assume that there is at the start of history an unanalyzable and irreducible agency, for example *Geist* in the system of Hegel or the material productive forces in that of Marx. And they further assume that this prime mover of history aims at a definite end, also unanalyzable and irreducible, for instance the Prussian state of about 1825 or socialism. Whatever one may think about the various systems of philosophy of history, it is obvious that they do not eliminate reference to individuality and irrationality. They merely shift it to another point of their interpretation.

Materialism wants to throw history overboard entirely. All ideas and actions should be explained as the necessary outcome of definite physiological processes. But this would not make it possible to reject any reference to irrationality. Like history, the natural sciences are ultimately faced with some data defying any further reduction to other data, that is, with something ultimately given.

2. *The Role of the Individual in History*

In the context of a philosophy of history there is no room left for any reference to individuality other than that of the prime mover and his plan determining the way events must go. All individual men are merely tools in the hand of ineluctable destiny. Whatever they may do, the outcome of their actions must necessarily fit into the preordained plan of Providence.

What would have happened if Lieutenant Napoleon Bonaparte had been killed in action at Toulon? Friedrich Engels knew the answer: "Another would have filled the place." For "the man has always been found as soon as he became necessary." [1] Necessary for whom and for what purpose? Obviously for the material productive forces to bring about, at a later date, socialism. It seems that the material productive forces always have a substitute at hand, just as a cautious opera manager has an understudy ready to sing the tenor's part in case the star should catch a cold. If Shakespeare had died in infancy, another man would have written *Hamlet* and the *Sonnets*. But, some people ask, how did this surrogate while away his time since Shakespeare's good health relieved him from this chore?

The issue has been purposely obfuscated by the champions of historical necessity, who confused it with other problems.

Looking backward upon the past, the historian must say that, all conditions having been as they were, everything that happened was inevitable. At any instant the state of affairs was the necessary consequence of the immediately preceding state. But among the elements determining any given state of historical affairs there

1. Letter to Starkenburg, Jan. 25, 1894, *Karl Marx and Friedrich Engels, Correspondence 1846–1895* (London, M. Lawrence, Ltd., 1934), p. 518.

are factors that cannot be traced back further than to the point at which the historian is faced with the ideas and actions of individuals.

When the historian says that the French Revolution of 1789 would not have happened if some things had been different, he is merely trying to establish the forces that brought about the event and the influence of each of these forces. Taine did not indulge in idle speculations as to what would have happened if the doctrines that he called *l'esprit revolutionnaire* and *l'esprit classique* had not been developed. He wanted to assign to each of them its relevance in the chain of events that resulted in the outbreak and the course of the Revolution.[2]

A second confusion concerns the limits drawn upon the influence of great men. Simplified accounts of history, adapted to the capacity of people slow of comprehension, have presented history as a product of the feats of great men. The older Hohenzollern made Prussia, Bismarck made the Second Reich, William II ruined it, Hitler made and ruined the Third Reich. No serious historian ever shared in such nonsense. It has never been contested that the part played even by the greatest figures of history was much more moderate. Every man, whether great or small, lives and acts within the frame of his age's historical circumstances. These circumstances are determined by all the ideas and events of the preceding ages as well as by those of his own age. The Titan may outweigh each of his contemporaries;

2. Taine, *Les Origines de la France contemporaine, 1,* Bk. III (16th ed. Paris, 1887), 221–328.

he is no match for the united forces of the dwarfs. A statesman can succeed only insofar as his plans are adjusted to the climate of opinion of his time, that is to the ideas that have got hold of his fellows' minds. He can become a leader only if he is prepared to guide people along the paths they want to walk and toward the goal they want to attain. A statesman who antagonizes public opinion is doomed to failure. No matter whether he is an autocrat or an officer of a democracy, the politician must give the people what they wish to get, very much as a businessman must supply the customers with the things they wish to acquire.

It is different with the pioneers of new ways of thinking and new modes of art and literature. The pathbreaker who disdains the applause he may get from the crowd of his contemporaries does not depend on his own age's ideas. He is free to say with Schiller's Marquis Posa: "This century is not ripe for my ideas; I live as a citizen of centuries to come." The genius' work too is embedded in the sequence of historical events, is conditioned by the achievements of preceding generations, and is merely a chapter in the evolution of ideas. But it adds something new and unheard of to the treasure of thoughts and may in this sense be called creative. The genuine history of mankind is the history of ideas. It is ideas that distinguish man from all other beings. Ideas engender social institutions, political changes, technological methods of production, and all that is called economic conditions. And in searching for their origin we inevitably come to a point at which all that can be asserted is that a man had an idea. Whether the name of this man is known or not is of secondary importance.

This is the meaning that history attaches to the notion of individuality. Ideas are the ultimate given of historical inquiry. All that can be said about ideas is that they came to pass. The historian may point out how a new idea fitted into the ideas developed by earlier generations and how it may be considered a continuation of these ideas and their logical sequel. New ideas do not originate in an ideological vacuum. They are called forth by the previously existing ideological structure; they are the response offered by a man's mind to the ideas developed by his predecessors. But it is an arbitrary surmise to assume that they were bound to come and that if A had not generated them a certain B or C would have performed the job.

In this sense what the limitations of our knowledge induce us to call chance plays a part in history. If Aristotle had died in childhood, intellectual history would have been affected. If Bismarck had died in 1860, world affairs would have taken a different course. To what extent and with what consequences nobody can know.

3. The Chimera of the Group Mind

In their eagerness to eliminate from history any reference to individuals and individual events, collectivist authors resorted to a chimerical construction, the group mind or social mind.

At the end of the eighteenth and beginning of the nineteenth centuries German philologists began to study German medieval poetry, which had long since fallen into oblivion. Most of the epics they edited from old manuscripts were imitations of French works. The names of their authors—most of them knightly warriors in the service of dukes or counts—were known. These epics were not much to boast of. But there were two epics of a quite different character, genuinely original works of high literary value, far surpassing the conventional products of the courtiers: the *Nibelungenlied* and the *Gudrun*. The former is one of the great books of world literature and undoubtedly the outstanding poem Germany produced before the days of Goethe and Schiller. The names of the authors of these masterpieces were not handed down to posterity. Perhaps the poets belonged to the class of professional entertainers (*Spielleute*), who not only were snubbed by the nobility but had to endure mortifying legal disabilities. Perhaps they were heretical or Jewish, and the clergy was eager to make people forget them. At any rate the philologists called these two works "people's epics" (*Volksepen*). This term suggested to naïve minds the idea that they were written not by individual authors but by the "people." The same mythical authorship was attributed to popular songs (*Volkslieder*) whose authors were unknown.

Again in Germany, in the years following the Napoleonic wars, the problem of comprehensive legislative codification was brought up for discussion. In this controversy the historical school of jurisprudence, led by Savigny, denied the competence of any age and any persons to write legislation. Like the Volksepen and the

Volkslieder, a nation's laws, they declared, are a spontaneous emanation of the *Volksgeist,* the nation's spirit and peculiar character. Genuine laws are not arbitrarily written by legislators; they spring up and thrive organically from the Volksgeist.

This Volksgeist doctrine was devised in Germany as a conscious reaction against the ideas of natural law and the "un-German" spirit of the French Revolution. But it was further developed and elevated to the dignity of a comprehensive social doctrine by the French positivists, many of whom not only were committed to the principles of the most radical among the revolutionary leaders but aimed at completing the "unfinished revolution" by a violent overthrow of the capitalistic mode of production. Émile Durkheim and his school deal with the group mind as if it were a real phenomenon, a distinct agency, thinking and acting. As they see it, not individuals but the group is the subject of history.

As a corrective of these fancies the truism must be stressed that only individuals think and act. In dealing with the thoughts and actions of individuals the historian establishes the fact that some individuals influence one another in their thinking and acting more strongly than they influence and are influenced by other individuals. He observes that cooperation and division of labor exist among some, while existing to a lesser extent or not at all among others. He employs the term "group" to signify an aggregation of individuals who cooperate together more closely. However, the distinction of groups is optional. The group is not an ontological entity like the biological species. The various group concepts intersect one another. The historian chooses, according to the special plan of his studies, the features and attributes that determine the classification of individuals into various groups. The grouping may integrate people speaking the same language or professing the same religion or practicing the same vocation or occupation or descended from the same ancestry. The group concept of Gobineau was different from that of Marx. In short, the group concept is an ideal type and as such is derived from the historian's understanding of the historical forces and events.

Only individuals think and act. Each individual's thinking and acting is influenced by his fellows' thinking and acting. These influences are variegated. The individual American's thoughts and conduct cannot be interpreted if one assigns him to a single group. He is not only an American but a member of a definite religious group or an agnostic or an atheist; he has a job, he belongs to a political party, he is affected by traditions inherited from his ancestors and conveyed to him by his upbringing, by the family, the school, the neighborhood, by the ideas prevailing in his town, state, and country. It is an enormous simplification to speak of the American mind. Every American has his own mind. It is absurd to ascribe any achievements and virtues or any misdeeds and vices of individual Americans to America as such.

Most people are common men. They do not have thoughts of their own; they are only receptive. They do not create new ideas; they repeat what they have heard and imitate what they have seen. If the world were peopled only by such as these, there would not be any change and any history. What produces change is new ideas and actions guided by them. What distinguishes one group from another is the effect of such innovations. These innovations are not accomplished by a group mind; they are always the achievements of individuals. What makes the American people different from any other people is the joint effect produced by the thoughts and actions of innumerable uncommon Americans.

We know the names of the men who invented and step by step perfected the motorcar. A historian can write a detailed history of the evolution of the automobile. We do not know the names of the men who, in the beginnings of civilization, made the greatest inventions —for example lighting a fire. But this ignorance does not permit us to ascribe this fundamental invention to a group mind. It is always an individual who starts a new method of doing things, and then other people imitate his example. Customs and fashions have always been inaugurated by individuals and spread through imitation by other people.

While the group-mind school tried to eliminate the individual by ascribing activity to the mythical Volksgeist, the Marxians were intent on the one hand upon depreciating the individual's contribution and on the other hand upon crediting innovations to common men. Thus Marx observed that a critical history of technology would demonstrate that none of the eighteenth century's inventions was the achievement of a single individual.[1] What does this prove? Nobody denies that technological progress is a gradual process, a chain of successive steps performed by long lines of men each of whom adds something to the accomplishments of his predecessors. The history of every technological contrivance, when completely told, leads back to the most primitive inventions made by cave dwellers in the earliest ages of mankind. To choose any later starting point is an arbitrary restriction of the whole tale. One may begin a history of wireless telegraphy with Maxwell and Hertz, but one may as well go back to the first experiments with electricity or to any previous technological feats that had necessarily to precede the construction of a radio network. All this does not in the least affect the truth that each step forward was made by an individual and not by some mythical impersonal agency. It does not detract from the contributions of Maxwell, Hertz, and Marconi to admit that they could be made only because others had previously made other contributions.

To illustrate the difference between the innovator and the dull crowd of routinists who cannot even imagine that any improvement is possible, we need only refer to a passage in Engels' most famous book.[2] Here, in 1878, Engels apodictically announced that military weapons are "now so perfected that no further progress of any revolutionizing influence is any longer possible." Henceforth "all further [technological] progress is by

1. *Das Kapital, 1*, 335, n. 89.
2. *Herrn Eugen Dührings Umwälzung der Wissenschaft*, 7th ed. Stuttgart, 1910.

and large indifferent for land warfare. The age of evolution is in this regard essentially closed." [3] This complacent conclusion shows in what the achievement of the innovator consists: he accomplishes what other people believe to be unthinkable and unfeasible.

Engels, who considered himself an expert in the art of warfare, liked to exemplify his doctrines by referring to strategy and tactics. Changes in military tactics, he declared, are not brought about by ingenious army leaders. They are achievements of privates who are usually cleverer than their officers. The privates invent them by dint of their instincts (*instinktmässig*) and put them into operation in spite of the reluctance of their commanders.[4]

Every doctrine denying to the "single paltry individual" [5] any role in history must finally ascribe changes and improvements to the operation of instincts. As those upholding such doctrines see it, man is an animal that has the instinct to produce poems, cathedrals, and airplanes. Civilization is the result of an unconscious and unpremeditated reaction of man to external stimuli. Each achievement is the automatic creation of an instinct with which man has been endowed especially for this purpose. There are as many instincts as there are human achievements. It is needless to enter into a critical examination of this fable invented by impotent people for slighting the achievements of better men

3. Ibid., pp. 176–7.
4. Ibid., pp. 172–6.
5. Engels, *Der Ursprung der Familie, des Privateigentums und des Staates* (6th ed. Stuttgart, 1894), p. 186.

and appealing to the resentment of the dull. Even on the basis of this makeshift doctrine one cannot negate the distinction between the man who had the instinct to write the book *On the Origin of Species* and those who lacked this instinct.

4. Planning History

Individuals act in order to bring about definite results. Whether they succeed or not depends on the suitability of the means applied and the response their actions encounter on the part of fellow individuals. Very often the outcome of an action differs considerably from what the actor was eager to achieve. The margin within which a man, however great, can act successfully is narrow. No man can through his actions direct the course of affairs for more than a comparatively short period of the future, still less for all time to come.

Yet every action adds something to history, affects the course of future events, and is in this sense a historical fact. The most trivial performance of daily routine by dull people is no less a historical datum than is the most startling innovation of the genius. The aggregate of the unvarying repetition of traditional modes of acting determines, as habits, customs and mores, the course of events. The common man's historical role consists in contributing a particle to the structure of the tremendous power of consuetude.

History is made by men. The conscious intentional actions of individuals, great and small, determine the course of events insofar as it is the result of the interaction of all men. But the historical process is not designed by individuals. It is the composite outcome of the intentional actions of all individuals. No man can plan history. All he can plan and try to put into effect is his own actions which, jointly with the actions of other men, constitute the historical process. The Pilgrim Fathers did not plan to found the United States.

Of course, there have always been men who planned for eternity. For the most part the failure of their designs appeared very soon. Sometimes their constructions lasted quite a while, but their effect was not what the builders had planned. The monumental tombs of the Egyptian kings still exist, but it was not the intention of their builders to make modern Egypt attractive for tourists and to supply present-day museums with mummies. Nothing demonstrates more emphatically the temporal limitations on human planning than the venerable ruins scattered about the surface of the earth.

Ideas live longer than walls and other material artifacts. We still enjoy the masterpieces of the poetry and philosophy of ancient India and Greece. But they do not mean for us what they meant to their authors. We may wonder whether Plato and Aristotle would have approved of the use later ages have made of their thoughts.

Planning for eternity, to substitute an everlasting state of stability, rigidity, and changelessness for historical evolution, is the theme of a special class of literature. The utopian author wants to arrange future conditions according to his own ideas and to deprive the rest of mankind once and for all of the faculty to choose and to act. One plan alone, viz., the author's plan, should be executed and all other people be silenced. The author, and after his death his successor, will henceforth alone determine the course of events. There will no longer be any history, as history is the composite effect of the interaction of all men. The superhuman dictator will rule the universe and reduce all other people to pawns in his plans. He will deal with them as the engineer deals with the raw materials out of which he builds, a method pertinently called social engineering.

Such projects are very popular nowadays. They enrapture the intellectuals. A few skeptics observe that their execution is contrary to human nature. But their supporters are confident that by suppressing all dissenters they can alter human nature. Then people will be as happy as the ants are supposed to be in their hills.

The essential question is: Will all men be prepared to yield to the dictator? Will nobody have the ambition to contest his supremacy? Will nobody develop ideas at variance with those underlying the dictator's plan? Will all men, after thousands of years of "anarchy" in thinking and acting, tacitly submit to the tyranny of one or a few despots?

It is possible that in a few years all nations will have adopted the system of all-round planning and totalitarian regimentation. The number of opponents is very small, and their direct political influence almost nil. But even a victory of planning will not mean the end of history. Atrocious wars among the candidates for the supreme office will break out. Totalitarianism may wipe out civilization, even the whole of the human race. Then, of course, history will have come to its end too.

Chapter 10. Historicism

1. *The Meaning of Historicism*

HISTORICISM developed from the end of the eighteenth century on as a reaction against the social philosophy of rationalism. To the reforms and policies advocated by various authors of the Enlightenment it opposed a program of preservation of existing institutions and, sometimes, even of a return to extinct institutions. Against the postulates of reason it appealed to the authority of tradition and the wisdom of ages gone by. The main target of its critique was the ideas that had inspired the American and the French Revolutions and kindred movements in other countries. Its champions proudly called themselves antirevolutionary and emphasized their rigid conservatism. But in later years the political orientation of historicism changed. It began to regard capitalism and free trade—both domestic and international—as the foremost evil, and joined hands with the "radical" or "leftist" foes of the market economy, aggressive nationalism on the one hand and revolutionary socialism on the other. As far as historicism still has actual political importance, it is ancillary to socialism and to nationalism. Its conservatism has almost withered away. It survives only in the doctrines of some religious groups.

People have again and again stressed the congeniality of historicism and artistic and literary romanticism.

The analogy is rather superficial. Both movements had in common a taste for the conditions of ages gone by and an extravagant overestimation of old customs and institutions. But this enthusiasm for the past is not the essential feature of historicism. Historicism is first of all an epistemological doctrine and must be viewed as such.

The fundamental thesis of historicism is the proposition that, apart from the natural sciences, mathematics, and logic, there is no knowledge but that provided by history. There is no regularity in the concatenation and sequence of phenomena and events in the sphere of human action. Consequently the attempts to develop a science of economics and to discover economic laws are vain. The only sensible method of dealing with human action, exploits, and institutions is the historical method. The historian traces every phenomenon back to its origins. He depicts the changes going on in human affairs. He approaches his material, the records of the past, without any prepossessions and preconceived ideas. The historian utilizes sometimes, in preliminary, merely technical, and ancillary examination of these sources, the results of the natural sciences, as for instance in determining the age of the material on which a document of disputed authenticity is written. But in his proper field, the exposition of past events, he does not rely upon any other branch of knowledge. The standards and general rules to which he resorts in dealing with the historical material are to be abstracted from this very material. They must not be borrowed from any other source.

The extravagance of these claims was later reduced to a more modest measure when Dilthey stressed the role psychology plays in the work of the historian.[1] The champions of historicism accepted this restriction and did not insist on their extreme description of the historical method. They were merely interested in the condemnation of economics and had no quarrel with psychology.

If the historicists had been consistent, they would have substituted economic history for the—in their opinion counterfeit—science of economics. (We may pass over the question how economic history could be treated without economic theory.) But this would not have served their political plans. What they wanted was to propagandize for their interventionist or socialist programs. The wholesale rejection of economics was only one item in their strategy. It relieved them from the embarrassment created by their inability to explode the economists' devastating critique of socialism and interventionism. But it did not in itself demonstrate the soundness of a prosocialist or interventionist policy. In order to justify their "unorthodox" leanings, the historicists developed a rather self-contradictory discipline to which various names were given such as realistic or institutional or ethical economics, or the economic aspects of political science (*wirtschaftliche Staatswissenschaften*).[2]

1. See below, p. 312.
2. For various other names suggested see Arthur Spiethoff in the Preface to the English edition of his treatise on "Business Cycles," *International Economic Papers*, No. 3 (New York, 1953), p. 75.

Most champions of these schools of thought did not bother about an epistemological explanation of their procedures. Only a few tried to justify their method. We may call their doctrine periodalism and their supporters periodalists.

The main idea underlying all these attempts to construct a quasi-economic doctrine that could be employed to justify policies fighting the market economy was borrowed from positivism. As historicists the periodalists talked indefatigably about something they called the historical method, and claimed to be historians. But they adopted the essential tenets of positivism, which rejected history as useless and meaningless chatter, and wanted to inaugurate in its place a new science to be modeled after the pattern of Newtonian mechanics. The periodalists accepted the thesis that it is possible to derive from historical experience a posteriori laws which, once they are discovered, will form a new—not yet existing—science of social physics or sociology or institutional economics.

Only in one regard did the periodalists' version of this thesis differ from that of the positivists. The positivists had laws in mind that would be valid universally. The periodalists believed that every period of history has its own economic laws different from those of other periods of economic history.

The periodalists distinguish various periods in the course of historical events. Obviously the criterion according to which this distinction is made is the characteristics of the economic laws determining economic becoming in each period. Thus the periodalists' argument moves in a circle. The periodization of economic history presupposes knowledge of the economic laws peculiar to each period, while these laws can only be discovered by examining each period without any reference to the events that happened in other periods.

The periodalists' image of the course of history is this: There are various periods or stages of economic evolution succeeding one another according to a definite order; throughout each of these periods the economic laws remain unchanged. Nothing is said about the transition from one period to the next one. If we assume that it is not brought about at one blow, we must assume that between two periods there is an interval of transition, a transition period as it were. What happens in this interval? What kind of economic laws are operative in it? Is it a time of lawlessness or has it its own laws? Besides, if one assumes that the laws of economic becoming are historical facts and therefore changing in the flux of historical events, it is manifestly contradictory to assert that there are periods in which there is no change, i.e., periods in which there is no history, and that between two such periods of rest there is a period of transition.

The same fallacy is also implied in the concept of a present age as resorted to by contemporary pseudo economics. Studies dealing with the economic history of the recent past are mislabeled as dealing with present economic conditions. If we refer to a definite length of time as the present, we mean that in regard to a special issue conditions remain unchanged throughout this period. The concept of the present is therefore different for various fields of action.[3] Besides, it is never certain how long this absence of change will last and consequently how much of the future has to be included. What a man can say about the future is always merely speculative anticipation. Dealing with some conditions of the recent past under the heading "present conditions" is a misnomer. The most that can be said is: Such were the conditions yesterday; we expect they will remain unchanged for some time to come.

Economics deals with a regularity in the concatenation and sequence of phenomena that is valid in the whole field of human action. It can therefore contribute to the elucidation of future events; it can predict within the limits drawn to praxeological prediction.[4] If one rejects the idea of an economic law necessarily valid for all ages, one no longer has the possibility of discovering any regularity that remains unchanged in the flux of events. Then one can say no more than: If conditions remain unchanged for some time, they will remain unchanged. But whether or not they really remain unchanged can only be known afterward.

The honest historicist would have to say: Nothing can be asserted about the future. Nobody can know how a definite policy will work in the future. All we believe to know is how similar policies worked in the past. Provided all relevant conditions remain unchanged, we may expect that the future effects will not widely differ from those of the past. But we do not know whether or not these relevant conditions will re-

3. Mises, *Human Action*, p. 101.
4. Ibid., pp. 117–18. See below, p. 309.

main unchanged. Hence we cannot make any prognostication about the—necessarily future—effects of any measure considered. We are dealing with the history of the past, not with the history of the future.

A dogma supported by many historicists asserts that tendencies of social and economic evolution as manifested in the past, and especially in the recent past, will prevail in the future too. Study of the past, they conclude, discloses therefore the shape of things to come.

Leaving aside all the metaphysical ideas with which this trend-philosophy has been loaded, we have only to realize that trends can change, have changed in the past, and will change in the future too.[5] The historicist does not know when the next change will occur. What he can announce about trends refers only to the past, never to the future.

Some of the German historicists liked to compare their periodization of economic history with the periodization of the history of art. As the history of art deals with the succession of various styles of artistic activities, economic history deals with the succession of various styles of economic activities (*Wirtschaftsstile*). This metaphor is neither better nor worse than other metaphors. But what the historicists who resorted to it failed to say was that the historians of art talk only about the styles of the past and do not develop doctrines about the art styles of the future. However, the historicists are writing and lecturing about the economic conditions of the past only in order to derive from them conclusions

5. Mises, *Planning for Freedom* (South Holland, Ill., 1952), pp. 163–9.

about economic policies that necessarily are directed toward the economic conditions of the future.

2. *The Rejection of Economics*

As historicism sees it, the essential error of economics consists in its assumption that man is invariably egoistic and aims exclusively at material well-being.

According to Gunnar Myrdal economics asserts that human actions are "solely motivated by economic interests" and considers as economic interests "the desire for higher incomes and lower prices and, in addition, perhaps stability of earnings and employment, reasonable time for leisure and an environment conducive to its satisfactory use, good working conditions, etc." This, he says, is an error. One does not completely account for human motivations by simply registering economic interests. What really determines human conduct is not interests alone but attitudes. "Attitude means the emotive disposition of an individual or a group to respond in certain ways to actual or potential situations." There are "fortunately many people whose attitudes are not identical with their interests." [1]

Now, the assertion that economics ever maintained that men are solely motivated by the striving after higher incomes and lower prices is false. Because of their failure to disentangle the apparent paradox of the use-value concept, the Classical economists and their

1. Gunnar Myrdal, *The Political Element in the Development of Economic Theory*, trans. by P. Streeten (Cambridge, Harvard University Press, 1954), pp. 199–200.

epigones were prevented from providing a satisfactory interpretation of the conduct of the consumers. They virtually dealt only with the conduct of the business-men who serve the consumers and for whom the valuations of their customers are the ultimate standard. When they referred to the principle of buying on the cheapest market and selling on the dearest market, they were trying to interpret the actions of the businessman in his capacity as a purveyor of the buyers, not in his capacity as a consumer and spender of his own income. They did not enter into an analysis of the motives prompting the individual consumers to buy and to consume. So they did not investigate whether individuals try only to fill their bellies or whether they also spend for other purposes, e.g., to perform what they consider to be their ethical and religious duties. When they distinguished between purely economic motives and other motives, the classical economists referred only to the acquisitive side of human behavior. They never thought of denying that men are also driven by other motives.

The approach of Classical economics appears highly unsatisfactory from the point of view of modern subjective economics. Modern economics rejects as entirely fallacious also the argument advanced for the epistemological justification of the Classical methods by their last followers, especially John Stuart Mill. According to this lame apology, pure economics deals only with the "economic" aspect of the operations of mankind, only with the phenomena of the production of wealth "as far as those phenomena are not modified by the pursuit of any other object." But, says Mill, in order to deal adequately with reality "the didactic writer on the subject will naturally combine in his exposition, with the truth of pure science, as many of the practical modifications as will, in his estimation, be most conducive to the usefulness of his work."[2] This certainly explodes Mr. Myrdal's assertion, so far as Classical economics is concerned.

Modern economics traces all human actions back to the value judgments of individuals. It never was so foolish, as Myrdal charges, as to believe that all that people are after is higher incomes and lower prices. Against this unjustified criticism which has been repeated a hundred times, Böhm-Bawerk already in his first contribution to the theory of value, and then later again and again, explicitly emphasized that the term "well-being" (*Wohlfahrtszwecke*) as he uses it in the exposition of the theory of value does not refer only to concerns commonly called egoistic but comprehends everything that appears to an individual as desirable and worthy of being aimed at (*erstrebenswert*).[3]

In acting man prefers some things to other things, and chooses between various modes of conduct. The result of the mental process that makes a man prefer one thing to another thing is called a judgment of value. In speaking of value and valuations economics refers to such judgments of value, whatever their content may

2. John Stuart Mill, *Essays on Some Unsettled Questions of Political Economy* (3d ed. London, 1877), pp. 140–1.

3. Böhm-Bawerk, "Grundzüge der Theorie des wirtschaftlichen Güterwerts," *Jahrbücher für Nationalökonomie und Statistik*, N.F., *13* (1886), 479, n. 1; *Kapital und Kapitalzins* (3d ed. Innsbruck, 1909), *2*, 316–17, n. 1.

be. It is irrelevant for economics, up to now the best developed part of praxeology, whether an individual aims like a member of a labor union at higher wages or like a saint at the best performance of religious duties. The "institutional" fact that most people are eager to get more tangible good is a datum of economic history, not a theorem of economics.

All brands of historicism—the German and the British historical schools of the social sciences, American institutionalism, the adepts of Sismondi, Le Play, and Veblen, and many kindred "unorthodox" sects—emphatically reject economics. But their writings are full of inferences drawn from general propositions about the effects of various modes of acting. It is, of course, impossible to deal with any "institutional" or historical problem without referring to such general propositions. Every historical report, no matter whether its theme is the conditions and events of a remote past or those of yesterday, is inevitably based on a definite kind of economic theory. The historicists do not eliminate economic reasoning from their treatises. While rejecting an economic doctrine they do not like, they resort in dealing with events to fallacious doctrines long since refuted by the economists.

The theorems of economics, say the historicists, are void because they are the product of a priori reasoning. Only historical experience can lead to realistic economics. They fail to see that historical experience is always the experience of complex phenomena, of the joint effects brought about by the operation of a multiplicity of elements. Such historical experience does not give the observer facts in the sense in which the natural sciences apply this term to the results obtained in laboratory experiments. (People who call their offices, studies, and libraries "laboratories" for research in economics, statistics, or the social sciences are hopelessly muddleheaded.) Historical facts need to be interpreted on the ground of previously available theorems. They do not comment upon themselves.

The antagonism between economics and historicism does not concern the historical facts. It concerns the interpretation of the facts. In investigating and narrating facts a scholar may provide a valuable contribution to history, but he does not contribute to the increase and perfection of economic knowledge.

Let us once more refer to the often repeated proposition that what the economists call economic laws are merely principles governing conditions under capitalism and of no avail for a differently organized society, especially not for the coming socialist management of affairs. As these critics see it, it is only the capitalists with their acquisitiveness who bother about costs and about profit. Once production for use has been substituted for production for profit, the categories of cost and profit will become meaningless. The primary error of economics consists in considering these and other categories as eternal principles determining action under any kind of institutional conditions.

However, cost is an element in any kind of human action, whatever the particular features of the individual case may be. Cost is the value of those things the actor renounces in order to attain what he wants to attain; it is the value he attaches to the most urgently desired satisfaction among those satisfactions which he cannot have because he preferred another to it. It is the price paid for a thing. If a young man says: "This examination cost me a week end with friends in the country," he means: "If I had not chosen to prepare for my examination, I would have spent this week end with friends in the country." Things it costs no sacrifice to attain are not economic goods but free goods and as such no objects of any action. Economics does not deal with them. Man does not have to choose between them and other satisfactions.

Profit is the difference between the higher value of the good obtained and the lower value of the good sacrificed for its obtainment. If the action, due to bungling, error, an unanticipated change in conditions, or to other circumstances, results in obtaining something to which the actor attaches a lower value than to the price paid, the action generates a loss. Since action invariably aims to substitute a state of affairs which the actor considers as more satisfactory for a state which he considers less satisfactory, action always aims at profit and never at loss. This is valid not only for the actions of individuals in a market economy but no less for the actions of the economic director of a socialist society.

3. The Quest for Laws of Historical Change

A widespread error confuses historicism and history. Yet the two have nothing in common. History is the presentation of the course of past events and conditions, a statement of facts and of their effects. Historicism is an epistemological doctrine.

Some schools of historicism have declared that history is the only way to deal with human action and have denied the adequacy, possibility, and meaningfulness of a general theoretical science of human action. Other schools have condemned history as unscientific and, paradoxically enough, have developed a sympathetic attitude toward the negative part of the doctrines of the positivists, who asked for a new science which, modeled on the pattern of Newtonian physics, should derive from historical experience laws of historical evolution and of "dynamic" change.

The natural sciences have developed, on the basis of Carnot's second law of thermodynamics, a doctrine about the course of the history of the universe. Free energy capable of work depends on thermodynamic instability. The process producing such energy is irreversible. Once all free energy produced by unstable systems is exhausted, life and civilization will cease. In the light of this cognition the universe as we know it appears as an evanescent episode in the flux of eternity. It moves toward its own extinction.

But the law from which this inference is drawn, Carnot's second law, is in itself not a historical or dynamic law. Like all other laws of the natural sciences, it is derived from the observation of phenomena and verified by experiments. We call it a law because it describes a process that repeats itself whenever the conditions for its operation are present. The process is irreversible, and from this fact scientists infer that the conditions for its operation will no longer be given once all thermo-dynamic instability has disappeared.

The notion of a law of historical change is self-contradictory. History is a sequence of phenomena that are characterized by their singularity. Those features which an event has in common with other events are not historical. What murder cases have in common refers to penal law, to psychology, to the technique of killing. As historical events the assassination of Julius Caesar and that of Henri IV of France are entirely different. The importance of an event for the production of further events is what counts for history. This effect of an event is unique and unrepeatable. Seen from the point of view of American constitutional law, the presidential elections of 1860 and of 1956 belong to the same class. For history they are two distinct events in the flux of affairs. If a historian compares them, he does so in order to elucidate the differences between them, not in order to discover laws that govern any instance of an American presidential election. Sometimes people formulate certain rules of thumb concerning such elections, as for instance: the party in power wins if business is booming. These rules are an attempt to understand the conduct of the voters. Nobody ascribes to them the necessity and apodictic validity which is the essential logical feature of a law of the natural sciences. Everybody is fully aware that the voters might proceed in a different way.

Carnot's second law is not the result of a study of the history of the universe. It is a proposition about phenomena that are repeated daily and hourly in precisely the way the law describes. From this law science deduces certain consequences concerning the future of the universe. This deduced knowledge is in itself not a law. It is the application of a law. It is a prognostication of future events made on the basis of a law that describes what is believed to be an inexorable necessity in the sequence of repeatable and repeated events.

Neither is Darwin's principle of natural selection a law of historical evolution. It tries to explain biological change as the outcome of the operation of a biological law. It interprets the past, it does not prognosticate things to come. Although the operation of the principle of natural selection may be considered as perennial, it is not permissible to infer that man must inevitably develop into a sort of superman. A line of evolutionary change may lead into a dead end beyond which there is no further change at all or a retrogression to previous states.

As it is impossible to deduce any general laws from the observation of historical change, the program of "dynamic" historicism could only be realized by discovering that the operation of one or several praxeological laws must inevitably result in the emergence of definite conditions of the future. Praxeology and its until now best-developed branch, economics, never claimed to know anything about such matters. Historicism, on account of its rejection of praxeology, was from the outset prevented from embarking upon such a study.

Everything that has been said about future historical events, inevitably bound to come, stems from prophecies elaborated by the metaphysical methods of the philosophy of history. By dint of intuition the author guesses the plans of the prime mover, and all uncertainty about the future disappears. The author of the Apocalypse, Hegel and, above all, Marx held themselves to be perfectly familiar with the laws of historical evolution. But the source of their knowledge was not science; it was the revelation of an inner voice.

4. *Historicist Relativism*

The ideas of historicism can be understood only if one takes into account that they sought exclusively one end: to negate everything that rationalist social philosophy and economics had established. In this pursuit many historicists did not shrink from any absurdity. Thus to the statement of the economists that there is an inevitable scarcity of nature-given factors upon which human well-being depends they opposed the fantastic assertion that there is abundance and plenty. What brings about poverty and want, they say, is the inadequacy of social institutions.

When the economists referred to progress, they looked upon conditions from the point of view of the ends sought by acting men. There was nothing metaphysical in their concept of progress. Most men want to live and to prolong their lives; they want to be healthy and to avoid sickness; they want to live comfortably and not to exist on the verge of starvation. In the eyes of acting men advance toward these goals means improvement, the reverse means impairment. This is the meaning of the terms "progress" and "retrogression" as applied by economists. In this sense they call a drop in infant mortality or success in fighting contagious diseases progress.

The question is not whether such progress makes people happy. It makes them happier than they would otherwise have been. Most mothers feel happier if their children survive, and most people feel happier without tuberculosis than with it. Looking upon conditions from his personal point of view, Nietzsche expressed misgivings about the "much too many." But the objects of his contempt thought differently.

In dealing with the means to which men resorted in their actions history as well as economics distinguishes between means which were fit to attain the ends sought and those which were not. In this sense progress is the substitution of more suitable methods of action for less suitable. Historicism takes offense at this terminology. All things are relative and must be viewed from the point of view of their age. Yet no champion of historicism has the boldness to contend that exorcism ever was a suitable means to cure sick cows. But the historicists are less cautious in dealing with economics. For instance, they declare that what economics teaches about the effects of price control is inapplicable to the conditions of the Middle Ages. The historical works of authors imbued with the ideas of historicism are muddled precisely on account of their rejection of economics.

While emphasizing that they do not want to judge the past by any preconceived standard, the historicists in fact try to justify the policies of the "good old days."

Instead of approaching the theme of their studies with the best mental equipment available, they rely upon the fables of pseudo economics. They cling to the superstition that decreeing and enforcing maximum prices below the height of the potential prices which the unhampered market would fix is a suitable means to improve the conditions of the buyers. They omit to mention the documentary evidence of the failure of the just price policy and of its effects which, from the point of view of the rulers who resorted to it, were more undesirable than the previous state of affairs which they were designed to alter.

One of the vain reproaches heaped by historicists on the economists is their alleged lack of historical sense. Economists, they say, believe that it would have been possible to improve the material conditions of earlier ages if only people had been familiar with the theories of modern economics. Now, there can be no doubt that the conditions of the Roman Empire would have been considerably affected if the emperors had not resorted to currency debasement and had not adopted a policy of price ceilings. It is no less obvious that the mass penury in Asia was caused by the fact that the despotic governments nipped in the bud all endeavors to accumulate capital. The Asiatics, unlike the Western Europeans, did not develop a legal and constitutional system which would have provided the opportunity for large-scale capital accumulation. And the public, actuated by the old fallacy that a businessman's wealth is the cause of other people's poverty, applauded whenever rulers confiscated the holdings of successful merchants.

The economists have always been aware that the evolution of ideas is a slow, time-consuming process. The history of knowledge is the account of a series of successive steps made by men each of whom adds something to the thoughts of his predecessors. It is not surprising that Democritus of Abdera did not develop the quantum theory or that the geometry of Pythagoras and Euclid is different from that of Hilbert. Nobody ever thought that a contemporary of Pericles could have created the free-trade philosophy of Hume, Adam Smith, and Ricardo and converted Athens into an emporium of capitalism.

There is no need to analyze the opinion of many historicists that to the soul of some nations the practices of capitalism appear so repulsive that they will never adopt them. If there are such peoples, they will forever remain poor. There is but one road that leads toward prosperity and freedom. Can any historicist on the ground of historical experience contest this truth?

No general rules about the effects of various modes of action and of definite social institutions can be derived from historical experience. In this sense the famous dictum is true that the study of history can teach only one thing: viz., that nothing can be learned from history. We could therefore agree with the historicists in not paying much attention to the indisputable fact that no people ever raised itself to a somewhat satisfactory state of welfare and civilization without the institution of private ownership of the means of production. It is not history but economics that clarifies our thoughts about the effects of property rights. But we must entirely reject the reasoning, very popular with many nineteenth-century writers, that the alleged fact that the institution of private property was unknown to peoples in primitive stages of civilization is a valid argument in favor of socialism. Having started as the harbingers of a future society which will wipe out all that is unsatisfactory and will transform the earth into a paradise, many socialists, for instance Engels, virtually became advocates of a return to the supposedly blissful conditions of a fabulous golden age of the remote past.

It never occurred to the historicists that man must pay a price for every achievement. People pay the price if they believe that the benefits derived from the thing to be acquired outweigh the disadvantages resulting from the sacrifice of something else. In dealing with this issue historicism adopts the illusions of romantic poetry. It sheds tears about the defacement of nature by civilization. How beautiful were the untouched virgin forests, the waterfalls, the solitary shores before the greed of acquisitive people spoiled their beauty! The romantic historicists pass over in silence the fact that the forests were cut down in order to win arable land and the falls were utilized to produce power and light. There is no doubt that Coney Island was more idyllic in the days of the Indians than it is today. But in its present state it gives millions of New Yorkers an opportunity to refresh themselves which they cannot get elsewhere. Talk about the magnificence of untouched nature is idle if it does not take into account what man has got by "desecrating" nature. The earth's marvels were certainly splendid when visitors seldom set foot upon them. Commercially organized tourist traffic made them accessible to the many. The man who thinks "What a pity not to be alone on this peak! Intruders spoil my pleasure," fails to remember that he himself probably would not be on the spot if business had not provided all the facilities required.

The technique of the historicists' indictment of capitalism is simple indeed. They take all its achievements for granted, but blame it for the disappearance of some enjoyments that are incompatible with it and for some imperfections which still may disfigure its products. They forget that mankind has had to pay a price for its achievements—a price paid willingly because people believe that the gain derived, e.g., the prolongation of the average length of life, is more to be desired.

5. Dissolving History

History is a sequence of changes. Every historical situation has its individuality, its own characteristics that distinguish it from any other situation. The stream of history never returns to a previously occupied point. History is not repetitious.

Stating this fact is not to express any opinion about the biological and anthropological problem of whether mankind is descended from a common *human* ancestry. There is no need to raise the question here whether the transformation of subhuman primates into the species Homo sapiens occurred only once at a definite time and in a definite part of the earth's surface or came to pass several times and resulted in the emergence of various original races. Neither does the establishment of this fact mean that there is such a thing as unity of civilization. Even if we assume that all men are scions of a common human ancestry, there remains the fact that the scarcity of the means of sustenance brought about a dispersal of people over the globe. This dispersal resulted in the segregation of various groups. Each of these groups had to solve for itself man's specific problem of life: how to pursue the conscious striving after improvement of conditions warranting survival. Thus various civilizations emerged. It will probably never be known to what extent definite civilizations were isolated and independent of one another. But it is certain that for thousands of years instances of such cultural isolation existed. It was only the explorations of European navigators and travelers that finally put an end to it.

Many civilizations came to an impasse. They either were destroyed by foreign conquerors or disintegrated from within. Next to the ruins of marvelous structures the progeny of their builders live in poverty and ignorance. The cultural achievements of their forefathers, their philosophy, technology, and often even their language have fallen into oblivion, and the people have relapsed into barbarism. In some cases the literature of the extinct civilization has been preserved and, rediscovered by scholars, has influenced later generations and civilizations.

Other civilizations developed to a certain point and then came to a standstill. They were arrested, as Bagehot said.[1] The people tried to preserve the achievements of the past but they no longer planned to add anything new to them.

A firm tenet of eighteenth-century social philosophy was meliorism. Once the superstitions, prejudices, and errors that caused the downfall of older civilizations have given way to the supremacy of reason, there will be a steady improvement of human conditions. The world will become better every day. Mankind will never return to the dark ages. Progress toward higher stages of well-being and knowledge is irresistible. All reactionary movements are doomed to failure. Present-day philosophy no longer indulges in such optimistic views. We realize that our civilization too is vulnerable. True, it is safe against external attacks on the part of foreign barbarians. But it could be destroyed from within by domestic barbarians.

Civilization is the product of human effort, the achievement of men eager to fight the forces adverse to their well-being. This achievement is dependent on men's using suitable means. If the means chosen are not fit to produce the ends sought, disaster results. Bad policies can disintegrate our civilization as they have destroyed many other civilizations. But neither reason nor experience warrants the assumption that we cannot avoid choosing bad policies and thereby wrecking our civilization.

There are doctrines hypostatizing the notion of civilization. In their view a civilization is a sort of living being. It comes into existence, thrives for some time,

1. Walter Bagehot, *Physics and Politics* (London, 1872), p. 212.

and finally dies. All civilizations, however different they may appear to the superficial observer, have the same structure. They must necessarily pass through the same sequence of successive stages. There is no history. What is mistakenly called history is in fact the repetition of events belonging to the same class; is, as Nietzsche put it, eternal recurrence.

The idea is very old and can be traced back to ancient philosophy. It was adumbrated by Giovanni Battista Vico. It played some role in the attempts of several economists to develop schemes of parallelisms of the economic history of various nations. It owes its present popularity to Oswald Spengler's *Decline of the West.* Softened to some extent and thereby rendered inconsistent, it is the main idea of the voluminous Study of History on which Arnold J. Toynbee is still working. There is no doubt that both Spengler and Toynbee were prompted by the widespread disparagement of capitalism. Spengler's motive clearly was to prognosticate the inevitable breakdown of our civilization. Although unaffected by the chiliastic prophecies of the Marxians, he was himself a socialist and entirely under the sway of the socialists' vilification of the market economy. He was judicious enough to see the disastrous implications of the policies of the German Marxians. But, lacking any economic knowledge and even full of contempt for economics, he came to the conclusion that our civilization has to choose between two evils each of which is bound to destroy it. The doctrines of both Spengler and Toynbee show clearly the poor results engendered by neglect of economics in any treatment of human concerns. True, Western civilization is decadent. But its decadence consists precisely in the endorsement of the anticapitalistic creed.

What we may call the Spengler doctrine dissolves history into the record of the life span of individual entities, the various civilizations. We are not told in precise terms what marks characterize an individual civilization as such and distinguish it from another civilization. All that we learn about this essential matter is metaphorical. A civilization is like a biological being; it is born, grows, matures, decays, and dies. Such analogies are no substitute for unambiguous clarification and definition.

Historical research cannot deal with all things together; it must divide and subdivide the totality of events. Out of the whole body of history it carves separate chapters. The principles applied in so doing are determined by the way the historian understands things and events, value judgments and the actions prompted by them and the relation of actions to the further course of affairs. Almost all historians agree in dealing separately with the history of various more or less isolated peoples and civilizations. Differences of opinion about the application of this procedure to definite problems must be decided by careful examination of each individual case. No epistemological objection can be raised to the idea of distinguishing various civilizations within the totality of history.

But what the Spengler doctrine means is something entirely different. In its context a civilization is a *Gestalt*, a whole, an individuality of a distinct nature. What determines its origin, changes, and extinction stems from its own nature. It is not the ideas and actions of the individuals that constitute the historical process. There is in fact no historical process. On the earth civilizations come into being, live for some time, and then die just as various specimens of every plant species are born, live, and wither away. Whatever men may do is irrelevant to the final outcome. Every civilization must decay and die.

There is no harm in comparing different historical events and different events that occurred in the history of various civilizations. But there is no justification whatever for the assertion that every civilization must pass through a sequence of inevitable stages.

Mr. Toynbee is inconsistent enough not to deprive us entirely of any hope for the survival of our civilization. While the whole and only content of his study is to point out that the process of civilization consists of periodic repetitive movements, he adds that this "does not imply that the process itself is of the same cyclical order as they are." Having taken pains to show that sixteen civilizations have perished already and nine others are at the point of death, he expresses a vague optimism concerning the future of the twenty-sixth civilization.[2]

History is the record of human action. Human action is the conscious effort of man to substitute more satisfactory conditions for less satisfactory ones. Ideas determine what are to be considered more and less satisfactory conditions and what means are to be re-

2. A. J. Toynbee, *A Study of History*, Abridgment of Volumes I–VI by D. C. Somervell (Oxford University Press, 1947), p. 254.

sorted to to alter them. Thus ideas are the main theme of
the study of history. Ideas are not an invariable stock
that existed from the very beginning of things and that
does not change. Every idea originated at a definite
point of time and space in the head of an individual.
(Of course, it has happened again and again that the
same idea originated independently in the heads of various individuals at various points of time and space.)
The genesis of every new idea is an innovation; it adds
something new and unheard of before to the course of
world affairs. The reason history does not repeat itself
is that every historical state is the consummation of the
operation of ideas different from those that operated in
other historical states.

Civilization differs from the mere biological and physiological aspects of life in being an offshoot of ideas.
The essence of civilization is ideas. If we try to distinguish different civilizations, the *differentia specifica* can
be found only in the different meanings of the ideas
that determined them. Civilizations differ from one another precisely in the quality of the substance that characterizes them as civilizations. In their essential structure they are unique individuals, not members of a class.
This forbids us to compare their vicissitudes with the
physiological process going on in an individual man's or
animal's life. In every animal body the same physiological changes come to pass. A child ripens in the mother's
womb, it is delivered, grows, matures, decays, and dies
in the consummation of the same cycle of life. It is
quite another thing with civilizations. In being civilizations they are disparate and incommensurable because

they are actuated by different ideas and therefore develop in different ways.

Ideas must not be classified without regard to the soundness of their content. Men have had different ideas concerning the cure of cancer. Up to now none of these ideas has produced fully satisfactory results. But this would not justify the inference that therefore future attempts to cure cancer will also be futile. The historian of past civilizations may declare: There was something wrong with the ideas upon which those civilizations that decayed from within were built. But he must not derive from this fact the conclusion that other civilizations, built on different ideas, are also doomed. Within the body of animals and plants forces are operating that are bound to disintegrate it eventually. No such forces could be discovered in the "body" of a civilization which would not be the outcome of its particular ideologies.

No less vain are efforts to search in the history of various civilizations for parallelisms or identical stages in their life span. We may compare the history of various peoples and civilizations. But such comparisons must deal not only with similarities but also with differences. The eagerness to discover similarities induces authors to neglect or even to conjure away discrepancies. The first task of the historian is to deal with historical events. Comparisons made afterward on the basis of a knowledge of events as perfect as possible may be harmless or sometimes even instructive. Comparisons that accompany or even precede study of the sources create confusion if not outright fables.

6. Undoing History

There have always been people who exalted the good old days and advocated a return to the happy past. The resistance offered to legal and constitutional innovations by those whom they hurt has frequently crystallized in programs that requested a reconstruction of old institutions or presumably old institutions. In some cases reforms that aimed at something essentially new have been recommended as a restoration of ancient law. An eminent example was provided by the role Magna Charta played in the ideologies of England's seventeenth-century anti-Stuart parties.

But it was historicism which for the first time frankly suggested unmaking historical changes and returning to extinct conditions of a remote past. We need not deal with the lunatic fringe of this movement, such as German attempts to revive the cult of Wodan. Neither do the sartorial aspects of these tendencies deserve more than ironical comments. (A magazine picture showing members of the Hanover-Coburg family parading in the garb of the Scottish clansmen who fought at Culloden would have startled the "Butcher" Cumberland.) Only the linguistic and economic issues involved require attention.

In the course of history many languages have been submerged. Some disappeared completely without leaving any trace. Others are preserved in old documents, books, and inscriptions and can be studied by scholars. Several of these "dead" languages—Sanskrit, Hebrew,

Greek, and Latin—influence contemporary thought through the philosophical and poetical value of the ideas expressed in their literature. Others are merely objects of philological research.

The process that resulted in the extinction of a language was in many cases merely linguistic growth and transformation of the spoken word. A long succession of slight changes altered the phonetic forms, the vocabulary, and the syntax so thoroughly that later generations could no longer read the documents bequeathed by their ancestors. The vernacular developed into a new distinct language. The old tongue could only be understood by those with special training. The death of the old language and the birth of the new one were the outcome of a slow, peaceful evolution.

But in many cases linguistic change was the outcome of political and military events. People speaking a foreign language acquired political and economic hegemony either by military conquest or by the superiority of their civilization. Those speaking the native tongue were relegated to a subordinate position. On account of their social and political disabilities it did not matter very much what they had to say and how they said it. Important business was transacted exclusively in the language of their masters. Rulers, courts, church, and schools employed only this language; it was the language of the laws and the literature. The old native tongue was used only by the uneducated populace. Whenever one of these underlings wanted to rise to a better position, he had first to learn the language of the masters. The vernacular was reserved to the dullest and the least ambitious; it fell into contempt and finally into oblivion. A foreign language superseded the native idiom.

The political and military events that actuated this linguistic process were in many cases characterized by tyrannical cruelty and pitiless persecution of all opponents. Such methods met with the approval of some philosophers and moralists of precapitalistic ages, as they have sometimes won the praise of contemporary "idealists" when the socialists resort to them. But to the "spurious rationalistic dogmatism of the orthodox liberal doctrinaires" they appear shocking. The historical writings of the latter lacked that lofty relativism which induced self-styled "realistic" historians to explain and to justify all that had happened in the past and to vindicate surviving oppressive institutions. (As one critic reproachfully observed, in the utilitarians "old institutions awake no thrill; they are simply embodiments of prejudice.") [1] It does not need any further explanation why the descendants of the victims of those persecutions and oppressions judged in a different way the experience of their ancestors, still less why they were intent upon abolishing those effects of past despotism which still hurt them. In some cases, not content with eliminating still existing oppression, they planned to undo also such changes as did not harm them any longer, however detrimental and malignant the proc-

1. Leslie Stephens, *The English Utilitarians* (London, 1900), 3, 70 (on J. Stuart Mill).

ess that had brought them about had been in a distant past. It is precisely this that the attempts to undo linguistic changes aim at.

The best example is provided by Ireland. Aliens had invaded and conquered the country, expropriated the landowners, destroyed its civilization, organized a despotic regime, and tried to convert the people by force of arms to a religious creed which they despised. The establishment of an alien church did not succeed in making the Irish abandon Roman Catholicism. But the English language superseded the native Gaelic idiom. When later the Irish succeeded step by step in curbing their foreign oppressors and finally acquiring political independence, most of them were no longer linguistically different from the English. They spoke English and their eminent writers wrote English books some of which are among the outstanding works of modern world literature.

This state of affairs hurts the feelings of many Irish. They want to induce their fellow citizens to return to the idiom their ancestors spoke in ages gone by. There is little open opposition to these pursuits. Few people have the courage to fight a popular movement openly, and radical nationalism is today, next to socialism, the most popular ideology. Nobody wants to risk being branded an enemy of his nation. But powerful forces are silently resisting the linguistic reform. People cling to the tongue they speak no matter whether those who want to suppress it are foreign despots or domestic zealots. The modern Irish are fully aware of the advantages they derive from the fact that English is the foremost language of contemporary civilization, which everyone has to learn in order to read many important books or to play a role in international trade, in world affairs, and in great ideological movements. Precisely because the Irish are a civilized nation whose authors write not for a limited audience but for all educated people, the chances of a substitution of Gaelic for English are slim. No nostalgic sentimentality can alter these circumstances.

It must be mentioned that the linguistic pursuits of Irish nationalism were prompted by one of the most widely adopted political doctrines of the nineteenth century. The principle of nationality as accepted by all the peoples of Europe postulates that every linguistic group must form an independent state and that this state must embrace all people speaking the same language.[2] From the point of view of this principle an English-speaking Ireland should belong to the United Kingdom of Great Britain and Ireland, and the mere existence of an independent Irish Free State appears irregular. The prestige which the principle of nationality enjoyed in Europe was so enormous that various peoples who desired to form a state of their own the independence of which was at variance with it tried to change their language in order to justify their aspirations in its light. This explains the attitude of the Irish nationalists, but it does not affect what has been said about the implications of their linguistic plans.

A language is not simply a collection of phonetic

2. Mises, *Omnipotent Government* (New Haven, Yale University Press, 1944), pp. 84–9.

signs. It is an instrument of thinking and acting. Its vocabulary and grammar are adjusted to the mentality of the individuals whom it serves. A living language—spoken, written, and read by living men—changes continually in conformity with changes occurring in the minds of those who use it. A language fallen into desuetude is dead because it no longer changes. It mirrors the mentality of people long since passed away. It is useless to the people of another age no matter whether these people are biologically the scions of those who once used it or merely believe themselves to be their descendants. The trouble is not with the terms signifying tangible things. Such terms could be supplemented by neologisms. It is the abstract terms that provide insoluble problems. The precipitate of a people's ideological controversies, of their ideas concerning issues of pure knowledge and religion, legal institutions, political organization, and economic activities, these terms reflect all the vicissitudes of their history. In learning their meaning the rising generation are initiated into the mental environment in which they have to live and to work. This meaning of the various words is in continual flux in response to changes in ideas and conditions.

Those who want to revive a dead language must in fact create out of its phonetic elements a new language whose vocabulary and syntax are adjusted to the conditions of the present age, entirely different from those of the old age. The tongue of their ancestors is of no use to the modern Irish. The laws of present-day Ireland could not be written in the old vocabulary; Shaw, Joyce, and Yeats could not have employed it in their plays, novels, and poems. One cannot wipe out history and return to the past.

Different from the attempts to revive dead idioms are the plans to elevate local dialects to the position of a language of literature and other manifestations of thinking and acting. When communication between the various parts of a nation's territory was infrequent on account of the paucity of the interlocal division of labor and the primitiveness of transportation facilities, there was a tendency toward a disintegration of linguistic unity. Different dialects developed out of the tongue spoken by the people who had settled in an area. Sometimes these dialects evolved into a distinct literary language, as was the case with the Dutch language. In other cases only one of the dialects became a literary language, while the others remained idioms employed in daily life but not used in the schools, the courts, in books, and in the conversation of educated people. Such was the outcome in Germany, for instance, where the writings of Luther and the Protestant theologians gave the idiom of the "Saxon Chancellery" a preponderant position and reduced all other dialects to subordinate rank.

Under the impact of historicism movements sprang up which aim at undoing this process by elevating dialects into literary languages. The most remarkable of these tendencies is Félibrige, the design to restore to the Provençal tongue the eminence it once enjoyed as Langue d'Oc. The Félibrists, led by the distinguished poet Mistral, were judicious enough not to plan a complete substitution of their idiom for French. But even the prospects of their more moderate ambition, to create a new Provençal poesy, seem to be inauspicious. One cannot imagine any of the modern French masterpieces composed in Provençal.

Local dialects of various languages have been employed in novels and plays depicting the life of the uneducated. There is often an inherent insincerity in such writings. The author condescendingly puts himself on a level with people whose mentality he never shared or has since outgrown. He behaves like an adult who condescends to write books for children. No present-day work of literature can withdraw itself from the impact of the ideologies of our age. Once having gone through the schools of these ideologies, an author cannot successfully masquerade as a simple common man and adopt his speech and his world view.

History is an irreversible process.

7. Undoing Economic History

The history of mankind is the record of a progressive intensification of the division of labor. Animals live in perfect autarky of each individual or of each quasi family. What made cooperation between men possible is the fact that work performed under the division of tasks is more productive than the isolated efforts of autarkic individuals and that man's reason is capable of conceiving this truth. But for these two facts men would have remained forever solitary food-seekers, forced by an inevitable law of nature to fight one another without pity and pardon. No social bonds, no feelings of sympathy, benevolence, and friendship, no civilization would have developed in a world in which everybody had to see in all other men rivals in the biological competition for a strictly limited supply of food.

One of the greatest achievements of eighteenth-century social philosophy is the disclosure of the role which the principle of higher productivity resulting from division of labor has played in history. It was against these teachings of Smith and Ricardo that the most passionate attacks of historicism were directed.

The operation of the principle of division of labor and its corollary, cooperation, tends ultimately toward a world-embracing system of production. Insofar as the geographical distribution of natural resources does not limit the tendencies toward specialization and integration in the processing trades, the unhampered market aims at the evolution of plants operating in a comparatively narrow field of specialized production but serving the whole population of the earth. From the point of view of people who prefer more and better merchandise to a smaller and poorer supply the ideal system would consist in the highest possible concentration of the production of each speciality. The same principle that brought about the emergence of such specialists as blacksmiths, carpenters, tailors, bakers and also physicians, teachers, artists and writers would finally result in the emergence of one factory supplying the whole oecumene with some particular article. Although the geographical factor mentioned above counteracts the full operation of this tendency, international division of labor came into existence and will move forward until it reaches the limits drawn by geography, geology, and climate.

Every step on the road toward intensification of the division of labor hurts in the short run the personal interests of some people. The expansion of the more efficient plant hurts the interests of less efficient competitors whom it forces to go out of business. Technological innovation hurts the interests of workers who can no longer make a living by clinging to the discarded inferior methods. The vested short-run interests of small business and of inefficient workers are adversely affected by any improvement. This is not a new phenomenon. Neither is it a new phenomenon that those prejudiced by economic improvement ask for privileges that will protect them against the competition of the more efficient. The history of mankind is a long record of obstacles placed in the way of the more efficient for the benefit of the less efficient.

It is customary to explain the obstinate efforts to stop economic improvement by referring to the "interests." The explanation is very unsatisfactory. Leaving aside the fact that an innovation hurts merely the short-run interests of some people, we must emphasize that it hurts only the interests of a small minority while favoring those of the immense majority. The bread factory certainly hurts the small bakers. But it hurts them solely because it improves the conditions of all people consuming bread. The importation of foreign sugar and watches hurts the interests of a small minority of Americans. But it is a boon for all those who want to eat sugar and to buy watches. The problem is precisely this: Why is an innovation unpopular although it favors the interests of the great majority of the people?

A privilege accorded to a special branch of business is in the short run advantageous to those who at the instant happen to be in this branch. But it hurts all other people to the same extent. If everybody is privileged to the same degree, he loses as much in his capacity as a consumer as he wins in his capacity as a producer. Moreover, everybody is hurt by the fact that productivity in all branches of domestic production drops on account of these privileges.[1] To the extent that American legislation is successful in its endeavors to curb big business, all are hurt because the products are produced at higher costs in plants which would have been wiped out in the absence of this policy. If the United States had gone as far as Austria did in its fight against big business, the average American would not be much better off than the average Austrian.

It is not the interests that motivate the struggle against the further intensification of the division of labor, but spurious ideas about alleged interests. As in any other regard, historicism in dealing with these problems too sees only the short-run disadvantages that result for some people and ignores the long-run advantages for all of the people. It recommends measures without mentioning the price that must be paid for them. What fun shoemaking was in the days of Hans Sachs and the Meistersinger! No need to analyze critically such romantic dreams. But how many people went barefoot in those days? What a disgrace the big chemi-

1. See above, pp. 32 f.

cal concerns are! But would it have been possible for pharmacists in their primitive laboratories to turn out the drugs that kill the bacilli?

Those who want to set the clock of history back ought to tell people what their policy would cost. Splitting up big business is all right if you are prepared to put up with the consequences. If the present American methods of taxing incomes and estates had been adopted fifty years ago, most of those new things which no American would like to do without today would not have been developed at all or, if they had, would have been inaccessible to the greater part of the nation. What such authors as Professors Sombart and Tawney say about the blissful conditions of the Middle Ages is mere fantasy. The effort "to achieve a continuous and unlimited increase in material wealth," says Professor Tawney, brings "ruin to the soul and confusion to society." [2] No need to stress the fact that some people may feel that a soul so sensitive it is ruined by the awareness that more infants survive the first year of their lives and fewer people die from starvation today than in the Middle Ages is worth being ruined. What brings confusion to society is not wealth but the efforts of historicists such as Professor Tawney to discredit "economic appetites." After all it was nature, not the capitalists, that implanted appetites in man and impels him to satisfy them. In the collectivist institutions of the Middle Ages, such as church, township, village community, clan, family, and guild, says Sombart, the individual "was kept

2. R. H. Tawney, *Religion and the Rise of Capitalism* (New York, Penguin Books, n.d.), pp. 38 and 234.

warm and sheltered like the fruit in its rind." [3] Is this
a faithful description of a time when the population
was harassed again and again by famines, plagues, wars,
the persecution of heretics, and other disasters?

It is certainly possible to stop the further progress of
capitalism or even to return to conditions in which small
business and more primitive methods of production prevail. A police apparatus organized after the pattern of
the Soviet constabulary can achieve many things. The
question is only whether the nations that have built
modern civilization will be ready to pay the price.

3. W. Sombart, *Der proletarische Sozialismus* (10th ed. Jena,
1924), *I*, 31.

Chapter 11. The Challenge of Scientism

1. Positivism and Behaviorism

WHAT differentiates the realm of the natural sciences from that of the sciences of human action is the categorial system resorted to in each in interpreting phenomena and constructing theories. The natural sciences do not know anything about final causes; inquiry and theorizing are entirely guided by the category of causality. The field of the sciences of human action is the orbit of purpose and of conscious aiming at ends; it is teleological.

Both categories were resorted to by primitive man and are resorted to today by everybody in daily thinking and acting. The most simple skills and techniques imply knowledge gathered by rudimentary research into causality. Where people did not know how to seek the relation of cause and effect, they looked for a teleological interpretation. They invented deities and devils to whose purposeful action certain phenomena were ascribed. A god emitted lightning and thunder. Another god, angry about some acts of men, killed the offenders by shooting arrows. A witch's evil eye made women barren and cows dry. Such beliefs generated definite methods of action. Conduct pleasing to the deity, offering of sacrifices and prayer were considered suitable means to appease the deity's anger and to

240

avert its revenge; magic rites were employed to neutralize witchcraft. Slowly people came to learn that meteorological events, disease, and the spread of plagues are natural phenomena and that lightning rods and antiseptic agents provide effective protection while magic rites are useless. It was only in the modern era that the natural sciences in all their fields substituted causal research for finalism.

The marvelous achievements of the experimental natural sciences prompted the emergence of a materialistic metaphysical doctrine, positivism. Positivism flatly denies that any field of inquiry is open for teleological research. The experimental methods of the natural sciences are the only appropriate methods for any kind of investigation. They alone are scientific, while the traditional methods of the sciences of human action are metaphysical, that is, in the terminology of positivism, superstitious and spurious. Positivism teaches that the task of science is exclusively the description and interpretation of sensory experience. It rejects the introspection of psychology as well as all historical disciplines. It is especially fanatical in its condemnation of economics. Auguste Comte, by no means the founder of positivism but merely the inventor of its name, suggested as a substitute for the traditional methods of dealing with human action a new branch of science, sociology. Sociology should be social physics, shaped according to the epistemological pattern of Newtonian mechanics. The plan was so shallow and impractical that no serious attempt was ever made to realize it. The first generation of Comte's followers turned instead toward what they believed to be biological and organic interpretation of social phenomena. They indulged freely in metaphorical language and quite seriously discussed such problems as what in the social "body" should be classed as "intercellular substance." When the absurdity of this biologism and organicism became obvious, the sociologists completely abandoned the ambitious pretensions of Comte. There was no longer any question of discovering a posteriori laws of social change. Various historical, ethnographical, and psychological studies were put out under the label sociology. Many of these publications were dilettantish and confused; some are acceptable contributions to various fields of historical research. Without any value, on the other hand, were the writings of those who termed sociology their arbitrary metaphysical effusions about the recondite meaning and end of the historical process which had been previously styled philosophy of history. Thus, Émile Durkheim and his school revived under the appellation group mind the old specter of romanticism and the German school of historical jurisprudence, the *Volksgeist*.

In spite of this manifest failure of the positivist program, a neopositivist movement has arisen. It stubbornly repeats all the fallacies of Comte. The same motive inspires these writers that inspired Comte. They are driven by an idiosyncratic abhorrence of the market economy and its political corollary: representative government, freedom of thought, speech, and the press. They long for totalitarianism, dictatorship, and the ruthless oppression of all dissenters, taking, of course, for granted that they themselves or their intimate friends will be vested with the supreme office and the power to silence all opponents. Comte without shame advocated suppression of all doctrines he disliked. The most obtrusive champion of the neopositivist program concerning the sciences of human action was Otto Neurath who, in 1919, was one of the outstanding leaders of the short-lived Soviet regime of Munich and later cooperated briefly in Moscow with the bureaucracy of the Bolsheviks.[1] Knowing they cannot advance any tenable argument against the economists' critique of their plans, these passionate communists try to discredit economics wholesale on epistemological grounds.

The two main varieties of the neopositivistic assault on economics are panphysicalism and behaviorism. Both claim to substitute a purely causal treatment of human action for the—as they declare unscientific— teleological treatment.

Panphysicalism teaches that the procedures of physics are the only scientific method of all branches of science. It denies that any essential differences exist between the natural sciences and the sciences of human action. This denial lies behind the panphysicalists' slogan "unified science." Sense experience, which conveys to man his information about physical events, provides him also with all information about the behavior of his fellow men. Study of the way his fellows react to various stimuli does not differ essentially from study of the way other objects react. The language of physics is the

1. Otto Neurath, "Foundations of the Social Sciences," *International Encyclopedia of Unified Science*, Vol. 2, No. 1.

universal language of all branches of knowledge, without exception. What cannot be rendered in the language of physics is metaphysical nonsense. It is arrogant pretension in man to believe that his role in the universe is different from that of other objects. In the eyes of the scientist all things are equal. All talk about consciousness, volition, and aiming at ends is empty. Man is just one of the elements in the universe. The applied science of social physics, social engineering, can deal with man in the same way technology deals with copper and hydrogen.

The panphysicalist might admit at least one essential difference between man and the objects of physics. The stones and the atoms reflect neither upon their own nature, properties, and behavior nor upon those of man. They do not engineer either themselves or man. Man is at least different from them insofar as he is a physicist and an engineer. It is difficult to conceive how one could deal with the activities of an engineer without realizing that he chooses between various possible lines of conduct and is intent upon attaining definite ends. Why does he build a bridge rather than a ferry? Why does he build one bridge with a capacity of ten tons and another with a capacity of twenty tons? Why is he intent upon constructing bridges that do not collapse? Or is it only an accident that most bridges do not collapse? If one eliminates from the treatment of human action the notion of conscious aiming at definite ends, one must replace it by the—really metaphysical—idea that some superhuman agency leads men, independently of their will, toward a predestined goal: that what put the bridge-builder into motion was the preordained plan of *Geist* or the material productive forces which mortal men are forced to execute.

To say that man reacts to stimuli and adjusts himself to the conditions of his environment does not provide a satisfactory answer. To the stimulus offered by the English Channel some people have reacted by staying at home; others have crossed it in rowboats, sailing ships, steamers, or, in modern times simply by swimming. Some fly over it in planes; others design schemes for tunneling under it. It is vain to ascribe the differences in reaction to differences in attendant circumstances such as the state of technological knowledge and the supply of labor and capital goods. These other conditions too are of human origin and can only be explained by resorting to teleological methods.

The approach of behaviorism is in some respects different from that of panphysicalism, but it resembles the latter in its hopeless attempt to deal with human action without reference to consciousness and aiming at ends. It bases its reasoning on the slogan "adjustment." Like any other being, man adjusts himself to the conditions of his environment. But behaviorism fails to explain why different people adjust themselves to the same conditions in different ways. Why do some people flee violent aggression while others resist it? Why did the peoples of Western Europe adjust themselves to the scarcity of all things on which human well-being depends in a way entirely different from that of the Orientals?

Behaviorism proposes to study human behavior according to the methods developed by animal and infant psychology. It seeks to investigate reflexes and instincts, automatisms and unconscious reactions. But it has told us nothing about the reflexes that have built cathedrals, railroads, and fortresses, the instincts that have produced philosophies, poems, and legal systems, the automatisms that have resulted in the growth and decline of empires, the unconscious reactions that are splitting atoms. Behaviorism wants to observe human behavior from without and to deal with it merely as reaction to a definite situation. It punctiliously avoids any reference to meaning and purpose. However, a situation cannot be described without analyzing the meaning which the man concerned finds in it. If one avoids dealing with this meaning, one neglects the essential factor that decisively determines the mode of reaction. This reaction is not automatic but depends entirely upon the interpretation and value judgments of the individual, who aims to bring about, if feasible, a situation which he prefers to the state of affairs that would prevail if he were not to interfere. Consider a behaviorist describing the situation which an offer to sell brings about without reference to the meaning each party attaches to it!

In fact, behaviorism would outlaw the study of human action and substitute physiology for it. The behaviorists never succeeded in making clear the difference between physiology and behaviorism. Watson declared that physiology is "particularly interested in the functioning of parts of the animal . . . , behaviorism, on the other hand, while it is intensely interested in all of the functioning of these parts, is intrinsically interested in what the whole animal will do." [2] However, such physiological phenomena as the resistance of the body to infection or the growth and aging of an individual can certainly not be called behavior of parts. On the other hand, if one wants to call such a gesture as the movement of an arm (either to strike or to caress) behavior of the whole human animal, the idea can only be that such a gesture cannot be imputed to any separate part of the being. But what else can this something to which it must be imputed be if not the meaning and the intention of the actor or that unnamed thing from which meaning and intention originate? Behaviorism asserts that it wants to predict human behavior. But it is impossible to predict the reaction of a man accosted by another with the words "you rat" without referring to the meaning that the man spoken to attaches to the epithet.

Both varieties of positivism decline to recognize the fact that men aim purposefully at definite ends. As they see it, all events must be interpreted in the relationship of stimulus and response, and there is no room left for a search for final causes. Against this rigid dogmatism it is necessary to stress the point that the rejection of finalism in dealing with events outside the sphere of human action is enjoined upon science only by the insufficiency of human reason. The natural sciences must refrain from dealing with final causes because they are unable to discover any final causes, not because they can prove that no final causes are operative. The cogni-

2. John B. Watson, *Behaviorism* (New York, W. W. Norton, 1930), p. 11.

zance of the interconnectedness of all phenomena and of the regularity in their concatenation and sequence, and the fact that causality research works and has enlarged human knowledge, do not peremptorily preclude the assumption that final causes are operative in the universe. The reason for the natural sciences' neglect of final causes and their exclusive preoccupation with causality research is that this method works. The contrivances designed according to the scientific theories run the way the theories predicted and thus provide a pragmatic verification for their correctness. On the other hand the magic devices did not come up to expectations and do not bear witness to the magic world view.

It is obvious that it is also impossible to demonstrate satisfactorily by ratiocination that the alter ego is a being that aims purposively at ends. But the same pragmatic proof that can be advanced in favor of the exclusive use of causal research in the field of nature can be advanced in favor of the exclusive use of teleological methods in the field of human action. It works, while the idea of dealing with men as if they were stones or mice does not work. It works not only in the search for knowledge and theories but no less in daily practice.

The positivist arrives at his point of view surreptitiously. He denies to his fellow men the faculty of choosing ends and the means to attain these ends, but at the same time he claims for himself the ability to choose consciously between various methods of scientific procedure. He shifts his ground as soon as it comes to problems of engineering, whether technological or "social." He designs plans and policies which cannot be interpreted as merely being automatic reactions to stimuli. He wants to deprive all his fellows of the right to act in order to reserve this privilege for himself alone. He is a virtual dictator.

As the behaviorist tells us, man can be thought of as "an assembled organic machine ready to run." [3] He disregards the fact that while machines run the way the engineer and the operator make them run, men run spontaneously here and there. "At birth human infants, regardless of their heredity, are as equal as Fords." [4] Starting from this manifest falsehood, the behaviorist proposes to operate the "human Ford" the way the operator drives his car. He acts as if he owned humanity and were called upon to control and to shape it according to his own designs. For he himself is above the law, the godsent ruler of mankind. [5]

3. Watson, p. 269.

4. Horace M. Kallen, "Behaviorism," *Encyclopaedia of the Social Sciences*, 2, 498.

5. Karl Mannheim developed a comprehensive plan to produce the "best possible" human types by "deliberately" reorganizing the various groups of social factors. "*We*," that is Karl Mannheim and his friends, will determine what "the highest good of society and the peace of mind of the individual" require. Then "*we*" will revamp mankind. For *our* vocation is "the planned guidance of people's lives." Mannheim, *Man and Society in an Age of Reconstruction* (London, Routledge & Kegan Paul, 1940), p. 222. The most remarkable thing about such ideas is that in the thirties and forties they were styled democratic, liberal, and progressive. Joseph Goebbels was more modest than Mannheim in that he wanted only to revamp the German people and not the whole of mankind. But in his approach to the problem he did not differ essentially from Mannheim. In a letter of April 12, 1933, to Wilhelm Furtwängler he referred to the "*we*" to

As long as positivism does not explain philosophies and theories, and the plans and policies derived from them, in terms of its stimulus-response scheme, it defeats itself.

2. The Collectivist Dogma

Modern collectivist philosophy is a coarse offshoot of the old doctrine of conceptual realism. It has severed itself from the general philosophical antagonism between realism and nominalism and hardly pays any attention to the continued conflict of the two schools. It is a political doctrine and as such employs a terminology that is seemingly different from that used in the scholastic debates concerning universals as well from that of contemporary neorealism. But the nucleus of its teachings does not differ from that of the medieval realists. It ascribes to the universals objective real existence, even an existence superior to that of individuals, sometimes, even, flatly denying the autonomous existence of individuals, the only real existence.

What distinguishes collectivism from conceptual realism as taught by philosophers is not the method of approach but the political tendencies implied. Collectivism transforms the epistemological doctrine into an

---

whom "the responsible task has been entrusted, to fashion out of the raw stuff of the masses the firm and well-shaped structure of the nation (denen die verantwortungsvolle Aufgabe anvertraut ist, aus dem rohen Stoff der Masse das feste und gestalthafte Gebilde des Volkes zu formen)." Berta Geissmar, *Musik im Schatten der Politik* (Zürich, Atlantis Verlag, 1945), pp. 97–9. Unfortunately neither Mannheim nor Goebbels told us who had entrusted them with the task of reconstructing and re-creating men.

ethical claim. It tells people what they ought to do. It distinguishes between the true collective entity to which people owe loyalty and spurious pseudo entities about which they ought not to bother at all. There is no uniform collectivist ideology, but many collectivist doctrines. Each of them extols a different collectivist entity and requests all decent people to submit to it. Each sect worships its own idol and is intolerant of all rival idols. Each ordains total subjection of the individual, each is totalitarian.

The particularist character of the various collectivist doctrines could easily be ignored because they regularly start with the opposition between society in general and individuals. In this antithesis there appears only one collective comprehending all individuals. There cannot therefore arise any rivalry among a multitude of collective entities. But in the further course of the analysis a special collective is imperceptibly substituted for the comprehensive image of the unique great society.

Let us first examine the concept of society in general.

Men cooperate with one another. The totality of interhuman relations engendered by such cooperation is called society. Society is not an entity in itself. It is an aspect of human action. It does not exist or live outside of the conduct of people. It is an orientation of human action. Society neither thinks nor acts. Individuals in thinking and acting constitute a complex of relations and facts that are called social relations and facts.

The issue has been confused by an arithmetical metaphor. Is society, people asked, merely a sum of individuals or is it more than this and thereby an entity endowed with independent reality? The question is nonsensical. Society is neither the sum of individuals nor more nor less. Arithmetical concepts cannot be applied to the matter.

Another confusion arises from the no less empty question whether society is—in logic and in time—anterior to individuals or not. The evolution of society and that of civilization were not two distinct processes but one and the same process. The biological passing of a species of primates beyond the level of a mere animal existence and their transformation into primitive men implied already the development of the first rudiments of social cooperation. Homo sapiens appeared on the stage of earthly events neither as a solitary food-seeker nor as a member of a gregarious flock, but as a being consciously cooperating with other beings of his own kind. Only in cooperation with his fellows could he develop language, the indispensable tool of thinking. We cannot even imagine a reasonable being living in perfect isolation and not cooperating at least with members of his family, clan, or tribe. Man as man is necessarily a social animal. Some sort of cooperation is an essential characteristic of his nature. But awareness of this fact does not justify dealing with social relations as if they were something else than relations or with society as if it were an independent entity outside or above the actions of individual men.

Finally there are the misconstructions caused by the organismic metaphor. We may compare society to a biological organism. The *tertium comparationis* is the fact that division of labor and cooperation exist among the various parts of a biological body as among the various members of society. But the biological evolution that resulted in the emergence of the structure-function systems of plant and animal bodies was a purely physiological process in which no trace of a conscious activity on the part of the cells can be discovered. On the other hand, human society is an intellectual and spiritual phenomenon. In cooperating with their fellows, individuals do not divest themselves of their individuality. They retain the power to act antisocially, and often make use of it. Its place in the structure of the body is invariably assigned to each cell. But individuals spontaneously choose the way in which they integrate themselves into social cooperation. Men have ideas and seek chosen ends, while the cells and organs of the body lack such autonomy.

Gestalt psychology passionately rejects the psychological doctrine of associationism. It ridicules the conception of "a sensory mosaic which nobody has ever observed" and teaches that "analysis if it wants to reveal the universe in its completeness has to stop at the wholes, whatever their size, which possess functional reality." [1] Whatever one may think about Gestalt psychology, it is obvious that it has no reference at all to the problems of society. It is manifest that nobody has ever observed society as a whole. What can be observed is always actions of individuals. In interpreting the various aspects of the individual's actions, the theorists

1. K. Koffka, "Gestalt," *Encyclopaedia of the Social Sciences*, 6, 644.

develop the concept of society. There cannot be any question of understanding "the properties of parts from the properties of wholes." [2] There are no properties of society that cannot be discovered in the conduct of its members.

In contrasting society and the individual and in denying to the latter any "true" reality, the collectivist doctrines look upon the individual merely as a refractory rebel. This sinful wretch has the impudence to give preference to his petty selfish interests as against the sublime interests of the great god society. Of course, the collectivist ascribes this eminence only to the rightful social idol, not to one of the pretenders.

> But who pretender is, and who is king,
> God bless us all—that's quite another thing.

When the collectivist extols the state, what he means is not every state but only that regime of which he approves, no matter whether this legitimate state exists already or has to be created. For the Czech irredentists in the old Austria and the Irish irredentists in the United Kingdom the states whose governments resided in Vienna and in London were usurpers; their rightful state did not yet exist. Especially remarkable is the terminology of the Marxians. Marx was bitterly hostile to the Prussian state of the Hohenzollern. To make it clear that the state which he wanted to see omnipotent and totalitarian was not that state whose rulers resided in Berlin, he called the future state of his program not state but society. The innovation was merely verbal.

2. Ibid., p. 645.

For what Marx aimed at was to abolish any sphere of the individual's initiative action by transferring the control of all economic activities to the social apparatus of compulsion and repression which is commonly called state or government. The hoax did not fail to beguile lots of people. Even today there are still dupes who think that there is a difference between state socialism and other types of socialism.

The confusion of the concepts of society and of state originated with Hegel and Schelling. It is customary to distinguish two schools of Hegelians: the left wing and the right wing. The distinction refers only to the attitude of these authors toward the Kingdom of Prussia and the doctrines of the Prussian Union Church. The political creed of both wings was essentially the same. Both advocated government omnipotence. It was a left-wing Hegelian, Ferdinand Lassalle, who most clearly expressed the fundamental thesis of Hegelianism: "The State is God." [3] Hegel himself had been a little more cautious. He only declared that it is "the course of God through the world that constitutes the State" and that in dealing with the State one must contemplate "the Idea, God as actual on earth." [4]

The collectivist philosophers fail to realize that what constitutes the state is the actions of individuals. The legislators, those enforcing the laws by force of arms, and those yielding to the dictates of the laws and the police constitute the state by their behavior. In this

3. Gustav Mayer, *Lassalleana, Archiv für Geschichte der Sozialismus*, 1, 196.
4. Hegel, *Philosophy of Right*, sec. 258.

sense alone is the state real. There is no state apart from such actions of individual men.

3. *The Concept of the Social Sciences*

The collectivist philosophy denies that there are such things as individuals and actions of individuals. The individual is merely a phantom without reality, an illusory image invented by the pseudo philosophy of the apologists of capitalism. Consequently collectivism rejects the concept of a science of human action. As it sees it, the only legitimate treatment of those problems that are not dealt with by the traditional natural sciences is provided by what they call the social sciences.

The social sciences are supposed to deal with group activities. In their context the individual counts only as a member of a group.[1] But this definition implies that there are actions in which the individual does not act as a member of a group and which therefore do not interest the social sciences. If this is so, it is obvious that the social sciences deal only with an arbitrarily selected fraction of the whole field of human action.

In acting, man must necessarily choose between various possible modes of acting. Limiting their analysis to one class of actions only, the social sciences renounce in advance any attempt to investigate the ideas that determine the individual's choice of a definite mode of conduct. They cannot deal with judgments of value which in any actual situation make a man prefer act-

1. E. R. A. Seligman, "What Are the Social Sciences?" *Encyclopaedia of the Social Sciences, 1,* 3.

ing as a group member to acting in a different manner. Neither can they deal with the judgments of value that prompt a man to act as a member of group A rather than as a member of any of the non-A groups.

Man is not the member of one group only and does not appear on the scene of human affairs solely in the role of a member of one definite group. In speaking of social groups it must be remembered that the members of one group are at the same time members of other groups. The conflict of groups is not a conflict between neatly integrated herds of men. It is a conflict between various concerns in the minds of individuals.

What constitutes group membership is the way a man acts in a concrete situation. Hence group membership is not something rigid and unchangeable. It may change from case to case. The same man may in the course of a single day perform actions each of which qualifies him as a member of a different group. He may contribute to the funds of his denomination and cast his ballot for a candidate who antagonizes that denomination in essential problems. He may act at one instant as a member of a labor union, at another as a member of a religious community, at another as a member of a political party, at another as a member of a linguistic or racial group, and so on. Or he may act as an individual working to earn more income, to get his son into college, to purchase a home, a car, or a refrigerator. In fact he always acts as an individual, always seeks ends of his own. In joining a group and acting as a member of it, he aims no less at the fulfillment of his own wishes than in acting without any reference to a group. He may join a religious community in order to seek the salvation of his soul or to attain peace of mind. He may join a labor union because he believes that this is the best means to get higher pay or to avoid being bodily injured by the members of the union. He may join a political party because he expects that the realization of its program will render conditions more satisfactory for himself and his family.

It is vain to deal with "the activities of the individual as a member of a group" [2] while omitting other activities of the individual. Group activities are essentially and necessarily activities of individuals who form groups in order to attain their ends. There are no social phenomena which would not originate from the activities of various individuals. What creates a group activity is a definite end sought by individuals and the belief of these individuals that cooperating in this group is a suitable means to attain the end sought. A group is a product of human wishes and the ideas about the means to realize these wishes. Its roots are in the value judgments of individuals and in the opinions held by individuals about the effects to be expected from definite means.

To deal with social groups adequately and completely, one must start from the actions of the individuals. No group activity can be understood without analyzing the ideology that forms the group and makes it live and work. The idea of dealing with group activities without dealing with all aspects of human action is preposterous. There is no field distinct from the field

2. Seligman, loc. cit.

of the sciences of human action that could be investigated by something called the social sciences.

What prompted those who suggested the substitution of the social sciences for the sciences of human action was, of course, a definite political program. In their eyes the social sciences were designed to obliterate the social philosophy of individualism. The champions of the social sciences invented and popularized the terminology that characterizes the market economy, in which every individual is intent upon the realization of his own plan, as a planless and therefore chaotic system and reserves the term "plan" for the designs of an agency which, supported by or identical with the government's police power, prevents all citizens from realizing their own plans and designs. One can hardly overrate the role which the association of ideas generated by this terminology plays in shaping the political tenets of our contemporaries.

4. *The Nature of Mass Phenomena*

Some people believe that the object of the social sciences is the study of mass phenomena. While the study of individual traits is of no special interest to them, they hope study of the behavior of social aggregates will reveal information of a really scientific character. For these people the chief defect of the traditional methods of historical research is that they deal with individuals. They esteem statistics precisely because, as they think, it observes and records the behavior of social groups.

In fact statistics records individual traits of the members of arbitrarily selected groups. Whatever the principle may be that determined the scientist to set up a group, the traits recorded refer primarily to the individuals that form the group and only indirectly to the group. The individual members of the group are the units of observation. What statistics provides is information about the behavior of individuals forming a group.

Modern statistics aims at discovering invariable connections between statistically established magnitudes by measuring their correlation. In the field of the sciences of human action this method is absurd. This has been clearly demonstrated by the fact that many coefficients of correlation of a high numerical value have been calculated which undoubtedly do not indicate any connection between the two groups of facts.[1]

Social phenomena and mass phenomena are not things outside and above individual phenomena. They are not the cause of individual phenomena. They are produced either by the cooperation of individuals or by parallel action. The latter may be either independent or imitative. This is valid also with regard to antisocial actions. The intentional killing of a man by another man is as such merely a human action and would have no other significance in a hypothetical (and irrealizable) state in which there was no cooperation between men. It becomes a crime, murder, in a state where social

1. M. R. Cohen and E. Nagel, *An Introduction to Logic and Scientific Method* (New York, Harcourt, Brace, 1934), p. 317.

cooperation precludes homicide except in cases strictly determined by the laws of this society.

What is commonly called a mass phenomenon is the frequent repetition and recurrence of a definite individual phenomenon. The proposition: In the West bread is an article of mass consumption, means: In the West the immense majority of men eat bread daily. They do not eat bread because it is an article of mass consumption. Bread is an article of mass consumption because practically everybody eats a piece of bread each day. From this point of view one may appreciate the endeavors of Gabriel Tarde to describe imitation and repetition as fundamental factors of social evolution.[2]

The champions of the social sciences criticize the historians for concentrating their attention upon the actions of individuals and neglecting the conduct of the many, the immense majority, the masses. The critique is spurious. A historian who deals with the spread of the Christian creed and of the various churches and denominations, with the events that resulted in the emergence of integrated linguistic groups, with the European colonization of the Western hemisphere, with the rise of modern capitalism certainly does not overlook the behavior of the many. However, the main task of history is to indicate the relation of the individuals' actions to the course of affairs. Different individuals influence historical change in different ways. There are pioneers who conceive new ideas and design new modes of thinking and acting; there are leaders who guide people along

2. G. Tarde, *Les lois de l'imitation,* 3d ed. Paris, 1900.

the way these people want to walk, and there are the anonymous masses who follow the leaders. There can be no question of writing history without the names of the pioneers and the leaders. The history of Christianity cannot pass over in silence such men as Saint Paul, Luther, and Calvin, nor can the history of seventeenth-century England fail to analyze the roles of Cromwell, Milton, and William III. To ascribe the ideas producing historical change to the mass psyche is a manifestation of arbitrary metaphysical prepossession. The intellectual innovations which August Comte and Buckle rightly considered the main theme of the study of history are not achievements of the masses. Mass movements are not inaugurated by anonymous nobodys but by individuals. We do not know the names of the men who in the early days of civilization accomplished the greatest exploits. But we are certain that also the technological and institutional innovations of those early ages were not the result of a sudden flash of inspiration that struck the masses but the work of some individuals who by far surpassed their fellow men.

There is no mass psyche and no mass mind but only ideas held and actions performed by the many in endorsing the opinions of the pioneers and leaders and imitating their conduct. Mobs and crowds too act only under the direction of ringleaders. The common men who constitute the masses are characterized by lack of initiative. They are not passive, they also act, but they act only at the instigation of abetters.

The emphasis laid by sociologists upon mass phenomena and their idolization of the common man are an offshoot of the myth that all men are biologically equal. Whatever differences exist between individuals are caused, it is maintained, by postnatal circumstances. If all people equally enjoyed the benefits of a good education, such differences would never appear. The supporters of this doctrine are at a loss to explain the differences among graduates of the same school and the fact that many who are self-taught far excel the doctors, masters, and bachelors of the most renowned universities. They fail to see that education cannot convey to pupils more than the knowledge of their teachers. Education rears disciples, imitators, and routinists, not pioneers of new ideas and creative geniuses. The schools are not nurseries of progress and improvement but conservatories of tradition and unvarying modes of thought. The mark of the creative mind is that it defies a part of what it has learned or, at least, adds something new to it. One utterly misconstrues the feats of the pioneer in reducing them to the instruction he got from his teachers. No matter how efficient school training may be, it would only produce stagnation, orthodoxy, and rigid pedantry if there were no uncommon men pushing forward beyond the wisdom of their tutors.

It is hardly possible to mistake more thoroughly the meaning of history and the evolution of civilization than by concentrating one's attention upon mass phenomena and neglecting individual men and their exploits. No mass phenomenon can be adequately treated without analyzing the ideas implied. And no new ideas spring from the mythical mind of the masses.

Chapter 12. Psychology and Thymology

1. Naturalistic Psychology and Thymology

MANY AUTHORS believe that psychology is basic to the social sciences, even that it comprehends them all.

Insofar as psychology proceeds with the experimental methods of physiology, these claims are manifestly unwarranted. The problems investigated in the laboratories of the various schools of experimental psychology have no more reference to the problems of the sciences of human action than those of any other scientific discipline. Most of them are even of no use to praxeology, economics, and all the branches of history. In fact, nobody ever tried to show how the findings of naturalistic psychology could be utilized for any of these sciences.

But the term "psychology" is applied in another sense too. It signifies the cognition of human emotions, motivations, ideas, judgments of value and volitions, a faculty indispensable to everybody in the conduct of daily affairs and no less indispensable to the authors of poems, novels, and plays as well as to historians. Modern epistemology calls this mental process of the historians the specific understanding of the historical sciences of human action. Its function is twofold: it establishes, on the one hand, the fact that, motivated by definite value judgments, people have engaged in definite actions and applied definite means to attain the ends they seek. It tries, on the other hand, to evaluate the effects and the intensity of the effects of an action, its bearing upon the further course of events.

The specific understanding of the historical disciplines is not a mental process exclusively resorted to by historians. It is applied by everybody in daily intercourse with all his fellows. It is a technique employed in all interhuman relations. It is practiced by children in the nursery and kindergarten, by businessmen in trade, by politicians and statesmen in affairs of state. All are eager to get information about other people's valuations and plans and to appraise them correctly. People as a rule call this insight into the minds of other men psychology. Thus, they say a salesman ought to be a good psychologist, and a political leader should be an expert in mass psychology. This popular use of the term "psychology" must not be confused with the psychology of any of the naturalistic schools. When Dilthey and other epistemologists declared that history must be based on psychology, what they had in mind was this mundane or common-sense meaning of the term.

To prevent mistakes resulting from the confusion of these two entirely different branches of knowledge it is expedient to reserve the term "psychology" for naturalistic psychology and to call the knowledge of human valuations and volitions "thymology." [1]

1. Some writers, for instance, Santayana, employed the term "literary psychology." See his book *Scepticism and Animal Faith*, ch. 24. However, the use of this term seems inadvisable, not only because it was employed in a pejorative sense by Santayana as well as by many representatives of naturalistic psychology, but because it is impossible to form a corresponding adjective. "Thymology" is derived from the

Thymology is on the one hand an offshoot of introspection and on the other a precipitate of historical experience. It is what everybody learns from intercourse with his fellows. It is what a man knows about the way in which people value different conditions, about their wishes and desires and their plans to realize these wishes and desires. It is the knowledge of the social environment in which a man lives and acts or, with historians, of a foreign milieu about which he has learned by studying special sources. If an epistemologist states that history has to be based on such knowledge as thymology, he simply expresses a truism.

While naturalistic psychology does not deal at all with the content of human thoughts, judgments, desires, and actions, the field of thymology is precisely the study of these phenomena.

The distinction between naturalistic psychology and physiology on the one hand and thymology on the other hand can best be illustrated by referring to the methods of psychiatry. Traditional psychopathology and neuropathology deal with the physiological aspects of the diseases of the nerves and the brain. Psychoa-

---

Greek θυμός, which Homer and other authors refer to as the seat of the emotions and as the mental faculty of the living body by means of which thinking, willing, and feeling are conducted. See Wilhelm von Volkmann, *Lehrbuch der Psychologie* (Cöthen, 1884), *1*, 57–9; Erwin Rohde, *Psyche*, trans. by W. B. Hillis (London, 1925), p. 50; Richard B. Onians, *The Origins of European Thought about the Body, the Mind, the Soul, the World, Time, and Fate* (Cambridge, 1951), pp. 49–56. Recently Professor Hermann Friedmann employed the term *Thymologie* with a somewhat different connotation. See his book *Das Gemüt, Gedanken zu einer Thymologie* (Munich, C. H. Beck, 1956), pp. 2–16.

nalysis deals with their thymological aspects. The object of its investigations is ideas and the conscious aiming at ends that come into conflict with physiological impulses. Ideas urge individuals to suppress certain natural drives, especially such as the sex impulse. But the attempts to repress them do not always succeed fully. The impulses are not eradicated, merely relegated to a hiding place, and take their vengeance. From the depth they exert a disturbing influence on the conscious life and conduct of the individual. Psychoanalytic therapy tries to remove these neurotic troubles by bringing the conflict into the full consciousness of the patient. It heals with ideas, not with drugs or surgical operations.

It is customary to assert that psychoanalysis deals with irrational factors influencing human conduct. This statement needs interpretation in order to prevent confusion. All ultimate ends aimed at by men are beyond the criticism of reason. Judgments of value can be neither justified nor refuted by reasoning. The terms "reasoning" and "rationality" always refer only to the suitability of means chosen for attaining ultimate ends. The choice of ultimate ends is in this sense always irrational.

The sex impulse and the urge to preserve one's own vital forces are inherent in the animal nature of man. If man were only an animal and not also a valuing person, he would always yield to the impulse that at the instant is most powerful. The eminence of man consists in the fact that he has ideas and, guided by them, chooses between incompatible ends. He chooses also between life and death, between eating and hunger, between coition and sexual abstinence.

In earlier days people were prepared to assume that there was no sense at all in the exceptional behavior of neurotics. Freud demonstrated that the seemingly senseless acts of the neurotic are designed to attain definite ends. The ends the neurotic wants to attain may differ from those for which normal people strive, and—very often—the means the neurotic resorts to are not suitable for their realization. But the fact that means chosen are not fit to attain the ends sought does not qualify an action as irrational.

To make mistakes in pursuing one's ends is a widespread human weakness. Some err less often than others, but no mortal man is omniscient and infallible. Error, inefficiency, and failure must not be confused with irrationality. He who shoots wants, as a rule, to hit the mark. If he misses it, he is not "irrational"; he is a poor marksman. The doctor who chooses the wrong method to treat a patient is not irrational; he may be an incompetent physician. The farmer who in earlier ages tried to increase his crop by resorting to magic rites acted no less rationally than the modern farmer who applies more fertilizer. He did what according to his—erroneous—opinion was appropriate to his purpose.

What characterizes the neurotic as such is not the fact that he resorts to unsuitable means but that he fails to come to grips with the conflicts that confront civilized man. Life in society requires that the individual suppress instinctive urges present in every animal. We may leave it undecided whether the impulse of aggression is one of these innate urges. There is no doubt that life in society is incompatible with indulgence in the animal habits of satisfying sexual appetites. Perhaps there are better methods of regulating sexual intercourse than those resorted to in actual society. However that may be, it is a fact that the adopted methods put too much strain upon the minds of some individuals. These men and women are at a loss to solve problems which luckier people get over. Their dilemma and embarrassment make them neurotic.

Many spurious objections have been raised to the philosophy of rationalism. Various nineteenth-century schools of thought completely misinterpreted the essence of the rationalist doctrine. As against these misinterpretations it is important to realize that eighteenth-century classical rationalism was defective only in the treatment of some subordinate and merely incidental issues and that these minor deficiencies could easily lead undiscerning critics astray.

The fundamental thesis of rationalism is unassailable. Man is a rational being; that is, his actions are guided by reason. The proposition: Man acts, is tantamount to the proposition: Man is eager to substitute a state of affairs that suits him better for a state of affairs that suits him less. In order to achieve this, he must employ suitable means. It is his reason that enables him to find out what is a suitable means for attaining his chosen end and what is not.

Rationalism was right furthermore in stressing that there is a far-reaching unanimity among people with regard to the choice of ultimate ends. With almost negligible exceptions, all people want to preserve their lives and health and improve the material conditions of their existence. It is this fact that determines both cooperation and competition among men. But in dealing with this point rationalist philosophers committed serious blunders.

In the first place they assumed that all men are endowed with the same power of reasoning. They ignored the difference between clever people and dullards, even that between the pioneering genius and the vast crowds of simple routinists who at best can espouse the doctrines developed by the great thinkers but more often are incapable of comprehending them. As the rationalists saw it, every sane adult was intelligent enough to grasp the meaning of the most complicated theory. If he failed to achieve it, the fault lay not in his intellect but in his education. Once all people have enjoyed a perfect education, all will be as wise and judicious as the most eminent sage.

The second shortcoming of rationalism was its neglect of the problem of erroneous thinking. Most of the rationalist philosophers failed to see that even honest men, sincerely devoted to the search for truth, could err. This prepossession prevented them from doing justice to the ideologies and the metaphysical doctrines of the past. A doctrine of which they disapproved could in their opinion have been prompted only by purposeful deceit. Many of them dismissed all religions as the product of the intentional fraud of wicked impostors.

Yet these shortcomings of classical rationalism do not

excuse any of the passionate attacks of modern irrationalism.

2. *Thymology and Praxeology*

Thymology has no special relation to praxeology and economics. The popular belief that modern subjective economics, the marginal utility school, is founded on or closely connected with "psychology" is mistaken.

The very act of valuing is a thymological phenomenon. But praxeology and economics do not deal with the thymological aspects of valuation. Their theme is acting in accordance with the choices made by the actor. The concrete choice is an offshoot of valuing. But praxeology is not concerned with the events which within a man's soul or mind or brain produce a definite decision between an *A* and a *B*. It takes it for granted that the nature of the universe enjoins upon man choosing between incompatible ends. Its subject is not the content of these acts of choosing but what results from them: action. It does not care about what a man chooses but about the fact that he chooses and acts in compliance with a choice made. It is neutral with regard to the factors that determine the choice and does not arrogate to itself the competence to examine, to revise, or to correct judgments of value. It is *wertfrei*.

Why one man chooses water and another man wine is a thymological (or, in the traditional terminology, psychological) problem. But it is of no concern to praxeology and economics.

The subject matter of praxeology and of that part of it which is so far the best developed—economics—is action as such and not the motives that impel a man to aim at definite ends.

3. *Thymology as a Historical Discipline*

Psychology in the sense in which the term is employed today by the discipline called psychology is a natural science. It is not the task of an epistemological treatise dealing with the sciences of human action to raise the question as to what distinguishes this branch of the natural sciences from general physiology.

Psychology in the sense of thymology is a branch of history. It derives its knowledge from historical experience. We shall deal in a later section with introspection. At this point is suffices to stress the fact that the thymological observation both of other people's choices and of the observer's own choosing necessarily always refers to the past, in the way that historical experience does. There is no method available which would produce in this field something analogous to what the natural sciences consider an experimentally established fact. All that thymology can tell us is that in the past definite men or groups of men were valuing and acting in a definite way. Whether they will in the future value and act in the same way remains uncertain. All that can be asserted about their future conduct is speculative anticipation of the future based on the specific understanding of the historical branches of the sciences of human action.

There is no difference in this regard between the thymology of individuals and that of groups. What is called *Völkerpsychologie* and mass psychology too are historical disciplines. What is called a nation's "character" is at best the traits displayed by members of that nation in the past. It remains uncertain whether or not the same traits will manifest themselves in the future too.

All animals are endowed with the impulse of self-preservation. They resist forces detrimental to their survival. If attacked, they defend themselves or counterattack or seek safety in flight. Biology is in a position to predict, on the basis of observation of the behavior of various species of animals, how a healthy individual of each species will respond to attack. No such apodictic forecast concerning the conduct of men is possible. True, the immense majority of men are driven by the animal impulse of self-preservation. But there are exceptions. There are men who are led by definite ideas to choose nonresistance. There are others whom hopelessness induces to abstain from any attempt to resist or to flee. Before the event it is impossible to know with certainty how an individual will react.

In retrospect historical analysis tries to show us that the outcome could not have been different from what it really was. Of course, the effect is always the necessary resultant of the factors operating. But it is impossible to deduce with certainty from thymological experience the future conduct of men, whether individuals or groups of individuals. All prognostications based on thymological knowledge are specific understanding of the future as practiced daily by everyone in their actions and especially also by statesmen, politicians, and businessmen.

What thymology achieves is the elaboration of a catalogue of human traits. It can moreover establish the fact that certain traits appeared in the past as a rule in connection with certain other traits. But it can never predict in the way the natural sciences can. It can never know in advance with what weight the various factors will be operative in a definite future event.

4. History and Fiction

History tries to describe past events as they really happened. It aims at faithful representation. Its concept of truth is correspondence with what was once reality.

Epic and dramatic fiction depict what is to be considered true from the point of view of thymological insight, no matter whether the story told really happened or not. It is not our task to deal with the effects the author wants to bring about by his work and with its metaphysical, aesthetic, and moral content. Many writers seek merely to entertain the public. Others are more ambitious. In telling a story, they try to suggest a general view of man's fate, of life and death, of human effort and suffering, of success and frustration. Their message differs radically from that of science as well as from that of philosophy. Science, in describing and interpreting the universe, relies entirely upon reason and experience. It shuns propositions which are not open to demonstration by means of logic (in the broadest sense of the term that includes mathematics and praxeology) and experience. It analyzes parts of the universe without making any statements about the totality of things. Philosophy tries to build upon the foundations laid by science a comprehensive world view. In striving after this end, it feels itself bound not to contradict any of the well-founded theses of contemporary science. Thus its path too is confined by reason and experience.

Poets and artists approach things and problems in another mood. In dealing with a single aspect of the universe they are always dealing with the whole. Narration and description, the portrayal of individual things and of particular events, is for them only a means. The essential feature of their work is beyond words, designs, and colors. It is in the ineffable feelings and ideas that activated the creator and move the reader and spectator. When Konrad Ferdinand Meyer described a Roman fountain and Rainer Maria Rilke a caged panther, they did not simply portray reality. They caught a glimpse of the universe. In Flaubert's novel it is not Madame Bovary's sad story that is of primary concern; it is something that reaches far beyond the fate of this poor woman. There is a fundamental difference between the most faithful photograph and a portrait painted by an artist. What characterizes a work of literature and art as such is not its reporting of facts but the way it reveals an aspect of the universe and man's attitude toward it. What makes an artist is not experience and knowledge as such. It is his particular reaction to the problems of human existence and fate. It is *Erlebnis,* a purely personal response to the reality of his environment and his experience.

Poets and artists have a message to tell. But this message refers to ineffable feelings and ideas. It is not open to utterance in an unambiguous way precisely because it is ineffable. We can never know whether what we experience—*erleben*—in enjoying their work is what they experienced in creating it. For their work is not simply a communication. Apart from what it communicates, it stirs up in the reader and spectator feelings and ideas which may differ from those of its author. It is a hopeless task to interpret a symphony, a painting, or a novel. The interpreter at best tries to tell us something about his reaction to the work. He cannot tell us with certainty what the creator's meaning was or what other people may see in it. Even if the creator himself provides a commentary on his work, as in the case of program-music, this uncertainty remains. There are no words to describe the ineffable.

What history and fiction have in common is the fact that both are based on knowledge concerning the human mind. They operate with thymological experience. Their method of approach is the specific understanding of human valuations, of the way people react to the challenge of their natural and social environment. But then their ways part. What the historian has to tell is completely expressed in his report. He communicates to the reader all he has established. His message is exoteric. There is nothing that would go beyond the content of his book as intelligible to competent readers.

It may happen that the study of history, or for that matter also the study of the natural sciences, rouses in the mind of a man those ineffable thoughts and views of the universe as a whole which are the mark of the empathic grasp of totality. But this does not alter the nature and character of the historian's work. History is unconditionally the search after facts and events that really happened.

Fiction is free to depict events that never occurred. The writer creates, as people say, an imaginary story. He is free to deviate from reality. The tests of truth that apply to the work of the historian do not apply to his work. Yet his freedom is limited. He is not free to defy the teachings of thymological experience. It is not a requirement of novels and plays that the things related should really have happened. It is not even necessary that they could happen at all; they may introduce heathen idols, fairies, animals acting in human manner, ghosts and other phantoms. But all the characters of a novel or a play must act in a thymologically intelligible way. The concepts of truth and falsehood as applied to epic and dramatic works refer to thymological plausibility. The author is free to create fictitious persons and plots but he must not try to invent a thymology—psychology—different from that derived from the observation of human conduct.

Fiction, like history, does not deal with average man or man in the abstract or general man—*homme général* [1]

1. P. Lacombe, *De l'histoire considérée comme science* (2d ed. Paris, 1930), pp. 35–41.

—but with individual men and individual events. Yet even here there is a conspicuous difference between history and fiction.

The individuals with whom history deals may be and often are groups of individuals, and the individual events with which it deals are events that affected such groups of individuals. The single individual is a subject of the historian's interest primarily from the point of view of the influence his actions exercised upon a multitude of people or as a typical specimen representative of whole groups of individuals. The historian does not bother about other people. But for the writer of fiction it is always only the individual as such that counts, no matter what his influence upon other people or whether or not he is to be considered typical.

This has been entirely misunderstood in some doctrines about literature developed in the second part of the nineteenth century. The authors of these doctrines were misled by contemporary changes in the treatment of history. While older historians wrote chiefly about great men and affairs of state, modern historians shifted to the history of ideas, institutions, and social conditions. At a time when the prestige of science far surpassed that of literature, and positivist zealots sneered at fiction as a useless pastime, writers tried to justify their profession by representing it as a branch of scientific research. In the opinion of Émile Zola the novel was a sort of descriptive economics and social psychology, to be based upon punctilious exploration of particular conditions and institutions. Other authors went even further and asserted that only the fate of classes, nations, and races, not that of individuals, is to be treated in novels and plays.They obliterated the distinction between a statistical report and a "social" novel or play.

The books and plays written in compliance with the precepts of this naturalistic aesthetics were clumsy pieces of work. No outstanding writer paid more than lip service to these principles. Zola himself was very restrained in the application of his doctrine.

The theme of novels and plays is individual man as he lives, feels, and acts, and not anonymous collective wholes. The milieu is the background of the portraits the author paints; it is the state of external affairs to which the characters respond by moves and acts. There is no such thing as a novel or play whose hero is an abstract concept such as a race, a nation, a caste, or a political party. Man alone is the perennial subject of literature, individual real man as he lives and acts.

The theories of the aprioristic sciences—logic, mathematics, and praxeology—and the experimental facts established by the natural sciences can be viewed without reference to the personality of their authors. In dealing with the problems of Euclidian geometry we are not concerned with the man Euclid and may forget that he ever lived. The work of the historian is necessarily colored by the historian's specific understanding of the problems involved, but it is still possible to discuss the various issues implied without referring to the historical fact that they originated from a definite author. No such objectivity is permitted in dealing with works of fiction. A novel or a play always has one hero more than the plot indicates. It is also a confession of the author and tells no less about him than about the persons in the story. It reveals his innermost soul.

It has sometimes been asserted that there is more truth in fiction than in history. Insofar as the novel or play is looked upon as a disclosure of the author's mind, this is certainly correct. The poet always writes about himself, always analyzes his own soul.

5. Rationalization

The thymological analysis of man is essential in the study of history. It conveys all we can know about ultimate ends and judgments of value. But as has been pointed out above, it is of no avail for praxeology and of little use in dealing with the means applied to attain ends sought.

With regard to the choice of means all that matters is their suitability to attain the ends sought. There is no other standard for appraising means. There are suitable means and unsuitable means. From the point of view of the actor the choice of unsuitable means is always erroneous, an inexcusable failure.

History is called upon to explain the origin of such errors by resorting to thymology and the specific understanding. As man is fallible and the search after appropriate means is very difficult, the course of human history is by and large a series of errors and frustration. Looking backward from the present state of our knowledge we are sometimes tempted to belittle past ages and boast of the efficiency of our time. However, even the pundits of the "atomic age" are not safe against error.

Shortcomings in the choice of means and in acting are not always caused by erroneous thinking and inefficiency. Frequently frustration is the result of irresoluteness with regard to the choice of ends. Wavering between various incompatible goals, the actor vacillates in his conduct of affairs. Indecision prevents him from marching straight toward one goal. He moves to and fro. He goes now toward the left, then toward the right. Thus he does not accomplish anything. Political, diplomatic, and military history has dealt amply with this type of irresolute action in the conduct of affairs of state. Freud has shown what role in the daily life of the individual subconscious repressed urges play in forgetting, mistakes, slips of the tongue or the pen, and accidents.

A man who is obliged to justify his handling of a matter in the eyes of other people often resorts to a pretext. As the motive of his deviation from the most suitable way of procedure he ascribes another reason than that which actually prompted him. He does not dare to admit his real motive because he knows that his critics would not accept it as a sufficient justification.

Rationalization is the name psychoanalysis gives to the construction of a pretext to justify conduct in the actor's own mind. Either the actor is loath to admit the real motive to himself or he is not aware of the repressed urge directing him. He disguises the subconscious impulse by attaching to his actions reasons acceptable to his superego. He is not consciously cheating and lying. He is himself a victim of his illusions and wishful thinking. He lacks the courage to look squarely at reality. As he dimly surmises that the cognition of the true state of affairs would be unpleasant, undermine his self-esteem, and weaken his resolution, he shrinks from analyzing the problems beyond a certain point. This is of course a rather dangerous attitude, a retreat from an unwelcome reality into an imaginary world of fancy that pleases better. A few steps further in the same direction may lead to insanity.

However, in the lives of individuals there are checks that prevent such rationalizations from becoming rampant and wreaking havoc. Precisely because rationalization is a type of behavior common to many, people are watchful and even often suspect it where it is absent. Some are always ready to unmask their neighbors' sly attempts to bolster their own self-respect. The most cleverly constructed legends of rationalization cannot in the long run withstand the repeated attacks of debunkers.

It is quite another thing with rationalization developed for the benefit of social groups. That can thrive luxuriantly because it encounters no criticism from the members of the group and because the criticism of outsiders is dismissed as obviously biased. One of the main tasks of historical analysis is to study the various manifestations of rationalization in all fields of political ideologies.

6. *Introspection*

The passionate quarrel of the introspectionists and anti-introspectionists refers to the problems of naturalistic psychology and does not affect thymology. None of the methods and procedures recommended by the anti-introspectionist schools could convey any information and knowledge about the phenomena which thymology explores.

Being himself a valuing and acting ego, every man knows the meaning of valuing and acting. He is aware that he is not neutral with regard to the various states of his environment, that he prefers certain states to others, and that he consciously tries, provided the conditions for such interference on his part are given, to substitute a state that he likes better for one he likes less. It is impossible to imagine a sane human being who lacks this insight. It is no less impossible to conceive how a being lacking this insight could acquire it by means of any experience or instruction. The categories of value and of action are primary and aprioristic elements present to every human mind. No science should or could attack the problems involved without prior knowledge of these categories.

Only because we are aware of these categories do we know what meaning means and have a key to interpret other people's activities. This awareness makes us distinguish in the external world two separate realms, that of human affairs and that of nonhuman things, or that of final causes and that of causality. It is not our task here to deal with causality. But we must emphasize that the concept of final causes does not stem from experience and observation of something external; it is present in the mind of every human being.

It is necessary to emphasize again and again that no statement or proposition concerning human action can be made that does not imply reference to ends aimed at. The very concept of action is finalistic and is devoid of any sense and meaning if there is no referring to conscious aiming at chosen ends. There is no experience in the field of human action that can be had without resorting to the category of means and ends. If the observer is not familiar with the ideology, the technology, and the therapeutics of the men whose behavior he observes, he cannot make head or tail of it. He sees people running here and there and moving their hands, but he begins to understand what it is all about only when he begins to discover what they want to achieve.

If in employing the term "introspection" the positivist refers to such statements as those expressed in the last four words of the sentence "Paul runs to catch the train," then we must say that no sane human being could do without resorting to introspection in every thought.

Chapter 13. Meaning and Use of the Study of History

1. The Why of History

IN THE EYES of the positivist philosopher the study of mathematics and of the natural sciences is a preparation for action. Technology vindicates the labors of the experimenter. No such justification can be advanced in favor of the traditional methods resorted to by the historians. They should abandon their unscientific antiquarianism, says the positivist, and turn to the study of social physics or sociology. This discipline will abstract from historical experience laws which could render to social "engineering" the same services the laws of physics render to technological engineering.

In the opinion of the historicist philosopher the study of history provides man with signposts showing him the ways he has to walk along. Man can succeed only if his actions fit into the trend of evolution. To discover these trend lines is the main task of history.

The bankruptcy of both positivism and historicism raises anew the question about the meaning, the value, and the use of historical studies.

Some self-styled idealists think that reference to a thirst for knowledge, inborn in all men or at least in the higher types of men, answers these questions satisfactorily. Yet the problem is to draw a boundary line between the thirst for knowledge that impels the philologist to investigate the language of an African tribe and the curiosity that stimulates people to peer into the private lives of movie stars. Many historical events interest the average man because hearing or reading about them or seeing them enacted on the stage or screen gives him pleasant, if sometimes shuddering, sensations. The masses who greedily absorb newspaper reports about crimes and trials are not driven by Ranke's eagerness to know events as they really happened. The passions that agitate them are to be dealt with by psychoanalysis, not by epistemology.

The idealist philosopher's justification of history as knowledge for the mere sake of knowing fails to take into account the fact that there are certainly things which are not worth knowing. History's task is not to record all past things and events but only those that are historically meaningful. It is therefore necessary to find a criterion that makes it possible to sift what is historically meaningful from what is not. This cannot be done from the point of view of a doctrine which deems meritorious the mere fact of knowing something.

2. The Historical Situation

Acting man is faced with a definite situation. His action is a response to the challenge offered by this situation; it is his re-action. He appraises the effects the situation may have upon himself, i.e., he tries to establish what it means to him. Then he chooses and acts in order to attain the end chosen.

As far as the situation can be completely described

by the methods of the natural sciences, as a rule the natural sciences also provide an interpretation that enables the individual to make his decision. If a leak in the pipe line is diagnosed, the course of action to be resorted to is in most cases plain. Where a full description of a situation requires more than reference to the teachings of the applied natural sciences, recourse to history is inevitable.

People have often failed to realize this because they were deceived by the illusion that there is, between the past and the future, an extended space of time that can be called the present. As I have pointed out before,[1] the concept of such a present is not an astronomical or chronometrical notion but a praxeological one. It refers to the continuation of the conditions making a definite kind of action possible. It is therefore different for various fields of action. It is, moreover, never possible to know in advance how much of the future, of the time not yet past, will have to be included in what we call today the present. This can only be decided in retrospect. If a man says "At present the relations between Ruritania and Lapputania are peaceful," it is uncertain whether a later retrospective recording will include what today is called tomorrow in this period of present time. This question can only be answered the day after tomorrow.

There is no such thing as a nonhistorical analysis of the present state of affairs. The examination and description of the present are necessarily a historical account of the past ending with the instant just passed.

1. Mises, *Human Action*, p. 101. See also above, pp. 202 f.

The description of the present state of politics or of business is inevitably the narration of the events that have brought about the present state. If, in business or in government, a new man takes the helm, his first task is to find out what has been done up to the last minute. The statesman as well as the businessman learns about the present situation from studying the records of the past.

Historicism was right in stressing the fact that in order to know something in the field of human affairs one has to familiarize oneself with the way in which it developed. The historicists' fateful error consisted in the belief that this analysis of the past in itself conveys information about the course future action has to take. What the historical account provides is the description of the situation; the reaction depends on the meaning the actor gives it, on the ends he wants to attain, and on the means he chooses for their attainment. In 1860 there was slavery in many states of the Union. The most careful and faithful record of the history of this institution in general and in the United States in particular did not map out the future policies of the nation with regard to slavery. The situation in the manufacturing and marketing of motorcars that Ford found on the eve of his embarking upon mass production did not indicate what had to be done in this field of business. The historical analysis gives a diagnosis. The reaction is determined, so far as the choice of ends is concerned, by judgments of value and, so far as the choice of means is concerned, by the whole body of teachings placed at man's disposal by praxeology and technology.

Let those who want to reject the preceding statements undertake to describe any present situation— in philosophy, in politics, on a battlefield, on the stock exchange, in an individual business enterprise—without reference to the past.

3. *History of the Remote Past*

A skeptic may object: Granted that some historical studies are descriptions of the present state of affairs, but this is not true of all historical investigations. One may concede that the history of Nazism contributes to a better understanding of various phenomena in the present political and ideological situation. But what reference to our present worries have books on the Mithras cult, on ancient Chaldea, or on the early dynasties of the kings of Egypt? Such studies are merely antiquarian, a display of curiosity. They are useless, a waste of time, money, and manpower.

Criticisms such as these are self-contradictory. On the one hand they admit that the present state can only be described by a full account of the events that have brought it about. On the other hand, they declare beforehand that certain events cannot possibly have influenced the course of affairs that has led to the present state. Yet this negative statement can only be made after careful examination of all the material available, not in advance on the ground of some hasty conclusions.

The mere fact that an event happened in a distant country and a remote age does not in itself prove that it has no bearing on the present. Jewish affairs of three thousand years ago influence the lives of millions of present-day Christian Americans more than what happened to the American Indians as late as in the second part of the nineteenth century. In the present-day conflict of the Roman Church and the Soviets there are elements that trace back to the great schism of the Eastern and Western churches that originated more than a thousand years ago. This schism cannot be examined thoroughly without reference to the whole history of Christianity from its early beginnings; the study of Christianity presupposes analysis of Judaism and the various influences—Chaldean, Egyptian, and so on—that shaped it. There is no point in history at which we can stop our investigation fully satisfied that we have not overlooked any important factor. Whether civilization must be considered a coherent process or we should rather distinguish a multitude of civilizations does not affect our problem. For there were mutual exchanges of ideas between these autonomous civilizations, the extent and weight of which must be established by historical research.

A superficial observer might think that the historians are merely repeating what their predecessors have already said, at best occasionally retouching minor details of the picture. Actually the understanding of the past is in perpetual flux. A historian's achievement consists in presenting the past in a new perspective of understanding. The process of historical change is actuated by, or rather consists in, the ceaseless transformation of the ideas determining human action. Among these ideological changes those concerning the specific historical understanding of the past play a conspicuous role. What distinguishes a later from an earlier age is, among other ideological changes, also the change in the understanding of the preceding ages. Continuously examining and reshaping our historical understanding, the historians contribute their share to what is called the spirit of the age.[1]

4. Falsifying History

Because history is not a useless pastime but a study of the utmost practical importance, people have been eager to falsify historical evidence and to misrepresent the course of events. The endeavors to mislead posterity about what really happened and to substitute a fabrication for a faithful recording are often inaugurated by the men who themselves played an active role in the events, and begin with the instant of their happening,

1. Sometimes historical research succeeds in unmasking inveterate errors and substituting a correct account of events for an inadequate record even in fields that had up to then been considered fully and satisfactorily explored and described. An outstanding example is the startling discoveries concerning the history of the Roman emperors Maxentius, Licinius, and Constantinus and the events that ended the persecution of the Christians and paved the way for the victory of the Christian Church. (See Henri Grégoire, *Les Persécutions dans l'Empire Romain* in Mémoires de l'Académie Royale de Belgique, Tome 46, Fascicule 1, 1951, especially pp. 79–89, 153–6.) But fundamental changes in the historical understanding of events are more often brought about without any or only slight revision of the description of external events.

or sometimes even precede their occurrence. To lie about historical facts and to destroy evidence has been in the opinion of hosts of statesmen, diplomats, politicians, and writers a legitimate part of the conduct of public affairs and of writing history. One of the main problems of historical research is to unmask such falsehoods.

The falsifiers were often prompted by the desire to justify their own or their party's actions from the point of view of the moral code of those whose support or at least neutrality they were eager to win. Such whitewashing is rather paradoxical if the actions concerned appeared unobjectionable from the point of view of the moral ideas of the time when they occurred, and are condemned only by the moral standards of the fabricator's contemporaries.

No serious obstacles to the efforts of the historians are created by the machinations of the forgers and falsifiers. What is much more difficult for the historian is to avoid being misled by spurious social and economic doctrines.

The historian approaches the records equipped with the knowledge he has acquired in the fields of logic, praxeology, and the natural sciences. If this knowledge is defective, the result of his examination and analysis of the material will be vitiated. A good part of the last eighty years' contributions to economic and social history is almost useless on account of the writers' insufficient grasp of economics. The historicist thesis that the historian needs no acquaintance with economics and should even spurn it has vitiated the work of several generations of historians. Still more devastating was the effect of historicism upon those who called their publications describing various social and business conditions of the recent past economic research.

5. History and Humanism

Pragmatic philosophy appreciates knowledge because it gives power and makes people fit to accomplish things. From this point of view the positivists reject history as useless. We have tried to demonstrate the service that history renders to acting man in making him understand the situation in which he has to act. We have tried to provide a practical justification of history.

But there is more than this in the study of history. It not only provides knowledge indispensable to preparing political decisions. It opens the mind toward an understanding of human nature and destiny. It increases wisdom. It is the very essence of that much misinterpreted concept, a liberal education. It is the foremost approach to humanism, the lore of the specifically human concerns that distinguish man from other living beings.

The newborn child has inherited from his ancestors the physiological features of the species. He does not inherit the ideological characteristics of human existence, the desire for learning and knowing. What distinguishes civilized man from a barbarian must be acquired by every individual anew. Protracted strenuous exertion is needed to take possession of man's spiritual legacy.

Personal culture is more than mere familiarity with the present state of science, technology, and civic affairs. It is more than acquaintance with books and paintings and the experience of travel and of visits to museums. It is the assimilation of the ideas that roused mankind from the inert routine of a merely animal existence to a life of reasoning and speculating. It is the individual's effort to humanize himself by partaking in the tradition of all the best that earlier generations have bequeathed.

The positivist detractors of history contend that preoccupation with things past diverts people's attention from the main task of mankind, the improvement of future conditions. No blame could be more undeserved. History looks backward into the past, but the lesson it teaches concerns things to come. It does not teach indolent quietism; it rouses man to emulate the deeds of earlier generations. It addresses men as Dante's Ulysses addressed his companions:

> Considerate la vostra semenza:
> Fatti non foste a viver come bruti,
> Ma per seguir virtude e conoscenza.[1]

The dark ages were not dark because people were committed to study of the intellectual treasures left by ancient Hellenic civilization; they were dark so long as these treasures were hidden and dormant. Once they

---

1. *L'Inferno*, XXVI, 118–20. In the translation by Longfellow:

> Consider ye the seed from which ye sprang;
> Ye were not made to live like unto brutes,
> But for pursuit of virtue and of knowledge.

came to light again and began to stimulate the minds of the most advanced thinkers, they contributed substantially to the inauguration of what is called today Western civilization. The much criticized term "Renaissance" is pertinent in that it stresses the part the legacy of antiquity played in the evolution of all the spiritual features of the West. (The question whether the beginning of the Renaissance should not be dated some centuries farther back than Burckhardt set it need not concern us here.)

The scions of the barbarian conquerors who first began to study the ancients seriously were struck with awe. They realized that they and their contemporaries were faced with ideas they themselves could not have developed. They could not help thinking of the philosophy, the literature, and the arts of the classical age of Greece and Rome as unsurpassable. They saw no road to knowledge and wisdom but that paved by the ancients. To qualify a spiritual achievement as modern had for them a pejorative connotation. But slowly, from the seventeenth century on, people became aware that the West was coming of age and creating a culture of its own. They no longer bemoaned the disappearance of a golden age of the arts and of learning, irretrievably lost, and no longer thought of the ancient masterpieces as models to be imitated but never equaled, still less surpassed. They came to substitute the idea of progressive improvement for the previously held idea of progressive degeneration.

In this intellectual development that taught modern Europe to know its own worth and produced the self-reliance of modern Western civilization, the study of history was paramount. The course of human affairs was no longer viewed as a mere struggle of ambitious princes and army leaders for power, wealth, and glory. The historians discovered in the flux of events the operation of other forces than those commonly styled political and military. They began to regard the historical process as actuated by man's urge toward betterment. They disagreed widely in their judgments of value and in their appraisal of the various ends aimed at by governments and reformers. But they were nearly unanimous in holding that the main concern of every generation is to render conditions more satisfactory than their ancestors left them. They announced progress toward a better state of civic affairs as the main theme of human endeavor.

Faithfulness to tradition means to the historian observance of the fundamental rule of human action, namely, ceaseless striving to improve conditions. It does not mean preservation of unsuitable old institutions and clinging to doctrines long since discredited by more tenable theories. It does not imply any concession to the point of view of historicism.

6. *History and the Rise of Aggressive Nationalism*

The historian should utilize in his studies all the knowledge that the other disciplines place at his disposal. Inadequacy in this knowledge affects the results of his work.

If we were to consider the Homeric epics merely as

historical narratives, we would have to judge them unsatisfactory on account of the theology or mythology used to interpret and explain facts. Personal and political conflicts between princes and heroes, the spread of a plague, meteorological conditions, and other happenings were attributed to the interference of gods. Modern historians refrain from tracing back earthly events to supernatural causes. They avoid propositions that would manifestly contradict the teachings of the natural sciences. But they are often ignorant of economics and committed to untenable doctrines concerning the problems of economic policies. Many cling to neomercantilism, the social philosophy adopted almost without exception by contemporary political parties and governments and taught at all universities. They approve the fundamental thesis of mercantilism that the gain of one nation is the damage of other nations; that no nation can win but by the loss of others. They think an irreconcilable conflict of interests prevails among nations. From this point of view many or even most historians interpret all events. The violent clash of nations is in their eyes a necessary consequence of a nature-given and inevitable antagonism. This antagonism cannot be removed by any arrangement of international relations. The advocates of integral free trade, the Manchester or laissez-faire Liberals, are, they think, unrealistic and do not see that free trade hurts the vital interests of any nation resorting to it.

It is not surprising that the average historian shares the fallacies and misconceptions prevailing among his contemporaries. It was, however, not the historians but

the anti-economists who developed the modern ideology of international conflict and aggressive nationalism. The historians merely adopted and applied it. It
is not especially remarkable that in their writings they
took the side of their own nation and tried to justify
its claims and pretensions.

Books on history, especially those on the history of
one's own country, appeal more to the general reader
than do tracts on economic policy. The audience of the
historians is broader than that of the authors of books
on the balance of payments, foreign exchange control,
and similar matters. This explains why historians are
often considered the leading fomenters of the revival
of the warlike spirit and of the resulting wars of our
age. Actually they have merely popularized the teachings of pseudo economists.

7. *History and Judgments of Value*

The subject of history is action and the judgments of
value directing action toward definite ends. History
deals with values, but it itself does not value. It looks
upon events with the eyes of an unaffected observer.
This is, of course, the characteristic mark of objective
thought and of the scientific search for truth. Truth
refers to what is or was, not to a state of affairs that
is not or was not but that would suit the wishes of the
truth-seeker better.

There is no need to add anything to what has been
said in the first part of this essay about the futility of
the search for absolute and eternal values. History is

no better able than any other science to provide standards of value that would be more than personal judgments pronounced then and there by mortal men and rejected then and there by other mortal men.

There are authors who assert that it is logically impossible to deal with historical facts without expressing judgments of value. As they see it, one cannot say anything relevant about these things without making one value judgment after another. If, for example, one deals with such phenomena as pressure groups or prostitution, one has to realize that these phenomena themselves "are, as it were, constituted by value judgments." [1] Now, it is true that many people employ such terms as "pressure group" and almost every one the term "prostitution" in a way that implies a judgment of value. But this does not mean that the phenomena to which these terms refer are constituted by value judgments. Prostitution is defined by Geoffrey May as "the practice of habitual or intermittent sexual union, more or less promiscuous, for mercenary inducement." [2] A pressure group is a group aiming to attain legislation thought favorable to the interests of the group members. There is no valuation whatever implied in the mere use of such terms or in the reference to such phenomena. It is not true that history, if it has to avoid value judgments, would not be permitted to speak of cruelty. [3] The first meaning of the word "cruel" in the

1. Leo Strauss, *Natural Right and History* (Chicago, University of Chicago Press, 1953), p. 53.

2. G. May, "Prostitution," *Encyclopaedia of the Social Sciences,* 12, 553.

3. Strauss, p. 52.

Concise Oxford Dictionary is "indifferent to, delighting in, another's pain." [4] This definition is no less objective and free from any valuation than that given by the same dictionary for sadism: "sexual perversion marked by love of cruelty." [5] As a psychiatrist employs the term "sadism" to describe the condition of a patient, a historian may refer to "cruelty" in describing certain actions. A dispute that may arise as to what causes pain and what not, or as to whether in a concrete case pain was inflicted because it gave pleasure to the actor or for other reasons, is concerned with establishing facts, not making judgments of value.

The problem of history's neutrality as to judgments of value must not be confused with that of the attempts to falsify the historical account. There have been historians who were eager to represent battles lost by their own nation's armed forces as victories and who claimed for their own people, race, party, or faith everything they regarded as meritorious and exculpated them from everything they regarded as objectionable. The textbooks of history prepared for the public schools are marked by a rather naïve parochialism and chauvinism. There is no need to dwell on such futilities. But it must be admitted that even for the most conscientious historian abstention from judgments of value may offer certain difficulties.

As a man and as a citizen the historian takes sides in many feuds and controversies of his age. It is not

4. 3d ed., 1934, p. 273.
5. Ibid., p. 1042.

easy to combine scientific aloofness in historical studies with partisanship in mundane interests. But that can and has been achieved by outstanding historians. The historian's world view may color his work. His representation of events may be interlarded with remarks that betray his feelings and wishes and divulge his party affiliation. However, the postulate of scientific history's abstention from value judgments is not infringed by occasional remarks expressing the preferences of the historian if the general purport of the study is not affected. If the writer, speaking of an inept commander of the forces of his own nation or party, says "unfortunately" the general was not equal to his task, he has not failed in his duty as a historian. The historian is free to lament the destruction of the masterpieces of Greek art provided his regret does not influence his report of the events that brought about this destruction.

The problem of *Wertfreiheit* must also be clearly distinguished from that of the choice of theories resorted to for the interpretation of facts. In dealing with the data available, the historian needs all the knowledge provided by the other disciplines, by logic, mathematics, praxeology, and the natural sciences. If what these disciplines teach is insufficient or if the historian chooses an erroneous theory out of several conflicting theories held by the specialists, his effort is misled and his performance is abortive. It may be that he chose an untenable theory because he was biased and this theory best suited his party spirit. But the acceptance of a faulty doctrine may often be merely the outcome of ignorance or of the fact that it enjoys greater popularity than more correct doctrines.

The main source of dissent among historians is divergence in regard to the teachings of all the other branches of knowledge upon which they base their presentation. To a historian of earlier days who believed in witchcraft, magic, and the devil's interference with human affairs, things had a different aspect than they have for an agnostic historian. The neomercantilist doctrines of the balance of payments and of the dollar shortage give an image of present-day world conditions very different from that provided by an examination of the situation from the point of view of modern subjectivist economics.

Chapter 14. The Epistemological Features of History

1. Prediction in the Natural Sciences

THE NATURAL SCIENCES have two modes of predicting future events: the sweeping prediction and the statistical prediction. The former says: b follows a. The latter says: In $x\%$ of all cases b follows a; in $(100-x)\%$ of all cases non-b follows a.

Neither of these predictions can be called apodictic. Both are based upon experience. Experience is necessarily of past events. It can be resorted to for the prediction of future events only with the aid of the assumption that an invariable uniformity prevails in the concatenation and succession of natural phenomena. Referring to this aprioristic assumption, the natural sciences proceed to ampliative induction, inferring from regularity observed in the past to the same regularity in future events.

Ampliative induction is the epistemological basis of the natural sciences. The fact that the various machines and gadgets designed in accordance with the theorems of the natural sciences run and work in the expected way provides practical confirmation both of the theorems concerned and of the inductive method. However, this corroboration too refers only to the past. It does not preclude the possibility that one day factors up to now unknown to us may produce effects that will make a shambles of our knowledge and technological skill. The philosopher has to admit that there is no way mortal man can acquire *certain* knowledge about the future. But acting man has no reason to attach any importance to the logical and epistemological precariousness of the natural sciences. They provide the only mental tool that can be used in the ceaseless struggle for life. They have proved their practical worth. As no other way to knowledge is open to man, no alternative is left to him. If he wants to survive and to render his life more agreeable, he must accept the natural sciences as guides toward technological and therapeutical success. He must behave *as if* the predictions of the natural sciences were truth, perhaps not eternal, unshakable truth, but at least truth for that period of time for which human action can plan to provide.

The assurance with which the natural sciences announce their findings is not founded solely upon this *as if*. It is also derived from the intersubjectivity and objectivity of the experience that is the raw material of the natural sciences and the starting point of their reasoning. The apprehension of external objects is such that among all those in a position to become aware of them agreement about the nature of that apprehension can easily be reached. There is no disagreement about pointer readings that cannot be brought to a final decision. Scientists may disagree about theories. They never lastingly disagree about the establishment of what is called pure facts. There can be no dispute as to whether a definite piece of stuff is copper or iron or its weight is two pounds or five.

It would be preposterous to fail to recognize the significance of the epistemological discussions concerning induction, truth, and the mathematical calculus of probability. Yet these philosophical disquisitions do not further our endeavors to analyze the epistemological problems of the sciences of human action. What the epistemology of the sciences of human action has to remember about the natural sciences is that their theorems, although abstracted from experience, i.e., from what happened in the past, have been used successfully for designing future action.

2. History and Prediction

In their logical aspect the procedures applied in the most elaborate investigations in the field of natural events do not differ from the mundane logic of everybody's daily business. The logic of science is not different from the logic resorted to by any individual in the meditations that precede his actions or weigh their effects afterward. There is only one a priori and only one logic conceivable to the human mind. There is consequently only one body of natural science that can stand critical examination by the logical analysis of available experience.

As there is only one mode of logical thinking, there is only one praxeology (and, for that matter, only one mathematics) valid for all. As there is no human thinking that would fail to distinguish between A and non-A, so there is no human action that would not distinguish between means and ends. This distinction implies that man values, i.e., that he prefers an A to a B.

For the natural sciences the limit of knowledge is the establishment of an ultimate given, that is, of a fact that cannot be traced back to another fact of which it would appear as the necessary consequence. For the sciences of human action the ultimate given is the judgments of value of the actors and the ideas that engender these judgments of value.

It is precisely this fact that precludes employing the methods of the natural sciences to solve problems of human action. Observing nature, man discovers an inexorable regularity in the reaction of objects to stimuli. He classifies things according to the pattern of their reaction. A concrete thing, for example copper, is something that reacts in the same way in which other specimens of the same class react. As the patterns of this reaction are known, the engineer knows what future reaction on the part of copper he has to expect. This foreknowledge, notwithstanding the epistemological reservations referred to in the preceding section, is considered apodictic. All our science and philosophy, all our civilization would at once be called into question if, in but one instance and for but one moment, the patterns of these reactions varied.

What distinguishes the sciences of human action is the fact that there is no such foreknowledge of the individuals' value judgments, of the ends they will aim at under the impact of these value judgments, of the means they will resort to in order to attain the ends sought and of the effects of their actions insofar as these are not entirely determined by factors the knowledge of which is conveyed by the natural sciences. We know something about these things, but our knowledge of them and about them is *categorially* different from the kind of knowledge the experimental natural sciences provide about natural events. We could call it historical knowledge if this term were not liable to misinterpretation in suggesting that this knowledge serves only or predominantly to elucidate past events. Yet its most important use is to be seen in the service it renders to the anticipation of future conditions and to the designing of action that necessarily always aims at affecting future conditions.

Something happens in the field of the nation's domestic politics. How will Senator X, the outstanding man of the green party, react? Many informed men may have an opinion about the senator's expected reaction. Perhaps one of these opinions will prove to be correct. But it may also happen that none of them was right and that the senator reacts in a way not prognosticated by anybody. And then a similar dilemma arises in weighing the effects brought about by the way the senator has reacted. This second dilemma cannot be resolved as the first one was, as soon as the senator's action becomes known. For centuries to come historians may disagree about the effects produced by certain actions.

Traditional epistemology, exclusively preoccupied with the logical problems of the natural sciences and wholly ignorant even of the existence of the field of praxeology, tried to deal with these problems from the point of view of its narrow-minded, dogmatic orthodoxy. It condemned all the sciences that were not experimental natural sciences as backward and committed to an outdated philosophical and metaphysical, i.e., in their usage, stupid, method. It confused probability as the term is used in colloquial expressions referring to history and practical everyday action with the concept of probability as employed in the mathematical calculus of probability. Finally sociology made its appearance. It promised to substitute true science for the rubbish and empty gossiping of the historians in developing an aposteriori science of "social laws" to be derived from historical experience.

This disparagement of the methods of history moved first Dilthey, then Windelband, Rickert, Max Weber, Croce, and Collingwood to opposition. Their interpretations were in many regards unsatisfactory. They were deluded by many of the fundamental errors of historicism. All but Collingwood failed entirely to recognize the unique epistemological character of economics. They were vague in their references to psychology. The first four moreover were not free from the chauvinistic bias which in the age of pan-Germanism induced even the most eminent German thinkers to belittle the teachings of what they called Western philosophy. But the fact remains that they succeeded brilliantly in elucidating the epistemological features of the study of history. They destroyed forever the prestige of those epistemological doctrines that blamed history for being history and for not being "social physics." They exposed the futility of the search after aposteriori laws of historical change or historical becoming that would make possible the prediction of future history in the way the physicists predict the future behavior of copper. They made history self-conscious.

3. *The Specific Understanding of History*

Praxeology, the a priori science of human action, and, more specifically, its up to now best-developed part, economics, provides in its field a consummate interpretation of past events recorded and a consummate anticipation of the effects to be expected from future actions of a definite kind. Neither this interpretation nor this anticipation tells anything about the actual content and quality of the acting individuals' judgments of value. Both presuppose that the individuals are valuing and acting, but their theorems are independent of and unaffected by the particular characteristics of this valuing and acting. These characteristics are for the sciences of human action ultimate data, they are what is called historical individuality.

However, there is a momentous difference between the ultimate given in the natural sciences and that in the field of human action. An ultimate given of nature is—for the time being, that is, until someone succeeds in exposing it as the necessary consequence of some other ultimate given—a stopping point for human reflection. It is as it is, that is all that man can say about it.

But it is different with the ultimate given of human action, with the value judgments of individuals and the actions induced by them. They are ultimately given as they cannot be traced back to something of which they would appear to be the necessary consequence. If this were not the case, it would not be permissible to call them an ultimate given. But they are not, like the ultimate given in the natural sciences, a stopping point for human reflection. They are the starting point of a specific mode of reflection, of the specific understanding of the historical sciences of human action.

If the experimenter in the laboratory has established a fact which, at least for the time being, cannot be traced back to another fact of which it would appear as a derivative, there is nothing more to be said about the issue. But if we are faced with a value judgment and the resulting action, we may try to understand how they originated in the mind of the actor.

This specific understanding of human action as it is practiced by everybody in all his interhuman relations and actions is a mental procedure that must not be confused with any of the logical schemes resorted to by the natural sciences and by everybody in purely technological or therapeutical activities.

The specific understanding aims at the cognition of other people's actions. It asks in retrospect: What was he doing, what was he aiming at? What did he mean in choosing this definite end? What was the outcome of his action? Or it asks analogous questions for the future: What ends will he choose? What will he do in order to attain them? What will the outcome of his action be?

In actual life all these questions are seldom asked in isolation. They are mostly connected with other questions referring to praxeology or to the natural sciences. The categorial distinctions that epistemology is bound to make are tools of our mental operations. The real events are complex phenomena and can be grasped by the mind only if each of the various tools available is employed for its proper purpose.

The main epistemological problem of the specific understanding is: How can a man have any knowledge of the future value judgments and actions of other people? The traditional method of dealing with this problem, commonly called the problem of the alter ego or *Fremdverstehen,* is unsatisfactory. It focused attention upon grasping the meaning of other people's behavior in the "present" or, more correctly, in the past. But the task with which acting man, that is, everybody, is faced in all relations with his fellows does not refer to the past; it refers to the future. To know the future reactions of other people is the first task of acting man. Knowledge of their past value judgments and actions, although indispensable, is only a means to this end.

It is obvious that this knowledge which provides a man with the ability to anticipate to some degree other people's future attitudes is not a priori knowledge. The a priori discipline of human action, praxeology, does not deal with the actual content of value judgments; it deals only with the fact that men value and then act according to their valuations. What we know about the actual content of judgments of value can be derived only from experience. We have experience of other people's past value judgments and actions; and we have experience of our own value judgments and actions.

The latter is commonly called introspection. To distinguish it from experimental psychology, the term thymology was suggested in an earlier chapter [1] for that branch of knowledge which deals with human judgments of values and ideas.

Wilhelm Dilthey stressed the role that thymology—of course he said psychology—plays in the *Geisteswissenschaften,* the mental or moral sciences, the sciences dealing with human thoughts, ideas, and value judgments, and their operation in the external world.[2] It is not our task to trace back Dilthey's ideas to earlier authors. There is little doubt that he owed much to predecessors, especially to David Hume. But the examination of these influences must be left to treatises dealing with the history of philosophy. Dilthey's chief contribution was his pointing out in what respect the kind of psychology he was referring to was epistemologically and methodologically different from the natural sciences and therefore also from experimental psychology.

4. *Thymological Experience*

Thymological experience is what we know about human value judgments, the actions determined by them, and the responses these actions arouse in other people. As has been said, this experience stems either from introspection or from intercourse with other men, from our acting in various interhuman relations.

1. See p. 265.
2. See especially Dilthey, *Einleitung in die Geisteswissenschaften,* Leipzig, 1883. See also H. A. Hodges, *The Philosophy of Wilhelm Dilthey* (London, 1952), pp. 170 ff.

Like all experience, thymological experience too is necessarily knowledge of things that happened in the past. For reasons made sufficiently clear in the earlier sections of this essay, it is not permitted to assign to it the meaning the natural sciences assign to the results of experimentation. What we learn from thymological experience never has the significance of what is called in the natural sciences an experimentally established fact. It always remains a historical fact. Thymology is a historical discipline.

For lack of any better tool, we must take recourse to thymology if we want to anticipate other people's future attitudes and actions. Out of our general thymological experience, acquired either directly from observing our fellow men and transacting business with them or indirectly from reading and from hearsay, as well as out of our special experience acquired in previous contacts with the individuals or groups concerned, we try to form an opinion about their future conduct. It is easy to see in what the fundamental difference consists between this kind of anticipation and that of an engineer designing the plan for the construction of a bridge.

Thymology tells no more than that man is driven by various innate instincts, various passions, and various ideas. The anticipating individual tries to set aside those factors that manifestly do not play any role in the concrete case under consideration. Then he chooses among the remaining ones.

It is usual to qualify such prognoses as more or less probable and to contrast them with the forecasts of the natural sciences which once were called certain and are still considered certain and exact by people not familiar with the problems of logic and epistemology. Setting aside these latter problems, we must emphasize that the probability of the prognoses concerning future human action has little in common with that category of probability which is dealt with in the mathematical calculus of probability. The former is case probability and not class probability.[1] In order to prevent confusion, it is advisable to refer to case probability as likelihood.

In the specific understanding of future events there are as a rule two orders of likelihood to be ascertained. The first refers to the enumeration of the factors that could possibly take or have taken effect in producing the outcome in question. The second refers to the influence of each of these factors in the production of the outcome. It can easily be seen that the likelihood that the enumeration of the operating factors will be correct and complete is much higher than the likelihood that the proper extent of participation will be attributed to each. Yet the correctness or incorrectness of a prognosis depends on the correctness or incorrectness of this latter evaluation. The precariousness of forecasting is mainly due to the intricacy of this second problem. It is not only a rather puzzling question in forecasting future events. It is no less puzzling in retrospect for the historian.

It is not enough for the statesman, the politician, the general, or the entrepreneur to know all the factors that can possibly contribute to the determination of a future

1. See above, p. 91.

event. In order to anticipate correctly they must also anticipate correctly the quantity as it were of each factor's contribution and the instant at which its contribution will become effective. And later the historians will have to face the same difficulty in analyzing and understanding the case in retrospect.

5. Real Types and Ideal Types

The natural sciences classify the things of the external world according to their reaction to stimuli. Since copper is something that reacts in a definite way, the name copper is denied to a thing that reacts in a different way. In establishing the fact that a thing is copper, we make a forecast about its future behavior. What is copper cannot be iron or oxygen.

In acting—in their daily routine, as well as in technology and therapeutics, and also in history—people employ "real types," that is, class concepts distinguishing people or institutions according to neatly definable traits. Such classification can be based on concepts of praxeology and economics, of jurisprudence, of technology, and of the natural sciences. It may refer to Italians, for example, either as the inhabitants of a definite area, or as people endowed with a special legal characteristic, viz., Italian nationality, or as a definite linguistic group. This kind of classification is independent of specific understanding. It points toward something that is common to all members of the class. All Italians in the geographic sense of the term are affected by geological or meteorological events that touch their country. All Italian citizens are concerned by legal acts relating to people of their nationality. All Italians in the linguistic sense of the term are in a position to make themselves understood to one another. Nothing more than this is meant when a man is called an Italian in one of these three connotations.

The characteristic mark of an "ideal type," on the other hand, is that it implies some proposition concerning valuing and acting. If an ideal type refers to people, it implies that in some respect these men are valuing and acting in a uniform or similar way. When it refers to institutions, it implies that these institutions are products of uniform or similar ways of valuing and acting or that they influence valuing and acting in a uniform or similar way.

Ideal types are constructed and employed on the basis of a definite mode of understanding the course of events, whether in order to forecast the future or to analyze the past. If in dealing with American elections one refers to the Italian vote, the implication is that there are voters of Italian descent whose voting is to some extent influenced by their Italian origin. That such a group of voters exists will hardly be denied; but people disagree widely as to the number of citizens included in this group and the degree to which their voting is determined by their Italian ideologies. It is this uncertainty about the power of the ideology concerned, this impossibility of finding out and measuring its effect upon the minds of the individual members of the group, that characterizes the ideal type as such and distinguishes it from real types. An ideal type is a conceptual tool of understanding and the service that it renders depends entirely on the serviceableness of the definite mode of understanding.

Ideal types must not be confused with the types referred to in moral or political "oughts," which we may call "ought types." The Marxians contend that all proletarians necessarily behave in a definite way, and the Nazis make the analogous statement with regard to all Germans. But neither of these parties can deny that its declaration is untenable as a proposition about what is, since there are proletarians and Germans who deviate from the modes of acting which these parties call proletarian and German respectively. What they really have in mind in announcing their dicta is a moral obligation. What they mean is: Every proletarian ought to act the way the party program and its legitimate expositors declare to be proletarian; every German ought to act the way the nationalist party considers genuinely German. Those proletarians or Germans whose conduct does not comply with the rules are smeared as traitors. The ought type belongs to the terminology of ethics and politics and not to that of the epistemology of the sciences of human action.

It is furthermore necessary to separate ideal types from organizations having the same name. In dealing with nineteenth-century French history we frequently encounter references to the Jesuits and to the Free Masons. These terms may refer to acts of the organizations designated by these names, e.g., "The Jesuit order opened a new school" or "The lodges of the Free Masons donated a sum of money for the relief of people who suffered in a fire." Or they may refer to ideal types, pointing out that members of these organizations and their friends are in definite respects acting under the sway of a definite Jesuit or Masonic ideology. There is a difference between stating that a political movement is organized, guided, and financed by the order or the lodges as such and saying that it is inspired by an ideology of which the order or the lodges are considered the typical or outstanding representatives. The first proposition has no reference to the specific understanding. It concerns facts that could be confirmed or disproved by the study of records and the hearing of witnesses. The second assertion regards understanding. In order to form a judgment on its adequacy or inadequacy one has to analyze ideas and doctrines and their bearing upon actions and events. Methodologically there is a fundamental difference between the analysis of the impact of the ideology of Marxian socialism upon the mentality and the conduct of our contemporaries and the study of the actions of the various communist and socialist governments, parties, and conspiracies.[1]

1. There is a distinction between the Communist party or a Communist party as an organized body on the one hand and the communist (Marxian) ideology on the other. In dealing with contemporary history and politics people often fail to realize the fact that many people who are not members—"card-bearing" or dues-paying members —of a party organization may be, either totally or in certain regards, under the sway of the party ideology. Especially in weighing the strength of the ideas of communism or of those of Nazism in Germany or of Fascism in Italy serious confusion resulted from this error. Furthermore it is necessary to know that an ideology may sometimes also influence the minds of those who believe that they are entirely untouched by it or who even consider themselves its deadly foes and are fighting it passionately. The success of Nazism in Germany in 1933

The service a definite ideal type renders to the acting man in his endeavors to anticipate future events and to the historian in his analysis of the past is dependent on the specific understanding that led to its construction. To question the usefulness of an ideal type for explaining a definite problem, one must criticize the mode of understanding involved.

In dealing with conditions in Latin America the ideal type "general" may be of some use. There have been definite ideologies current which in some respects determined the role played by many—not by all—army leaders who became important in politics. In France too ideas prevailed that by and large circumscribed the position of generals in politics and the role of such men as Cavaignac, MacMahon, Boulanger, Pétain, and de Gaulle. But in the United States it would make no sense to employ the ideal type of a political general or a general in politics. No American ideology exists that would consider the armed forces as a separate entity distinguished from and opposed to the "civilian" population. There is consequently no political *esprit de corps* in the army and its leaders have no authoritarian prestige among "civilians." A general who becomes president ceases not only legally but also politically to be a member of the army.

---

was due to the fact that the immense majority of the Germans, even of those voting the ticket of the Marxist parties, of the Catholic Centrum party, and of the various "bourgeois" splinter parties, were committed to the ideas of radical aggressive nationalism, while the Nazis themselves had adopted the basic principles of the socialist program. Great Britain would not have gone socialist if the Conservatives, not to speak of the "Liberals," had not virtually endorsed socialist ideas.

In referring to ideal types the historian of the past as well as the historian of the future, i.e., acting man, must never forget that there is a fundamental difference between the reactions of the objects of the natural sciences and those of men. It is this difference that people have wanted to bring into relief in speaking of the opposition of mind and matter, of freedom of the will, and of individuality. Ideal types are expedients to simplify the treatment of the puzzling multiplicity and variety of human affairs. In employing them one must always be aware of the deficiencies of any kind of simplification. The exuberance and variability of human life and action cannot be fully seized by concepts and definitions. Some unanswered or even unanswerable questions always remain, some problems whose solution passes the ability even of the greatest minds.

PART FOUR. THE COURSE OF HISTORY

Chapter 15. Philosophical Interpretations of History

1. Philosophies of History and Philosophical Interpretations of History

THE ATTEMPTS to provide a philosophical interpretation of history must not be confused with any of the various schemes of philosophy of history. They do not aim at the discovery of the end toward which the process of human history is tending. They try to bring into relief factors that play a momentous part in determining the course of historical events. They deal with the ends individuals and groups of individuals are aiming at, but they abstain from any opinion about the end and the meaning of the historical process as a whole or about a preordained destiny of mankind. They rely not upon intuition but upon a study of history. They try to demonstrate the correctness of their interpretation by referring to historical facts. In this sense they can be called discursive and scientific.

It is useless to enter into a discussion about the merits and demerits of a definite brand of philosophy of history. A philosophy of history has to be accepted as a whole or rejected as a whole. No logical arguments and no reference to facts can be advanced either for or against a philosophy of history. There is no question of reasoning about it; what matters is solely belief or disbelief. It is possible that in a few years the entire earth will be subject to socialism. If this occurs, it will by no means confirm the Marxian variety of philosophy of history. Socialism will not be the outcome of a law operating "independently of the will of men" with "the inexorability of a law of nature." It will be precisely the outcome of the ideas that got into the heads of men, of the conviction shared by the majority that socialism will be more beneficial to them than capitalism.

A philosophical interpretation of history can be misused for political propaganda. However, it is easy to separate the scientific core of the doctrine from its political adaptation and modification.

2. Environmentalism

Environmentalism is the doctrine that explains historical changes as produced by the environment in which people are living. There are two varieties of this doctrine: the doctrine of physical or geographical environmentalism and the doctrine of social or cultural environmentalism.

The former doctrine asserts that the essential features of a people's civilization are brought about by geographical factors. The physical, geological, and climatic conditions and the flora and fauna of a region determine the thoughts and the actions of its inhabitants. In the most radical formulation of their thesis, anthropogeographical authors are eager to trace back all differences between races, nations, and civilizations to the operation of man's natural environment.

The inherent misconception of this interpretation is

that it looks upon geography as an active and upon human action as a passive factor. However, the geographical environment is only one of the components of the situation in which man is placed by his birth, that makes him feel uneasy and causes him to employ his reason and his bodily forces to get rid of this uneasiness as best he may. Geography (nature) provides on the one hand a provocation to act and on the other hand both means that can be utilized in acting and insurmountable limits imposed upon the human striving for betterment. It provides a stimulus but not the response. Geography sets a task, but man has to solve it. Man lives in a definite geographical environment and is forced to adjust his action to the conditions of this environment. But the way in which he adjusts himself, the methods of his social, technological, and moral adaptation, are not determined by the external physical factors. The North American continent produced neither the civilization of the Indian aborigines nor that of the Americans of European extraction.

Human action is conscious reaction to the stimulus offered by the conditions under which man lives. As some of the components of the situation in which he lives and is called upon to act vary in different parts of the globe, there are also geographical differences in civilization. The wooden shoes of the Dutch fishermen would not be useful to the mountaineers of Switzerland. Fur coats are practical in Canada but less so in Tahiti.

The doctrine of social and cultural environmentalism merely stresses the fact that there is—necessarily—continuity in human civilization. The rising generation does not create a new civilization from the grass roots. It enters into the social and cultural milieu that the preceding generations have created. The individual is born at a definite date in history into a definite situation determined by geography, history, social institutions, mores, and ideologies. He has daily to face the alteration in the structure of this traditional surrounding effected by the actions of his contemporaries. He does not simply live in the world. He lives in a circumscribed spot. He is both furthered and hampered in his acting by all that is peculiar to this spot. But he is not determined by it.

The truth contained in environmentalism is the cognition that every individual lives at a definite epoch in a definite geographical space and acts under the conditions determined by this environment. The environment determines the situation but not the response. To the same situation different modes of reacting are thinkable and feasible. Which one the actors choose depends on their individuality.

3. *The Egalitarians' Interpretation of History*

Most biologists maintain that there is but one species of man. The fact that all people can interbreed and produce fertile offspring is taken as evidence of the zoological unity of mankind. Yet within the species Homo sapiens there are numerous variations which make it imperative to distinguish subspecies or races.

There are considerable bodily differences between

the members of various races; there are also remarkable although less momentous differences between members of the same race, subrace, tribe, or family, even between brothers and sisters, even between nonidentical twins. Every individual is already at birth different bodily from all other specimens, is characterized by individual traits of his own. But no matter how great these differences may be, they do not affect the logical structure of the human mind. There is not the slightest evidence for the thesis developed by various schools of thought that the logic and thinking of different races are categorially different.

The scientific treatment of the inborn differences between individuals and of their biological and physiological inheritance has been grossly muddled and twisted by political prepossessions. Behavioristic psychology maintains that all differences in mental traits among men are caused by environmental factors. It denies all influence of bodily build upon mental activities. It holds that equalizing the outer conditions of human life and education could wipe out all cultural differences between individuals, whatever their racial or family affiliation might be. Observation contradicts these assertions. It shows that there is a degree of correlation between bodily structure and mental traits. An individual inherits from his parents and indirectly from his parents' ancestors not only the specific biological characteristics of his body but also a constitution of mental powers that circumscribes the potentialities of his mental achievements and his personality. Some peo-

ple are endowed with an innate ability for definite kinds
of activities while others lack this gift entirely or possess
it only to a lesser degree.

The behavioristic doctrine was used to support the
program of socialism of the egalitarian variety. Egalitarian socialism attacks the classical liberal principle of
equality before the law. In its opinion the inequalities
of income and wealth existing in the market economy
are in their origin and their social significance not different from those existing in a status society. They are
the outcome of usurpations and expropriations and the
resulting exploitation of the masses brought about by
arbitrary violence. The beneficiaries of this violence
form a dominating class as the instrument of which the
state forcibly holds down the exploited. What distinguishes the "capitalist" from the "common man" is the
fact that he has joined the gang of the unscrupulous exploiters. The only quality required in an entrepreneur
is villainy. His business, says Lenin, is accounting and
the control of production and distribution, and these
things have been "simplified by capitalism to the utmost till they have become the extraordinarily simple
operations of watching, recording and issuing receipts,
within the reach of anybody who can read and write
and knows the first four rules of arithmetic." [1] Thus the
"property privileges" of the "capitalists" are no less
superfluous and therefore parasitic than the status privileges of the aristocratic landowners were on the eve of
the Industrial Revolution. In establishing a spurious

1. Lenin, *State and Revolution* (New York, International Publishers,
1932), pp. 83 f.

equality before the law and preserving the most iniquitous of all privileges, private property, the bourgeoisie has duped the unsuspecting people and robbed them of the fruits of the revolution.

This doctrine, already dimly present in the writings of some earlier authors and popularized by Jean Jacques Rousseau and by Babeuf, was transformed in the Marxian class-struggle doctrine into an interpretation of the whole process of human history from the point of view of usurpation. In the context of the Marxian philosophy of history the emergence of status and class distinctions was a necessary and historically inevitable result of the evolution of the material productive forces. The members of the dominating castes and classes were not individually responsible for the acts of oppression and exploitation. They were not morally inferior to those they held in subservience. They were simply the men inscrutable destiny singled out to perform a socially, economically, and historically necessary task. As the state of the material productive forces determined each individual's role in the consummation of the historical process, it was their part to carry out all they accomplished.

But quite a different description of the march of human affairs is provided by those writings in which Marx and Engels deal with historical problems or with political issues of their own time. There they unreservedly espouse the popular doctrine of the inherent moral corruption of the "exploiters." Human history appears as a process of progressive moral corruption that started when the blissful conditions of primeval village communities were disrupted by the greed of selfish individuals. Private ownership of land is the original sin which step by step brought about all the disasters that have plagued mankind. What elevates an "exploiter" above the level of his fellow men is merely villainy. In the three volumes of *Das Kapital* unscrupulousness is the only quality alluded to as required in an "exploiter." The improvement of technology and the accumulation of wealth that Marx considered prerequisite for the realization of socialism are described as a result of the spontaneous evolution of the mythical material productive forces. The "capitalists" do not get any credit for these achievements. All that these villains do is to expropriate those who should by rights have the fruits of the operation of the material productive forces. They appropriate to themselves "surplus value." They are merely parasites, and mankind can do without them.

This interpretation of history from the egalitarian point of view is the official philosophy of our age. It assumes that an automatic process of historical evolution tends to improve technological methods of production, to accumulate wealth, and to provide the means for improving the standard of living of the masses. Looking back upon conditions in the capitalistic West as they developed in the last century or two, statisticians see a trend of rising productivity and blithely surmise that this trend will continue, whatever society's economic organization may be. As they see it, a trend of historical evolution is something above the level of the actions of men, a "scientifically" established fact which cannot be affected by men and by the social system. Hence no harm can result from institutions— such as the contemporary tax legislation—which aim at ultimately wiping out the inequalities of income and wealth.

The egalitarian doctrine is manifestly contrary to all the facts established by biology and by history. Only fanatical partisans of this theory can contend that what distinguishes the genius from the dullard is entirely the effect of postnatal influences. The presumption that civilization, progress, and improvement emanate from the operation of some mythical factor—in the Marxian philosophy, the material productive forces—shaping the minds of men in such a way that certain ideas are successively produced contemporaneously in them, is an absurd fable.

There has been a lot of empty talk about the non-existence of differences among men. But there has never been an attempt to organize society according to the egalitarian principle. The author of an egalitarian tract and the leader of an egalitarian party by their very activity contradict the principle to which they pay lip service. The historical role played by the egalitarian creed was to disguise the most abject forms of despotic oppression. In Soviet Russia egalitarianism is proclaimed as one of the main dogmas of the official creed. But Lenin was deified after his death, and Stalin was worshiped in life as no ruler has been since the days of the declining Roman Empire.

The egalitarian fables do not explain the course of

past history, they are out of place in an analysis of economic problems, and useless in planning future political action.

4. *The Racial Interpretation of History*

It is a historical fact that the civilizations developed by various races are different. In earlier ages it was possible to establish this truth without attempting to distinguish between higher and lower civilizations. Each race, one could contend, develops a culture that conforms to its wishes, wants, and ideals. The character of a race finds its adequate expression in its achievements. A race may imitate accomplishments and institutions developed by other races, but it does not long to abandon its own cultural pattern entirely and to substitute an imported alien system for it. If about two thousand years ago the Greco-Romans and the Chinese had learned about each other's civilizations, neither race would have admitted the superiority of the other's civilization.

But it is different in our age. The non-Caucasians may hate and despise the white man, they may plot his destruction and take pleasure in extravagant praise of their own civilizations. But they yearn for the tangible achievements of the West, for its science, technology, therapeutics, its methods of administration and of industrial management. Many of their spokesmen declare that they want only to imitate the material culture of the West, and to do even that only so far as it does not conflict with their indigenous ideologies or jeopardize their religious beliefs and observances. They fail to see that the adoption of what they disparagingly call the merely material achievements of the West is incompatible with preserving their traditional rites and taboos and their customary style of life. They indulge in the illusion that their peoples could borrow the technology of the West and attain a higher material standard of living without having first in a *Kulturkampf* divested themselves of the world view and the mores handed down from their ancestors. They are confirmed in this error by the socialist doctrine, which also fails to recognize that the material and technological achievements of the West were brought about by the philosophies of rationalism, individualism, and utilitarianism and are bound to disappear if the collectivist and totalitarian tenets substitute socialism for capitalism.

Whatever people may say about Western civilization, the fact remains that all peoples look with envy upon its achievements, want to reproduce them, and thereby implicitly admit its superiority. It is this state of affairs that has generated the modern doctrine of race differences and its political offshoot, racism.

The doctrine of race differences maintains that some races have succeeded better than others in the pursuit of those aims that are common to all men. All men want to resist the operation of the factors detrimental to the preservation of their lives, their health, and their well-being. It cannot be denied that modern Western capitalism has succeeded best in these endeavors. It has increased the average length of life and raised the average standard of living unprecedentedly. It has made

accessible to the common man those higher human accomplishments—philosophy, science, art—which in the
past were everywhere, and today outside the countries
of Western capitalism still are, accessible only to a small
minority. Grumblers may blame Western civilization
for its materialism and may assert that it gratified nobody but a small class of rugged exploiters. But their
laments cannot wipe out the facts. Millions of mothers
have been made happier by the drop in infant mortality.
Famines have disappeared and epidemics have been
curbed. The average man lives in more satisfactory conditions than his ancestors or his fellows in the noncapi-
talistic countries. And one must not dismiss as merely
materialistic a civilization which makes it possible for
practically everybody to enjoy a Beethoven symphony
performed by an orchestra conducted by an eminent
master.

The thesis that some races have been more successful
than others in their efforts to develop a civilization is
unassailable as a statement about historical experience.
As a résumé of what has happened in the past it is quite
correct to assert that modern civilization is the white
man's achievement. However, the establishment of this
fact justifies neither the white man's racial self-conceit
nor the political doctrines of racism.

Many people take pride in the fact that their ancestors or their relatives have performed great things. It
gives some men a special satisfaction to know that they
belong to a family, clan, nation, or race that has distinguished itself in the past. But this innocuous vanity
easily turns into scorn of those who do not belong to

the same distinguished group and into attempts to humiliate and to insult them. The diplomats, soldiers, bureaucrats, and businessmen of the Western nations who in their contacts with the colored races have displayed overbearing effrontery had no claim at all to boast of the deeds of Western civilization. They were not the makers of this culture which they compromised by their behavior. Their insolence which found its expression in such signs as "Entrance forbidden to dogs and natives" has poisoned the relations between the races for ages to come. But we do not have to deal with these sad facts in an analysis of racial doctrines.

Historical experience warrants the statement that in the past the efforts of some subdivisions of the Caucasian race to develop a civilization have eclipsed those of the members of other races. It does not warrant any statement about the future. It does not permit us to assume that this superiority of the white stock will persist in the future. Nothing can be predicted from historical experience with a likelihood that can be compared with the probability of predictions made in the natural sciences on the basis of facts established by laboratory experiments. In 1760 a historian would have been right in declaring that Western civilization was mainly an achievement of the Latins and the British and that the Germans had contributed little to it. It was permissible at that time to maintain that German science, art, literature, philosophy, and technology were insignificant compared to the accomplishments of the members of some other nations. One could fairly contend that those Germans who had distinguished themselves in these

fields—foremost among them the astronomers Copernicus [1] and Kepler and the philosopher Leibniz—could
succeed only because they had fully absorbed what
non-Germans had contributed, that intellectually they
did not belong to Germany, that for a long time they
had no German followers, and that those who first appreciated their doctrines were predominantly non-German.
But if somebody had inferred from these facts that the
Germans are culturally inferior and would rank in the
future far below the French and the British, his conclusion would have been disproved by the course of later
history.

A prediction about the future behavior of those races
which today are considered culturally backward could
only be made by biological science. If biology were to
discover some anatomical characteristics of the members of the non-Caucasian races which necessarily curb
their mental faculties, one could venture such a prediction. But so far biology has not discovered any such
characteristics.

It is not the task of this essay to deal with the biological issues of the racial doctrine. It must therefore
abstain from analysis of the controversial problems of
racial purity and miscegenation. Nor is it our task to
investigate the merits of the political program of racism.
This is for praxeology and economics.

All that can be said about racial issues on the ground
of historical experience boils down to two statements.
First, the prevailing differences between the various

1. We need not go into the question whether Copernicus was a
German or a Pole. See Mises, *Omnipotent Government*, p. 15.

biological strains of men are reflected in the civiliza-
tory achievements of the group members. Second, in
our age the main achievements in civilization of some
subdivisions of the white Caucasian race are viewed by
the immense majority of the members of all other races
as more desirable than characteristic features of the
civilization produced by the members of their respective own races.

5. *The Secularism of Western Civilization*

An almost universally accepted interpretation of
modern civilization distinguishes between the spiritual
and material aspects. The distinction is suspect, as it
originated not from a dispassionate observation of facts
but from resentment. Every race, nation, or linguistic
group boasts of its members' achievements in spiritual
matters even while admitting its backwardness in material matters. It is assumed that there is little connection between the two aspects of civilization, that the
spiritual is more sublime, deserving, and praiseworthy
than the "merely" material, and that preoccupation
with material improvement prevents a people from be-
stowing sufficient attention on spiritual matters.

Such were in the nineteenth century the ideas of the
leaders of the Eastern peoples who were eager to reproduce in their own countries the achievements of the
West. The study of Western civilization made them
subconsciously despise the institutions and ideologies of
their native countries and left them feeling inferior.
They re-established their mental equilibrium by means

of the doctrine that depreciated Western civilization as merely materialistic. The Rumanians or Turks who longed for railroads and factories to be built by Western capital consoled themselves by exalting the spiritual culture of their own nations. The Hindus and the Chinese were of course on firmer ground when referring to the literature and art of their ancestors. But it seems not to have occurred to them that many hundreds of years separated them from the generations that had excelled in philosophy and poetry, and that in the age of these famous ancestors their nations were, if not ahead of, certainly not second in material civilization to any of their contemporaries.

In recent decades the doctrine that belittles modern Western civilization as merely materialistic has been almost universally endorsed by the nations which brought about this civilization. It comforts Europeans when they compare the economic prosperity of the United States with present-day conditions in their own countries. It serves the American socialists as a leading argument in their endeavor to depict American capitalism as a curse of mankind. Reluctantly forced to admit that capitalism pours a horn of plenty upon people and that the Marxian prediction of the masses' progressive impoverishment has been spectacularly disproved by the facts, they try to salvage their detraction of capitalism by describing contemporary civilization as merely materialistic and sham.

Bitter attacks upon modern civilization are launched by writers who think that they are pleading the cause of religion. They reprimand our age for its secularism.

They bemoan the passing of a way of life in which, they would have us believe, people were not preoccupied with the pursuit of earthly ambitions but were first of all concerned about the strict observance of their religious duties. They ascribe all evils to the spread of skepticism and agnosticism and passionately advocate a return to the orthodoxy of ages gone by.

It is hard to find a doctrine which distorts history more radically than this antisecularism. There have always been devout men, pure in heart and dedicated to a pious life. But the religiousness of these sincere believers had nothing in common with the established system of devotion. It is a myth that the political and social institutions of the ages preceding modern individualistic philosophy and modern capitalism were imbued with a genuine Christian spirit. The teachings of the Gospels did not determine the official attitude of the governments toward religion. It was, on the contrary, this-worldly concerns of the secular rulers—absolute kings and aristocratic oligarchies, but occasionally also revolting peasants and urban mobs—that transformed religion into an instrument of profane political ambitions.

Nothing could be less compatible with true religion than the ruthless persecution of dissenters and the horrors of religious crusades and wars. No historian ever denied that very little of the spirit of Christ was to be found in the churches of the sixteenth century which were criticized by the theologians of the Reformation and in those of the eighteenth century which the philosophers of the Enlightenment attacked.

The ideology of individualism and utilitarianism which inaugurated modern capitalism brought freedom also to the religious longings of man. It shattered the pretension of those in power to impose their own creed upon their subjects. Religion is no longer the observance of articles enforced by constables and executioners. It is what a man, guided by his conscience, spontaneously espouses as his own faith. Modern Western civilization is this-worldly. But it was precisely its secularism, its religious indifference, that gave rein to the renascence of genuine religious feeling. Those who worship today in a free country are not driven by the secular arm but by their conscience. In complying with the precepts of their persuasion, they are not intent upon avoiding punishment on the part of the earthly authorities but upon salvation and peace of mind.

6. *The Rejection of Capitalism by Antisecularism*

The hostility displayed by the champions of antisecularism to modern ways of life manifests itself in the condemnation of capitalism as an unjust system.

In the opinion of the socialists as well as of the interventionists the market economy impedes the full utilization of the achievements of technology and thus checks the evolution of production and restricts the quantity of goods produced and available for consumption. In earlier days these critics of capitalism did not deny that an equal distribution of the social product among all would hardly bring about a noticeable improvement in the material conditions of the immense majority of

people. In their plans equal distribution played a subordinate role. Prosperity and abundance for all which
they promised was, as they thought, to be expected
from the freeing of the productive forces from the fetters allegedly imposed upon them by the selfishness of
the capitalists. The purpose of the reforms they suggested was to replace capitalism by a more efficient
system of production and thereby to inaugurate an age
of riches for all.

Now that economic analysis has exposed the illusions
and fallacies in the socialists' and interventionists' condemnation of capitalism, they try to salvage their programs by resorting to another method. The Marxians
have developed the doctrine of the inevitability of socialism, and the interventionists, following in their wake,
speak of the irreversibility of the trend toward more
and more government interference with economic affairs. It is obvious that these makeshifts are designed
merely to cover their intellectual defeat and to divert
the public's attention from the disastrous consequences
of the socialist and interventionist policies.

Similar motives prompt those who advocate socialism
and interventionism for moral and religious reasons.
They consider it supererogatory to examine the economic problems involved, and they try to shift the
discussion of the pros and cons of the market economy
from the field of economic analysis to what they call
a higher sphere. They reject capitalism as an unfair
system and advocate either socialism or interventionism
as being in accord with their moral or religious principles. It is vile, they say, to look upon human affairs

from the point of view of productivity, profits and a materialistic concern about wealth and a plentiful supply of material goods. Man ought to strive after justice, not wealth.

This mode of argumentation would be consistent if it were openly to ascribe inherent moral value to poverty and to condemn altogether any effort to raise the standard of living above the level of mere subsistence. Science could not object to such a judgment of value, since judgments of value are ultimate choices on the part of the individual who utters them.

However, those rejecting capitalism from a moral and religious point of view do not prefer penury to well-being. On the contrary, they tell their flock they want to improve man's material well-being. They see it as capitalism's chief weakness that it does not provide the masses with that degree of well-being which, as they believe, socialism or interventionism could provide. Their condemnation of capitalism and their recommendation of social reforms imply the thesis that socialism or interventionism will raise, not lower, the standard of living of the common man. Thus these critics of capitalism endorse altogether the teachings of the socialists and interventionists without bothering to scrutinize what the economists have brought forward to discredit them. The only fault they find with the tenets of the Marxian socialists and the secular parties of interventionism is their commitment to atheism or secularism.

It is obvious that the question whether material well-being is best served by capitalism, socialism, or interventionism can be decided only by careful analysis of the operation of each of these systems. This is what economics is accomplishing. There is no point in dealing with these issues without taking full account of all that economics has to say about them.

It is justifiable if ethics and religion tell people that they ought to make better use of the well-being that capitalism brings them; if they try to induce the faithful to substitute better ways of spending for the objectionable habits of feasting, drinking, and gambling; if they condemn lying and cheating and praise the moral values implied in purity of family relations and in charity to those in need. But it is irresponsible to condemn one social system and to recommend its replacement by another system without having fully investigated the economic consequences of each.

There is nothing in any ethical doctrine or in the teachings of any of the creeds based on the Ten Commandments that could justify the condemnation of an economic system which has multiplied the population and provides the masses in the capitalistic countries with the highest standard of living ever attained in history. From the religious point of view, too, the drop in infant mortality, the prolongation of the average length of life, the successful fight against plagues and disease, the disappearance of famines, illiteracy, and superstition tell in favor of capitalism. The churches are right to lament the destitution of the masses in the economically backward countries. But they are badly mistaken when they assume that anything can wipe out the poverty of these wretched people but unconditional adoption of the system of profit-seeking big business, that is, mass production for the satisfaction of the needs of the many.

A conscientious moralist or churchman would not consider meddling in controversies concerning technological or therapeutical methods without having sufficiently familiarized himself with all the physical, chemical and physiological problems involved. Yet many of them think that ignorance of economics is no bar to handling economic issues. They even take pride in their ignorance. They hold that problems of the economic organization of society are to be considered exclusively from the point of view of a preconceived idea of justice and without taking account of what they call the shabby materialistic concern for a comfortable life. They recommend some policies, reject others, and do not bother about the effects that must result from the adoption of their suggestions.

This neglect of the effects of policies, whether rejected or recommended, is absurd. For the moralists and the Christian proponents of anticapitalism do not concern themselves with the economic organization of society from sheer caprice. They seek reform of existing conditions because they want to bring about definite effects. What they call the injustice of capitalism is the alleged fact that it causes widespread poverty and destitution. They advocate reforms which, as they expect, will wipe out poverty and destitution. They are therefore, from the point of view of their own valuations and the ends they themselves are eager to attain, inconsistent in referring merely to something which they call the higher standard of justice and morality and ignoring the economic analysis of both capitalism and the anticapitalistic policies. Their terming capitalism unjust and anticapitalistic measures just is quite arbitrary since it has no relation to the effect of each of these sets of economic policies.

The truth is that those fighting capitalism as a system contrary to the principles of morals and religion have uncritically and lightheartedly adopted all the economic teachings of the socialists and communists. Like the Maxians, they ascribe all ills—economic crises, unemployment, poverty, crime, and many other evils —to the operation of capitalism, and everything that is satisfactory—the higher standard of living in the capitalistic countries, the progress of technology, the drop in mortality rates, and so on—to the operation of government and of the labor unions. They have unwittingly espoused all the tenets of Marxism minus its —merely incidental—atheism. This surrender of philosophical ethics and of religion to the anticapitalistic teachings is the greatest triumph of socialist and interventionist propaganda. It is bound to degrade philosophical ethics and religion to mere auxiliaries of the forces seeking the destruction of Western civilization. In calling capitalism unjust and declaring that its abolition will establish justice, moralists and churchmen render a priceless service to the cause of the socialists and interventionists and relieve them of their greatest embarrassment, the impossibility of refuting the economists' criticism of their plans by discursive reasoning.

It must be reiterated that no reasoning founded on the principles of philosophical ethics or of the Christian creed can reject as fundamentally unjust an economic system that succeeds in improving the material conditions of all people, and assign the epithet "just" to a system that tends to spread poverty and starvation. The evaluation of any economic system must be made by careful analysis of its effects upon the welfare of people, not by an appeal to an arbitrary concept of justice which neglects to take these effects into full account.

Chapter 16. Present-Day Trends and the Future

1. The Reversal of the Trend toward Freedom

FROM THE SEVENTEENTH CENTURY ON, philosophers in dealing with the essential content of history began to stress the problems of liberty and bondage. Their concepts of both were rather vague, borrowed from the political philosophy of ancient Greece and influenced by the prevailing interpretation of the conditions of the Germanic tribes whose invasions had destroyed Rome's Western empire. As these thinkers saw it, freedom was the original state of mankind and the rule of kings emerged only in the course of later history. In the scriptural relation of the inauguration of the kingship of Saul they found confirmation of their doctrine as well as a rather unsympathetic description of the characteristic marks of royal government.[1] Historical evolution, they concluded, had deprived man of his inalienable right of freedom.

The philosophers of the Enlightenment were almost unanimous in rejecting the claims of hereditary royalty and in recommending the republican form of government. The royal police forced them to be cautious in the expression of their ideas, but the public could read between the lines. On the eve of the American and the French revolutions monarchy had lost its age-old hold

1. I Samuel 8:11–18.

on men's minds. The enormous prestige enjoyed by England, then the world's richest and most powerful nation, suggested the compromise between the two incompatible principles of government which had worked rather satisfactorily in the United Kingdom. But the old indigenous dynasties of continental Europe were not prepared to acquiesce in their reduction to a merely ceremonial position such as the alien dynasty of Great Britain had finally accepted, though only after some resistance. They lost their crowns because they disdained the role of what the Count of Chambord had called "the legitimate king of the revolution."

In the heyday of liberalism the opinion prevailed that the trend toward government by the people is irresistible. Even the conservatives who advocated a return to monarchical absolutism, status privileges for the nobility, and censorship were more or less convinced that they were fighting for a lost cause. Hegel, the champion of Prussian absolutism, found it convenient to pay lip service to the universally accepted philosophical doctrine in defining history as "progress in the consciousness of freedom."

But then arose a new generation that rejected all the ideals of the liberal movement without, like Hegel, concealing their true intentions behind a hypocritical reverence for the word freedom. In spite of his sympathies with the tenets of these self-styled social reformers, John Stuart Mill could not help branding their projects—and especially those of Auguste Comte—liberticide.[2] In the

2. Letter to Harriet Mill, Jan. 15, 1855. F. A. Hayek, *John Stuart Mill and Harriet Taylor* (Chicago, University of Chicago Press, 1951), p. 216.

eyes of these new radicals the most depraved enemies of mankind were not the despots but the "bourgeois" who had evicted them. The bourgeoisie, they said, had deceived the people by proclaiming sham slogans of liberty, equality under the law, and representative government. What the bourgeois were really intent upon was reckless exploitation of the immense majority of honest men. Democracy was in fact plutodemocracy, a blind to disguise the unlimited dictatorship of the capitalists. What the masses needed was not freedom and a share in the administration of government affairs but the omnipotence of the "true friends" of the people, of the "vanguard" of the proletariat or of the charismatic Führer. No reader of the books and pamphlets of revolutionary socialism could fail to realize that their authors sought not freedom but unlimited totalitarian despotism. But so long as the socialists had not yet seized power, they badly needed for their propaganda the institutions and the bills of rights of "plutocratic" liberalism. As an opposition party they could not do without the publicity the parliamentary forum offered them, nor without freedom of speech, conscience, and the press. Thus willy-nilly they had to include temporarily in their program the liberties and civil rights which they were firmly resolved to abolish as soon as they seized power. For, as Bukharin declared *after* the conquest of Russia by the Bolshevists, it would have been ridiculous to demand from the capitalists liberty for the workers' movement in any other way than by demanding liberty for all.[3]

3. Bukharin, *Programme of the Communists* (*Bolsheviks*), ed. by the Group of English Speaking Communists in Russia (1919), pp. 28-9.

In the first years of their regime the Soviets did not bother to conceal their abhorrence of popular government and civil liberties, and openly praised their dictatorial methods. But in the later thirties they realized that an undisguised antifreedom program was unpopular in Western Europe and North America. As, frightened by German rearmament, they wanted to establish friendly relations with the West, they suddenly changed their attitude toward the terms (not the ideas) of democracy, constitutional government, and civil liberties. They proclaimed the slogan of the "popular front" and entered into alliance with the rival socialist factions which up to that moment they had branded social traitors. Russia got a constitution, which all over the world was praised by servile scribblers as the most perfect document in history in spite of its being based on the one-party principle, the negation of all civic liberties. From that time on the most barbaric and despotic of governments began to claim for itself the appellation "people's democracy."

The history of the nineteenth and twentieth centuries has discredited the hopes and the prognostications of the philosophers of the Enlightenment. The peoples did not proceed on the road toward freedom, constitutional government, civil rights, free trade, peace, and good will among nations. Instead the trend is toward totalitarianism, toward socialism. And once more there are people who assert that this trend is the ultimate phase of history and that it will never give way to another trend.

2. *The Rise of the Ideology of Equality in Wealth and Income*

From time immemorial the living philosophy of the plain man has unquestioningly accepted the fact of status differences as well as the necessity of subordination to those in power. Man's primary need is protection against malicious onslaughts on the part of other men and groups of men. Only when safe from hostile attacks can he gather food, build a home, rear a family, in short, survive. Life is the first of all goods, and no price to be paid for its preservation appeared too high to people harassed by predatory raids. To remain alive as a slave, they thought, is still better than to be killed. Lucky are those who enjoy the patronage of a benevolent master, but even a harsh overlord is to be preferred to no protection at all. Men are born unequal. Some are stronger and smarter, some are weaker and clumsier. The latter had no choice but to surrender to the former and link their own destiny with that of a mighty suzerain. God, declared the priests, ordained it this way.

This was the ideology that animated the social organization which Ferguson, Saint-Simon, and Herbert Spencer called militaristic and which present-day American writers call feudal. Its prestige began to decline when the warriors who fought the warlord's battles became aware that the preservation of their chieftain's power depended on their own gallantry and, made self-reliant by this insight, asked a share in the conduct of the affairs of state. The conflicts resulting from this claim of the aristocrats engendered ideas which were bound to question and finally to demolish the doctrine of the social necessity of status and caste distinctions. Why, asked the commoners, should the noblemen enjoy privileges and rights that are denied to us? Does not the flowering of the commonwealth depend on our toil and trouble? Do the affairs of state concern only the king and the barons and not the great majority of us? We pay the taxes and our sons bleed on the battlefields, but we have no voice in the councils in which the king and the representatives of the nobility determine our fate.

No tenable argument could be opposed to these pretensions of the *tiers état*. It was anachronistic to preserve status privileges that had originated from a type of military organization which had long since been abandoned. The discrimination practiced against commoners by the princely courts and "good society" was merely a nuisance. But the disdainful treatment, in the armies and in the diplomatic and civil service, of those who were not of noble extraction caused disasters. Led by aristocratic nincompoops, the French royal armies were routed; yet there were many commoners in France who later proved their brilliancy in the armies of the Revolution and the Empire. England's diplomatic, military, and naval accomplishments were evidently due in part to the fact that it had opened virtually all careers to every citizen. The demolition of the Bastille and the abolition of the privileges of the French nobility were hailed all over the world by the élite, in Germany by Kant, Goethe, and Schiller, among others. In imperial Vienna Beethoven wrote a symphony to honor the commander of the armies of the Revolution who had defeated the Austrian forces, and was deeply grieved when the news came that his hero had overthrown the republican form of government. The principles of freedom, equality of all men under the law, and constitutional government were with little opposition approved by public opinion in all Western countries. Guided by these principles, it was held, mankind was marching forward into a new age of justice and prosperity.

However, there was no unanimity in the interpretation of the concept of equality. For all of its champions it meant the abolition of status and caste privileges and the legal disabilities of the "lower" strata, and especially of slavery and serfdom. But there were some who advocated the leveling of differences in wealth and income.

To understand the origin and the power of this egalitarian ideology one must realize that is was stimulated by the resumption of an idea which for thousands of years all over the world had inspired reform movements as well as the merely academic writings of utopian authors: the idea of equal ownership of land. All the evils that plagued mankind were ascribed to the fact that some people had appropriated more land than they needed for the support of their families. The corollary of the abundance of the lord of the manor was the penury of the landless. This iniquity was seen as the cause of crime, robbery, conflict, and bloodshed. All these mischiefs would disappear in a society consisting exclusively of farmers who could produce in their own household what they needed for the support of their families, and neither more nor less. In such a commonwealth there would be no temptations. Neither individuals nor nations would covet what by rights belongs to others. There would be neither tyrants nor conquerors, for neither aggression nor conquest would pay. There would be eternal peace.

Equal distribution of land was the program that prompted the Gracchi in ancient Rome, the peasant revolts which again and again disturbed all European countries, the agrarian reforms aimed at by various Protestant sects and by the Jesuits in the organization of their famous Indian community in what is now Paraguay. The fascination of this utopia enticed many of the most noble minds, among them Thomas Jefferson. It influenced the program of the Social Revolutionaries, the party which recruited the immense majority of the people in Imperial Russia. It is the program today of hundreds of millions in Asia, Africa, and Latin America whose endeavors meet, paradoxically enough, with the support of the foreign policy of the United States.

Yet, the idea of equal distribution of land is a pernicious illusion. Its execution would plunge mankind into misery and starvation, and would in fact wipe out civilization itself.

There is no room in the context of this program for any kind of division of labor but regional specialization according to the particular geographical conditions of the various territories. The scheme, when consistently carried to its ultimate consequences, does not even provide for doctors and blacksmiths. It fails to take into account the fact that the present state of the productivity of land in the economically advanced countries is a result of the division of labor which supplies tools and machines, fertilizer, electric current, gasoline, and many other things that multiply the quantity and improve the quality of the produce. Under the system of the division of labor the farmer does not grow what he can make direct use of for himself and his family, but concentrates upon those crops for which his piece of soil offers comparatively the most favorable opportunities. He sells the produce on the market and buys on the market what he and his family need. The optimum size of a farm no longer has any relation to the size of the farmer's family. It is determined by technological considerations: the highest possible output per unit of input. Like other entrepreneurs the farmer produces for profit, i.e., he grows what is most urgently needed by every member of society for his use, and not what he and his family alone can directly use for their own consumption. But those who desire equal distribution of land stubbornly refuse to take notice of all these results of an evolution of many thousands of years, and dream of returning land utilization to a state long ago rendered obsolete. They would undo the whole of economic history, regardless of consequences. They disregard the fact that under the primitive methods of land tenure which they recommend our globe could not support more than a fraction of the population now inhabiting it, and even this fraction only at a much lower standard of living.

It is understandable that ignorant paupers in backward countries cannot think of any other way for the improvement of their conditions than the acquisition of a piece of land. But it is unpardonable that they are confirmed in their illusions by representatives of advanced nations who call themselves experts and should know very well what state of agriculture is required to make a people prosperous. The poverty of the backward countries can be eradicated only by industrialization and its agricultural corollary, the replacement of land utilization for the direct benefit of the farmer's household by land utilization to supply the market.

The sympathetic support with which schemes for land distribution meet today and have met in the past from people enjoying all the advantages of life under the division of labor has never been based in any realistic regard for the inexorable nature-given state of affairs. It is rather the outcome of romantic illusions. The corrupt society of decaying Rome, deprived of any share in the conduct of public affairs, bored and frustrated, fell into reveries about the imagined happiness of the simple life of self-sufficient farmers and shepherds. The still more idle, corrupt, and bored aristocrats of the ancien régime in France found pleasure in a pastime they chose to call dairy farming. Present-day American millionaires pursue farming as a hobby which has the added advantage that its costs reduce the amount of income tax due. These people look upon farming less as a branch of production than as a distraction.

A seemingly plausible plea for expropriation of the landholdings of the aristocracy could be made out at the time the civil privileges of the nobility were revoked. Feudal estates were princely gifts to the ancestors of the aristocratic owners in compensation for military services rendered in the past and to be rendered in the future. They provided the means to support the king's armed retinue, and the size of the holding allotted to the individual liegeman was determined by his rank and position in the forces. But as military conditions changed and the armies were no longer composed of vassals called up, the prevailing system of land distribution became anachronistic. There seemed to be no reason to let the squires keep revenues accorded as compensation for services they no longer rendered. It seemed justifiable to take back the fiefs.

Such arguments could not be refuted form the point of view of the doctrine to which the aristocrats themselves resorted in defense of their status privileges. They stood on their traditional rights, pointing to the value of the services their forbears had rendered to the nation. But as it was obvious that they themselves no longer rendered such indispensable services, it was correct to infer that all the benefits received as reward for these services should be canceled. This included revocation of the land grants.

From the point of view of the liberal economists, however, such confiscation appeared an unnecessary and dangerous disruption of the continuity of economic evolution. What was needed was the abolition of all those legal institutions that sheltered the inefficient proprietor against the competition of more efficient people who could utilize the soil to produce better and more cheaply. The laws that withdrew the estates of the noblemen from the market and the supremacy of the consumers—such as entails and the legal inability of commoners to acquire ownership by purchase—must be repealed. Then the supremacy of the market would shift control of land into the hands of those who know how to supply the consumers in the most efficient way with what they ask for most urgently.

Unimpressed by the dreams of the utopians, the economists looked upon the soil as a factor of production. The rightly understood interests of all the people demanded that the soil, like all other material factors of production, should be controlled by the most efficient entrepreneurs. The economists had no arbitrary preference for any special size of the farms: that size was best which secured the most efficient utilization. They did not let themselves be fooled by the myth that it was in the interest of the nation to have as many of its members as possible employed in agriculture. On the contrary, they were fully aware that is was beneficial not only to the rest of the nation but also to those employed in agriculture if waste of manpower was avoided in this as in all other branches of production. The increase in material well-being was due to the fact that, thanks to technological progress, a continually shrinking percentage of the whole population was sufficient to turn out all the farm products needed. Attempts to meddle with this secular evolution which more and more reduced the ratio of the farm population as against the nonfarm population were bound to lower the average standard of living. Mankind is the more prosperous the smaller the percentage of its total numbers employed in producing all the quantities of food and raw materials required. If any sense can be attached to the term "reactionary," then the endeavors to preserve by special measures those small-size farms which cannot hold their own in the competition of the market are certainly to be called reactionary. They tend to substitute a lower degree of the division of labor for a higher degree and thus slow down or entirely stop economic improvement. Let the consumers determine what size of farm best suits their interests.

The economists' critique of the agrarian utopia was highly unpopular. Nevertheless the weight of their arguments succeeded for a time in checking the zeal of the reformers. Only after the end of the first World War did the ideal of an agriculture predominantly or even exclusively operated by small farmers again attain the role it plays today in world politics.

The great historical and political importance of the idea of equal distribution of land is to be seen in the fact that it paved the way for the acceptance of socialism and communism. The Marxian socialists were academically opposed to it and advocated the nationalization of agriculture. But they used the slogan "equal distribution of land ownership" as a lever to incite the masses in the economically underdeveloped countries. For the illiterate rural population of these nations the nostrum "socialization of business" was meaningless. But all their instincts of envy and hatred were aroused when politicians promised them the land of the kulaks and the owners of big estates. When during F. D. Roosevelt's administration pro-communists in the United States government and the American press asserted that the Chinese "leftists" were not communists but "merely agrarian reformers," they were right insofar as the Chinese agents of the Soviets had adopted Lenin's clever trick of inaugurating the socialist revolution by resorting to the most popular slogans and concealing one's own real intentions. Today we see how in all economically under-developed countries the scheme of land confiscation and redistribution makes the most effective propaganda for the Soviets.

The scheme is manifestly inapplicable to the countries of Western civilization. The urban population of an industrialized nation cannot be lured by the prospect of such an agrarian reform. Its sinister effect upon the thinking of the masses in the capitalistic countries con-sists in its rendering sympathetic the program of wealth and income equality. It thus makes popular interven-tionist policies which must inevitably lead to full social-ism. To stress this fact does not mean that any socialist or communist regime would ever really bring about equalization of income. It is merely to point out that what makes socialism and communism popular is not only the illusory belief that they will give enormous riches to everybody but the no less illusory expectation that nobody will get more than anybody else. Envy is of course one of the deepest human emotions.

The American "progressives" who are stirring up their countrymen as well as all foreigners to envy and hatred and are vehemently asking for the equalization of wealth and incomes do not see how these ideas are interpreted by the rest of the world. Foreign nations look upon all Americans, including the workers, with the same jeal-ousy and hostility with which the typical American union member looks upon those whose income exceeds his own. In the eyes of foreigners, the American taxpayers have been motivated merely by bad conscience and fear when they spent billions to improve conditions abroad. Public opinion in Asia, Africa, Latin America, and many European countries views this system of foreign aid as socialist agitators do money laid out by the rich for charity: a pittance meant to bribe the poor and prevent them from taking what by rights belongs to them. Statesmen and writers who recommend that their nations should side with the United States against Russia are no less unpopular with their countrymen than those few Americans who have the courage to speak for capitalism and to reject socialism are with their fellow citizens. In Gerhard Hauptmann's play *Die Weber,* one of the most effective pieces of German anti-capitalistic literature, the wife of a businessman is startled when she realizes that people behave as if it were a crime to be rich. Except for an insignificant minority, everyone today is prepared to take this condemnation of wealth for granted. This mentality spells the doom of American foreign policy. The United States is condemned and hated because it is prosperous.

The almost uncontested triumph of the egalitarian ideology has entirely obliterated all other political ideals. The envy-driven masses do not care a whit for what the demagogues call the "bourgeois" concern for freedom of conscience, of thought, of the press, for habeas corpus, trial by jury, and all the rest. They long for the earthly paradise which the socialist leaders promise them. Like these leaders, they are convinced that the "liquidation of the bourgeois" will bring them back into the Garden of Eden. The irony is that nowadays they are calling this program the *liberal* program.

3. *The Chimera of a Perfect State of Mankind*

All doctrines that have sought to discover in the course of human history some definite trend in the sequence of changes have disagreed, in reference to the past, with the historically established facts, and where they tried to predict the future have been spectacularly proved wrong by later events.

Most of these doctrines were characterized by reference to a state of perfection in human affairs. They placed this perfect state either at the beginning of history or at its end or at both its beginning and its end. Consequently, history appeared in their interpretation as a progressive deterioration or a progressive improvement or as a period of progressive deterioration to be followed by one of progressive improvement. With some of these doctrines the idea of a perfect state was rooted in religious beliefs and dogmas. However, it is not the task of secular science to enter into an analysis of these theological aspects of the matter.

It is obvious that in a perfect state of human affairs there cannot be any history. History is the record of changes. But the very concept of perfection implies the absence of any change, as a perfect state can only be transformed into a less perfect state, i.e., can only be impaired by any alteration. If one places the state of perfection only at the supposed beginning of history, one asserts that the age of history was preceded by an age in which there was no history and that one day some events which disturbed the perfection of this original age inaugurated the age of history. If one assumes that history tends toward the realization of a perfect state, one asserts that history will one day come to an end.

It is man's nature to strive ceaselessly after the substitution of more satisfactory conditions for less satisfactory. This motive stimulates his mental energies and prompts him to act. Life in a perfect frame would reduce man to a purely vegetative existence.

History did not begin with a golden age. The conditions under which primitive man lived appear in the eyes of later ages rather unsatisfactory. He was surrounded by innumerable dangers that do not threaten civilized man at all, or at least not to the same degree. Compared with later generations, he was extremely poor and barbaric. He would have been delighted if opportunity had been given to him to take advantage of any of the achievements of our age, as for instance the methods of healing wounds.

Neither can mankind ever reach a state of perfection. The idea that a state of aimlessness and indifference is desirable and the most happy condition that mankind could ever attain permeates utopian literature. The authors of these plans depict a society in which no further changes are required because everything has reached the best possible form. In utopia there will no longer be any reason to strive for improvement because everything is already perfect. History has been brought to a close. Henceforth all people will be thoroughly happy.[1] It never occurred to one of these writers that those whom they were eager to benefit by the reform might have different opinions about what is desirable and what not.

A new sophisticated version of the image of the perfect society has arisen lately out of a crass misinterpretation of the procedure of economics. In order to deal with the effects of changes in the market situation, the endeavors to adjust production to these changes, and

1. In this sense Karl Marx too must be called a utopian. He too aimed at a state of affairs in which history will come to a standstill. For history is, in the scheme of Marx, the history of class struggles. Once classes and the class struggle are abolished, there can no longer be any history. It is true, that the Communist Manifesto merely declares that the history of all hitherto existing society, or, as Engels later added, more precisely, the history after the dissolution of the golden age of primeval communism, is the history of class struggles and thus does not exclude the interpretation that after the establishment of the socialist millennium some new content of history could emerge. But the other writings of Marx, Engels, and their disciples do not provide any indication that such a new type of historical changes, radically different in nature from those of the preceding ages of class struggles, could possibly come into being. What further changes can be expected once the higher phase of communism is attained, in which everybody gets all he needs?—The distinction that Marx made between his own "scientific" socialism and the socialist plans of older authors whom he branded as utopians refers not only to the nature and organization of the socialist commonwealth but also to the way in which this commonwealth is supposed to come into existence. Those whom Marx disparaged as utopians constructed the design of a socialist paradise and tried to convince people that its realization is highly desirable. Marx rejected this procedure. He pretended to have discovered the law of historical evolution according to which the coming of socialism is inevitable. He saw the shortcomings of the utopian socialists, their utopian character, in the fact that they expected the coming of socialism from the will of people, i.e., their conscious action, while his own scientific socialism asserted that socialism will come, independently of the will of men, by the evolution of the material productive forces.

the phenomena of profit and loss, the economist constructs the image of a hypothetical, although unattainable, state of affairs in which production is always fully adjusted to the realizable wishes of the consumers and no further changes whatever occur. In this imaginary world tomorrow does not differ from today, no maladjustments can arise, and no need for any entrepreneurial action emerges. The conduct of business does not require any initiative, it is a self-acting process unconsciously performed by automatons impelled by mysterious quasi-instincts. There is for economists (and, for that matter, also for laymen discussing economic issues), no other way to conceive what is going on in the real, continually changing world than to contrast it in this way with a fictitious world of stability and absence of change. But the economists are fully aware that the elaboration of this image of an evenly rotating economy is merely a mental tool that has no counterpart in the real world in which man lives and is called to act. They did not even suspect that anybody could fail to grasp the merely hypothetical and ancillary character of their concept.

Yet some people misunderstood the meaning and significance of this mental tool. In a metaphor borrowed from the theory of mechanics, the mathematical economists call the evenly rotating economy the static state, the conditions prevailing in it equilibrium, and any deviation from equilibrium disequilibrium. This language suggests that there is something vicious in the very fact that there is always disequilibrium in the real economy and that the state of equilibrium never becomes actual.

The merely imagined hypothetical state of undisturbed equilibrium appears as the most desirable state of reality. In this sense some authors call competition as it prevails in the changing economy imperfect competition. The truth is that competition can exist only in a changing economy. Its function is precisely to wipe out disequilibrium and to generate a tendency toward the attainment of equilibrium. There cannot be any competition in a state of static equilibrium because in such a state there is no point at which a competitor could interfere in order to perform something that satisfies the consumers better than what is already performed anyway. The very definition of equilibrium implies that there is no maladjustment anywhere in the economic system, and consequently no need for any action to wipe out maladjustments, no entrepreneurial activity, no entrepreneurial profits and losses. It is precisely the absence of the profits that prompts mathematical economists to consider the state of undisturbed static equilibrium as the ideal state, for they are inspired by the prepossession that entrepreneurs are useless parasites and profits are unfair lucre.

The equilibrium enthusiasts are also deluded by ambiguous thymological connotations of the term "equilibrium," which of course have no reference whatever to the way in which economics employs the imaginary construction of a state of equilibrium. The popular notion of a man's mental equilibrium is vague and cannot be particularized without including arbitrary judgments of value. All that can be said about such a state of mental or moral equilibrium is that it cannot prompt a man toward any action. For action presupposes some uneasiness felt, as its only aim can be the removal of uneasiness. The analogy with the state of perfection is obvious. The fully satisfied individual is purposeless, he does not act, he has no incentive to think, he spends his days in leisurely enjoyment of life. Whether such a fairy-like existence is desirable may be left undecided. It is certain that living men can never attain such a state of perfection and equilibrium. It is no less certain that, sorely tried by the imperfections of real life, people will dream of such a thorough fulfillment of all their wishes. This explains the sources of the emotional praise of equilibrium and condemnation of disequilibrium.

However, economists must not confuse this thymological notion of equilibrium with the use of the imaginary construction of a static economy. The only service that this imaginary construction renders is to set off in sharp relief the ceaseless striving of living and acting men after the best possible improvement of their conditions. There is for the unaffected scientific observer nothing objectionable in his description of disequilibrium. It is only the passionate pro-socialist zeal of mathematical pseudo-economists that transforms a purely analytical tool of logical economics into an utopian image of the good and most desirable state of affairs.

4. *The Alleged Unbroken Trend toward Progress*

A realistic philosophical interpretation of history must abstain from any reference to the chimerical notion of a perfect state of human affairs. The only basis from which a realistic interpretation can start is the fact that man, like all other living beings, is driven by the impulse to preserve his own existence and to remove, as far as possible, any uneasiness he feels. It is from this point of view that the immense majority of people appraise the conditions under which they have to live. It would be erroneous to scorn their attitude as materialism in the ethical connotation of the term. The pursuit of all those nobler aims which the moralists contrast with what they disparage as merely materialistic satisfactions presupposes a certain degree of material well-being.

The controversy about the monogenetic or polygenetic origin of Homo sapiens is, as has been pointed out above,[1] of little importance for history. Even if we assume that all men are the descendants of one group of primates, which alone evolved into the human species, we have to take account of the fact that at a very early date dispersion over the surface of the earth broke up this original unity into more or less isolated parts. For thousands of years each of these parts lived its own life with little or no intercourse with other parts. It was finally the development of the modern methods of marketing and transportation that put an end to the isolation of various groups of men.

To maintain that the evolution of mankind from its original conditions to the present state followed a definite line is to distort historical fact. There was neither uniformity nor continuity in the succession of historical events. It is still less permissible to apply to historical changes the terms growth and decay, progress and

1. See above, pp. 219 f.

retrogression, improvement and deterioration if the historian or philosopher does not arbitrarily pretend to know what the end of human endeavor ought to be. There is no agreement among people on a standard by which the achievements of civilization can be said to be good or bad, better or worse.

Mankind is almost unanimous in its appraisal of the material accomplishments of modern capitalistic civilization. The immense majority considers the higher standard of living which this civilization secures to the average man highly desirable. It would be difficult to discover, outside of the small and continually shrinking group of consistent ascetics, people who do not wish for themselves and their families and friends the enjoyment of the material paraphernalia of Western capitalism. If, from this point of view, people assert that "we" have progressed beyond the conditions of earlier ages, their judgment of value agrees with that of the majority. But if they assume that what they call progress is a necessary phenomenon and that there prevails in the course of events a law that makes progress in this sense go on forever, they are badly mistaken.

To disprove this doctrine of an inherent tendency toward progress that operates automatically, as it were, there is no need to refer to those older civilizations in which periods of material improvement were followed by periods of material decay or by periods of standstill. There is no reason whatever to assume that a law of historical evolution operates necessarily toward the improvement of material conditions or that trends which prevailed in the recent past will go on in the future too.

What is called economic progress is the effect of an accumulation of capital goods exceeding the increase in population. If this trend gives way to a standstill in the further accumulation of capital or to capital decumulation, there will no longer be progress in this sense of the term.

Everyone but the most bigoted socialists agrees that the unprecedented improvement in economic conditions which has occurred in the last two hundred years is an achievement of capitalism. It is, to say the least, premature to assume that the tendency toward progressive economic improvement will continue under a different economic organization of society. The champions of socialism reject as ill-considered all that economics has advanced to show that a socialist system, being unable to establish any kind of economic calculation, would entirely disintegrate the system of production. Even if the socialists were right in their disregard for the economic analysis of socialism, this would not yet prove that the trend toward economic improvement will or could go on under a socialist regime.

5. *The Suppression of "Economic" Freedom*

A civilization is the product of a definite world view, and its philosophy manifests itself in each of its accomplishments. The artifacts produced by men may be called material. But the methods resorted to in the arrangement of production activities are mental, the outcome of ideas that determine what should be done and how. All the branches of a civilization are animated by the spirit that permeates its ideology.

The philosophy that is the characteristic mark of the West and whose consistent elaboration has in the last centuries transformed all social institutions has been called individualism. It maintains that ideas, the good ones as well as the bad, originate in the mind of an individual man. Only a few men are endowed with the capacity to conceive new ideas. But as political ideas can work only if they are accepted by society, it rests with the crowd of those who themselves are unable to develop new ways of thinking to approve or disapprove the innovations of the pioneers. There is no guarantee that these masses of followers and routinists will make wise use of the power vested in them. They may reject the good ideas, those whose adoption would benefit them, and espouse bad ideas that will seriously hurt them. But if they choose what is worse, the fault is not theirs alone. It is no less the fault of the pioneers of the good causes in not having succeeded in bringing forward their thoughts in a more convincing form. The favorable evolution of human affairs depends ultimately on the ability of the human race to beget not only authors but also heralds and disseminators of beneficial ideas.

One may lament the fact that the fate of mankind is determined by the—certainly not infallible—minds of men. But such regret cannot change reality. In fact, the eminence of man is to be seen in his power to choose between good and evil. It is precisely this that the theologians had in view when they praised God for having bestowed upon man the discretion to make his choice between virtue and vice.

The dangers inherent in the masses' incompetence are not eliminated by transferring the authority to make ultimate decisions to the dictatorship of one or a few men, however excellent. It is an illusion to expect that despotism will always side with the good causes. It is characteristic of despotism that it tries to curb the endeavors of pioneers to improve the lot of their fellow men. The foremost aim of despotic government is to prevent any innovations that could endanger its own supremacy. Its very nature pushes it toward extreme conservatism, the tendency to retain what is, no matter how desirable for the welfare of the people a change might be. It is opposed to new ideas and to any spontaneity on the part of the subjects.

In the long run even the most despotic governments with all their brutality and cruelty are no match for ideas. Eventually the ideology that has won the support of the majority will prevail and cut the ground from under the tyrant's feet. Then the oppressed many will rise in rebellion and overthrow their masters. However, this may be slow to come about, and in the meantime irreparable damage may have been inflicted upon the common weal. In addition a revolution necessarily means a violent disturbance of social cooperation, produces irreconcilable rifts and hatreds among the citizens, and may engender bitterness that even centuries cannot entirely wipe out. The main excellence and worth of what is called constitutional institutions, democracy and government by the people is to be seen in the fact that they make possible peaceful change in the methods and personnel of government. Where there is representative government, no revolutions and civil wars are required to remove an unpopular ruler and his system. If the men in office and their methods of conducting public affairs no longer please the majority of the nation, they are replaced in the next election by other men and another system.

In this way the philosophy of individualism demolished the doctrine of absolutism, which ascribed heavenly dispensation to princes and tyrants. To the alleged divine right of the anointed kings it opposed the inalienable rights bestowed upon man by his Creator. As against the claim of the state to enforce orthodoxy and to exterminate what it considered heresy, it proclaimed freedom of conscience. Against the unyielding preservation of old institutions become obnoxious with the passing of time, it appealed to reason. Thus it inaugurated an age of freedom and progress toward prosperity.

It did not occur to the liberal philosophers of the eighteenth and early nineteenth centuries that a new ideology would arise which would resolutely reject all the principles of liberty and individualism and would proclaim the total subjection of the individual to the tutelage of a paternal authority as the most desirable goal of political action, the most noble end of history and the consummation of all the plans God had in view in creating man. Not only Hume, Condorcet, and Bentham but even Hegel and John Stuart Mill would have refused to believe it if some of their contemporaries had prophesied that in the twentieth century most of the writers and scientists of France and the Anglo-Saxon nations would wax enthusiastic about a system of government that eclipses all tyrannies of the past in pitiless persecution of dissenters and in endeavors to deprive the individual of all opportunity for spontaneous activity. They would have considered that man a lunatic who told them that the abolition of freedom, of all civil rights, and of government based on the consent of the governed would be called liberation. Yet all this has happened.

The historian may understand and give thymological explanations for this radical and sudden change in ideology. But such an interpretation in no way disproves the philosophers' and the economists' analysis and critique of the counterfeit doctrines that engendered this movement.

The key stone of Western civilization is the sphere of spontaneous action it secures to the individual. There have always been attempts to curb the individual's initiative, but the power of the persecutors and inquisitors has not been absolute. It could not prevent the rise of Greek philosophy and its Roman offshoot or the development of modern science and philosophy. Driven by their inborn genius, pioneers have accomplished their work in spite of all hostility and opposition. The innovator did not have to wait for invitation or order from anybody. He could step forward of his own accord and defy traditional teachings. In the orbit of ideas the West has by and large always enjoyed the blessings of freedom.

Then came the emancipation of the individual in the field of business, an achievement of that new branch of philosophy, economics. A free hand was given to the enterprising man who knew how to enrich his fellows by improving the methods of production. A horn of plenty was poured upon the common men by the capitalistic business principle of mass production for the satisfaction of the needs of the masses.

In order to appraise justly the effects of the Western idea of freedom we must contrast the West with conditions prevailing in those parts of the world that have never grasped the meaning of freedom.

Some oriental peoples developed philosophy and science long before the ancestors of the representatives of modern Western civilization emerged from primitive barbarism. There are good reasons to assume that Greek astronomy and mathematics got their first impulse from acquaintance with what had been accomplished in the East. When later the Arabs acquired a knowledge of Greek literature from the nations they had conquered, a remarkable Muslim culture began to flourish in Persia, Mesopotamia, and Spain. Up to the thirteenth century Arabian learning was not inferior to the contemporary achievements of the West. But then religious orthodoxy enforced unswerving conformity and put an end to all intellectual activity and independent thinking in the Muslim countries, as had happened before in China, in India, and in the orbit of Eastern Christianity. The forces of orthodoxy and persecution of dissenters, on the other hand, could not silence the voices of Western science and philosophy, for the spirit of freedom and individualism was already strong enough in the West to survive all persecutions. From the thirteenth century on all intellectual, political, and economic innovations originated in the West. Until the East, a few decades ago, was fructified by contact with the West, history in recording the great names in philosophy, science, literature, technology, government, and business could hardly mention any Orientals. There was stagnation and rigid conservatism in the East until Western ideas began to filter in. To the Orientals themselves slavery, serfdom, untouchability, customs like sutteeism or the crippling of the feet of girls, barbaric punishments, mass misery, ignorance, superstition, and disregard of hygiene did not give any offence. Unable to grasp the meaning of freedom and individualism, today they are enraptured with the program of collectivism.

Although these facts are well known, millions today enthusiastically support policies that aim at the substitution of planning by an authority for autonomous planning by each individual. They are longing for slavery.

Of course, the champions of totalitarianism protest that what they want to abolish is "only economic freedom" and that all "other freedoms" will remain untouched. But freedom is indivisible. The distinction between an economic sphere of human life and activity and a noneconomic sphere is the worst of their fallacies. If an omnipotent authority has the power to assign to every individual the tasks he has to perform, nothing that can be called freedom and autonomy is left to him.

He has only the choice between strict obedience and death by starvation.[1]

Committees of experts may be called to advise the planning authority whether or not a young man should be given the opportunity to prepare himself for and to work in an intellectual or artistic field. But such an arrangement can merely rear disciples committed to the parrot-like repetition of the ideas of the preceding generation. It would bar innovators who disagree with the accepted ways of thought. No innovation would ever have been accomplished if its originator had been in need of an authorization by those from whose doctrines and methods he wanted to deviate. Hegel would not have ordained Schopenhauer or Feuerbach, nor would Professor Rau have ordained Marx or Carl Menger. If the supreme planning board is ultimately to determine which books are to be printed, who is to experiment in the laboratories and who is to paint or to sculpture, and which alterations in technological methods should be undertaken, there will be neither improvement nor progress. Individual man will become a pawn in the hands of the rulers, who in their "social engineering" will handle him as engineers handle the stuff of which they construct buildings, bridges, and machines. In every sphere of human activity an innovation is a challenge not only to all routinists and to the experts and practitioners of traditional methods but even more to those who have in the past themselves been innovators.

1. Hayek, *The Road to Serfdom* (London, 1944), pp. 66 ff.; Mises, *Socialism*, p. 589.

It meets at the beginning chiefly stubborn opposition. Such obstacles can be overcome in a society where there is economic freedom. They are insurmountable in a socialist system.

The essence of an individual's freedom is the opportunity to deviate from traditional ways of thinking and of doing things. Planning by an established authority precludes planning on the part of individuals.

6. The Uncertainty of the Future

The outstanding fact about history is that it is a succession of events that nobody anticipated before they occurred. What the most far-seeing statesmen and businessmen divine is at most conditions as they will develop in the near future, in a period in which by and large no radical changes in ideologies and in general conditions will take place. The British and French philosophers whose writings actuated the French Revolution, and the thinkers and poets of all Western nations who enthusiastically hailed the first steps in this great transformation, foresaw neither the reign of terror nor the way Babeuf and his followers would very soon interpret the principle of equality. None of the economists whose theories demolished the precapitalistic methods of restricting economic freedom and none of the businessmen whose operations inaugurated the Industrial Revolution anticipated either the unprecedented achievements of free enterprise or the hostility with which those most benefited by capitalism would react to it. Those idealists who greeted as a panacea President

Wilson's policy of "making the world safe for democracy" did not foresee what the effects would be.

The fallacy inherent in predicting the course of history is that the prophets assume no ideas will ever possess the minds of men but those they themselves already know of. Hegel, Comte, and Marx, to name only the most popular of these soothsayers, never doubted their own omniscience. Each was fully convinced that he was the man whom the mysterious powers providently directing all human affairs had elected to consummate the evolution of historical change. Henceforth nothing of importance could ever happen. There was no longer any need for people to think. Only one task was left to coming generations—to arrange all things according to the precepts devised by the messenger of Providence. In this regard there was no difference between Mohammed and Marx, between the inquisitors and Auguste Comte.

Up to now in the West none of the apostles of stabilization and petrification has succeeded in wiping out the individual's innate disposition to think and to apply to all problems the yardstick of reason. This alone, and no more, history and philosophy can assert in dealing with doctrines that claim to know exactly what the future has in store for mankind.

Index